Deniable Memories

Vanessa Pearse

VULPINE

PRESS

Published by Vulpine Press in the United Kingdom in 2020

ISBN: 978-1-83919-032-2

Cover by Claire Wood

www.vulpine-press.com

For
Brian, Sarah, Naoise, Fionn and Martha
You really are the best

For
All the displaced people in the world
May you find homes.

Acknowledgements

My experiences in Sudan gave me a backdrop, but the seed for Martha's story came from a tale told to me many years ago by my dear and passionate friend, Suzanne O'Connell. I am forever grateful to Suzanne and other dear friends who spurred me on and supported me in my writing over recent years, especially Fiona Tierney, Marion Roche, Pauline Brennan, Ita Hicks, Eimear Shanahan, Eimear Gallagher – to name but a few. It would not have been possible for me to drop everything and go to Sudan if I had not been given the support of my then employer, Pricewaterhouse, and I am very grateful to them for this support.

My road to putting sentences on paper to create stories began with a Wild Women Writing course with Magi Gibson as part of the Bantry Literary Festival. Magi has a very special touch; we wrote, we laughed and we cried. After that I did a number of other great writing courses, including one with Claire Hennessy of Big Smoke who gave excellent individual feedback. My last course was with Conor Kostick in the Irish Writers Centre and I owe Conor major thanks for his sound direction and support in getting me to this point.

Probably like most debut authors, I felt nervous at the thought of working with an editor, but Sarah Hembrow of Vulpine Press has been a dream to work with. She gives me wise and valuable feedback that I know is just what my writing needs. Thank you, Sarah, for your kindness and your wisdom. Thank you Vulpine for all your great work in getting my novel published.

I am very lucky and very grateful to have a husband who has been supportive of me in whatever endeavours I have chosen over the years. He was a brave man when he married me but we have weathered it well and he is truly my best friend. To my children, I say thank you for being yourselves and for allowing me the freedom to indulge myself in this writing thing.

Author's Note

As I write, Ireland is in partial lockdown as Covid-19 seeks to spread itself across the world's population. Right now, some 20,000 people have died from the virus and nobody knows how many will die over the next months before an effective vaccine or treatment is developed. Everyone is at risk; rich and poor; the powerful and the powerless. And because this is the case, the world is taking action and will not stop taking action until the pandemic is addressed. By contrast, every year some nine million people die of hunger or hunger-related illnesses. People associate hunger with famine as a natural disaster, but so much of the world's hunger is actually man made, either directly attributable to war or state action or inaction which create both massive displacement of people and famine; the people who suffer are powerless, not powerful. Because of this, the action the world takes to address hunger is limited and stops so far short of seeking to address the hunger pandemic that it would be laughable if it wasn't so tragic.

In 1989/1990, I spent time in Sudan where over one million people were internally displaced by the war in the south. I saw the lengths to which a mother would go to care for her child; a child is a child and a mother is a mother wherever they are. I wondered at the inequality of it all, the sense that in the western world we value western lives more than lives outside this world. I saw the love and strength of Sudanese mothers in dreadful situations and I am grateful to these wonderful people for showing me what really matters.

Chapter 1

Airport

On the flight to Khartoum the voice in Martha's head grew louder and louder. By the time the plane had landed it was screaming, *Martha, what effin' planet were you on when you thought Sudan was a good idea?*

She stepped off the plane onto the tarmac of the hot, sandy airport and took a deep breath. She was hoping to calm her nerves by drawing in the warm floral aroma of the late-night air in this new country. But there were no warm floral aromas. Instead, her nostrils were assaulted by the pungent smells of fuel and tyres mingled with the stale human scents of her overheated fellow passengers. Yuck. She threw her backpack over her shoulder and nervously felt for two money belts worn under her heavy top. The top was another bad choice, ideal for the Irish winter, not the Saharan heat. Its only consolation was that it served well to hide the dreaded money belts. The belt to the front contained her own three hundred dollars cash; the one to the back contained ten thousand dollars that the charity's head office had handed to her with the abrupt instruction, "Do not declare this at the airport." Her silent response, apparently, implied willing consent.

She followed the other passengers into the bustling building, rating her body a two or three on the Richter scale – a noticeable tremor. How the hell did other people walk into busy airports or other public places carrying drugs or weapons without their nerves alone giving them away?

"*Salaam alaykum,*" the man at the first desk barked at her, taking her out of her internal, rapidly unsettling ramblings.

She shuddered and stared open-mouthed at his dark face, his military khakis and his old, but threatening, machine gun. He put a form into her

1

shaking hand and she squinted at its indecipherable Arabic. She looked up at him, pleading for help. He turned it over and pointed to the top of the page, where it read "Foreign Currency Declaration Form" in plain English.

She took the pen he offered and declared three hundred dollars for personal use. She rummaged in her brain for reassurance that she was doing the right thing. Was she about to smuggle, yes *smuggle*, ten thousand dollars through an airport teeming with security? They hadn't told her about all the security. She should have worked it out for herself after her previous experience of pedantic foreign exchange procedures with Patrick in Harare airport in Zimbabwe, and more particularly, from the information she had hastily extracted from an expat returning from Sudan. She knew Sudan was a military controlled country – what was she to expect? Using her imperfect accountant's logic, she had come to the conclusion that the continuation of Sudan's war depended on the millions of dollars of foreign aid that poured into it each year, all of which were exchanged at a contemptible government-enforced exchange rate. The war that caused the starvation, displacement and misery of millions of Sudanese people resulted in a need for foreign aid which in turn was financed by foreign aid dollars that enabled the war to continue. It was a never-ending cycle. The exchange rate, in Martha's opinion, was at the crux of the problem.

Taking this logic to a personal level, what did she think she was doing, going to Sudan as a volunteer accountant for a small Irish charity that had started in some obscure village in west Cork? Was her apparent benevolence nothing more than a self-serving need to do something different and escape the drudgery and trials of her personal life? *For feck's sake, Martha, what were you thinking?* Avoiding the punitive government exchange rate for some of the charity's expenditure was why she was expected to smuggle in ten thousand dollars, but where was this going to leave her?

As the many queues, including hers, moved along at a snail's pace, she observed no women amongst the airport personnel. Whose hands might pat her body in search of hidden items? Would she be taken into a cubicle and strip-searched? Would that be when they would find the money? If she was strip-searched, would it be by a woman?

She made her way to the carousel and dragged her large suitcase off it. For the main airport of one of the largest countries in Africa, Khartoum was small, old and crumbling. Everything was various shades of well-worn white or green. No computers or technology were visible. It didn't look ready for the fast approaching nineties but felt stuck in the sixties or seventies, not at all like the modern European or American airports Martha was used to. But the most unsettling difference was the extensive military presence; men armed with a range of guns of various shapes and sizes lurked at every turn. Martha had heard that some of the guns were so old and flawed they had been known to randomly go off in the heat of the Khartoum streets. The thought sent a slow shiver down her spine.

How was she going to adjust to this strange country, that is if she was somehow able to get through the airport without being arrested?

Apart from the airport personnel, the other men were dressed in loose, white turbans and almost full-length white dresses which she later learned were called *jallabiyahs*. These were worn over normal western attire, consisting of a white shirt with dark trousers. The few female passengers that she saw were mainly wearing barely visible western dresses covered by long lengths of light fabric, worn almost like a sari, going around their torso, up over their heads and tucked under their arms. She marvelled at how the women wore these colourful swaths of cloth with relative ease and elegance, somehow managing to achieve normal movement while maintaining their modesty.

Finally, it was her turn at a security table.

"*Salaam alaykum*," a tall dark army officer said as he put out his hand to take her passport and entrance visa. He took a long look at both documents, examining each page of her passport, and comparing the photo to Martha's white-washed face, exhausted by twenty-five hours of nervous travelling. The uniformed man took down some details in his book, stamped her passport and handed it back to her. She nodded and gave him a half-smile.

She joined the queue for baggage inspection and watched nervously as each person handed in their foreign exchange form and had their bags checked. She got lost in thought staring at two large women in the queue in front of her. They were dressed in full-length black burqas with their faces hidden behind rectangular cloth grids. She hadn't noticed these women in London. Had they boarded the plane in complete Muslim attire and, if so, how did they get through British security? The women's suitcases were as big

3

as any Martha had ever seen and the baggage security men struggled to lift them onto the tables. A female member of security appeared, dressed as many of the female passengers were, wrapped in a long length of cloth that Martha came to know as a *thobe*. She went through the women's bulging bags, lifting items up for closer inspection. The suitcases contained an array of fashionable clothes including strappy dresses, T-shirts and even shorts. They looked as if they were all in sizes big enough to fit the ample bodies that were evident under the burqas. Martha was fascinated. Did the women keep these clothes for when they were abroad? Did they wear them under their burqas? Did they wear them for their girlfriends or their husbands? She was pondering their fashion choices when a man, in full military attire including badges that covered half his chest, startled her by taking the Foreign Currency Declaration Form from her hand and slapping it down on the table. Parked for examination later, Martha assumed. He got her to lift her large suitcase up onto the table and proceeded to go through it. He pulled out various items of her clothing: long-sleeved tops, loose calf-length skirts, boring light-weight dresses, all of which had been carefully selected for their ability to cover shoulders, elbows and knees, in full anticipation of Sudanese modesty requirements.

She had packed for the year that she planned to be away and that included one year's supply of tampons which, to save space, she had taken out of their packaging. As she remembered this, to her horror, the man took one tampon out of her case, then another, until he had about twenty of them set neatly on the table. He turned and addressed Martha.

"I…I don't speak Arabic," she mumbled.

The officer pointed at the tampons. Martha inhaled his stale cigarette breath as he brought his face close to hers. She met his gaze, coughed, and backed away. She looked from his dark eyes to his finger pointing at the tampons. He was asking her to explain them. He seemed willing to wait however long it took. She stared back at him, her mind whirling in mortification and fear. How do you explain tampons without words? She cursed the absence of the little leaflets that would have explained everything with their simple pictures. The officer then picked up one tampon and proceeded to sniff it from end to end like a large cigar. Martha envisaged him smoking it and was scared that he would try. Thankfully, he stopped short of putting it in his mouth and lighting it. When he seemed to have grown bored with the game, if it was a game, he smiled at her and indicated for her to move on. He stamped her currency form and handed it back. He lifted her case off the table sending ten or more tampons rolling to the floor. She considered leaving them there but thought the better of it and bent down to pick them up.

"Thanks," she said sheepishly, as a *jallabiyahed* man retrieved one from under the table and handed it to her. He smiled at her and she averted her eyes, peering deliberately down at the ground in search of more. He took her lead and retrieved another one from under the next table.

"*Shokran*," Martha mumbled uncertainly, keeping her head down, surprised that her brain, in its muddle of terror, found one of the Arabic words that she had read. She repacked the tampons and her other items into her now chaotic suitcase. She felt the sweat run down her back as she struggled to zip it closed. In the end she took some of the clothes and shoved them into her backpack. The quicker she could get out the better.

She walked between an array of faded screens and through a doorway into the arrivals area with the undeclared ten thousand dollars. She released a slow, deep sigh rising up from the depth of her tight torso and out her mouth like air being released from a half-tied balloon, leaving some tension and knots lurking in the pit of her stomach. She'd made it.

After a few long minutes she spotted a small white woman in her early thirties, about five years older than her, waving in the waiting crowd: she was one white face amongst a sea of dark faces. In Ireland, a person who was not white – white being a misnomer, Martha had always thought – a person of colour, stood out loud, rare and different amongst the monochrome of the pasty Irish. Here in Khartoum airport, as the only white westerners, they had no trouble finding each other. Shelley immediately introduced herself as, "The person in charge, or better known as Help Sudan's Head of Mission."

She was physically many things that Martha was not: petite and pretty with long, slightly wavy auburn hair loosely pulled back with a thick white cotton hairband. Her hair almost reached her tiny waist which, in turn, accentuated her surprisingly large bust. In contrast, Martha was tall and thin with short, straight dark hair and, in her own opinion, was on the plain side and was distinctly under resourced in the bust. Shelley's white hairband and long hair framed her face and neck like a veil. Her neat dark shirt was buttoned up to give a tiny hint of her cleavage, and this, together with her long, fitted skirt managed to show off her incredible figure. The overall effect was that of a voluptuous nun. Her accent was plummy south Dublin, probably Dublin 4. Shelley oozed matter-of-fact confidence, in that irritating way that small, almost cute, yappy dogs did. The sort of dogs that, much to Martha's bafflement, many people loved, but she found got up her nose.

"So, you're here to replace Liam," Shelley stated as they made their way in virtual darkness to her pickup.

"Yes. Yes, I am. I am glad he asked me to come over and meet him before he left, and get a smooth handover, though it was a struggle trying to wrap up work, get my injections and get here before Christmas."

After the stress of getting through security, Martha's words came rushing out, as they sometimes did when she was feeling uncomfortable and she would have been better advised to say little or nothing. Having arrived on Sudanese sand – not soil – there was none of the happy anticipation that she had felt when she had landed in Zimbabwe, it was as if any sense of African magic that she might have been anticipating had been stolen by fear and apprehension.

"Yes, well, he's gone on holiday, be back in a couple of weeks," Shelley said in a clipped voice as she opened the boot of the small pickup to allow Martha to put her bags in.

"Oh," Martha muttered. *Well feck him anyway, he insisted that I come over before Christmas and now he's skedaddled off, leaving me high and dry, to do what?*

"Is there anyone else who I might do a bit of work with then?" she asked.

"There is always the bookkeeper, Dawit. Sure you can just use the time to get to know the place," Shelley responded curtly.

They headed off, with no further conversation, through unlit sandy streets of low, flat-roofed buildings. Martha stared out the side passenger window seeking solace in this new city. But in the darkness, there was little she could see; only a few other vehicles moved on the streets and she saw no people walking along the way. There was a strangeness to it all that gave her no comfort.

Her introspection was interrupted by moving lights up ahead, flagging them down. Behind the torches, Martha saw men manning a roadblock, rifles on the ready. The pickup was quickly surrounded by six men in khakis aiming their guns directly at them. Martha froze in her seat. Shelley wound down her window as one man approached the vehicle.

"*Salaam alaykum,*" he said, putting out his hand. "Curfew permit."

"*Alaykum Salaam,*" Shelley said, handing him a piece of paper.

He glanced quickly at it, handed it back and without a further word nodded at the other men who lifted the barrier and waved them through with a salute.

Soon after that Shelley parked on the street outside a three-storey building.

"This is where the Help volunteers live," she said, as they stepped out of the pickup onto sandy ground.

Martha looked up at the grey building and was instantly reminded of the old low-rise blocks of flats she had seen in poorer areas on the outskirts of many European cities.

"We have three flats. Your one is here to the front. You have it to yourself for now. The rest of us are in two more flats at the back, all at ground floor level."

The building was dusty and dated but to Martha's surprise, the lights worked: there was electricity. Shelley opened the door to the first flat on the left and they walked straight into a dreary, windowless sitting room. The entire space was a dirty off-white. Nothing hung on the walls. The furniture was from bygone days and was probably garden furniture as it was heavy wrought iron with ripped filthy yellow-and-brown cushion covers. Off the sitting room Martha could see a small dark kitchen and a shower room.

"This is your room," Shelley said, opening the door to an equally miserable-looking bedroom.

There was a narrow bed, a small cupboard, a doctor's examination table – which could surely have been given better use elsewhere – a desk, a chair and, thankfully, a window with shutters and, another surprise, a dusty air-conditioning unit. *It's a pretty depressing place, but it could be worse; I have my own bedroom.*

Shelley got down on her hunkers and opened a small safe under the bed.

"Have you some dollars for me?" she asked, putting out her hand.

"Yes." Martha sighed with frustration at Shelley's unfriendliness as she reached under her T-shirt and brought the opening of the large money belt around to the front. She pulled out the wads of hundred-dollar bills and handed them to Shelley.

Shelley deposited the notes in the safe alongside small bundles of other dollars already there, closed the door, turned the key and stood up. Martha opened her mouth to finally ask about the implications if the money was found by the wrong people. Her fuzzy, tired brain sought the words to tell Shelley that she did not want to sleep in the company of such hot money, especially not in a country which functioned under strict military rule.

"Well it's late so I'll be off. Goodnight."

She was gone before Martha could open her mouth. Martha sighed, a long, frustrated sigh before setting about unpacking her belongings, wondering if she had enough clothes to get her through the year, putting most of them away neatly in the small cupboard. She put her clock, tapes, Walkman, wash bag and writing material out on the desk and plugged her new speakers into the Walkman. She put the pile of post and parcels that she had for the other volunteers out on the examination table beside her alarm clock. She left the tampons, the bag of Christmas goodies from head office, some going-out clothes that she didn't expect to need, and the treats that she had brought from home in the suitcase. She closed it up and put it under the bed.

As she unpacked, it struck Martha that Shelley had collected her out of necessity rather than kindness. She had made no effort to make her feel welcome or to brief her in anyway on what to expect. Martha would have made it her business to make a newcomer feel comfortable and would have been empathetic to the ordeal of getting through an airport teeming with military, not least carrying ten thousand undeclared dollars. But life had taught Martha that just because she would naturally look out for others, especially at a vulnerable time, they would not always look out for her. Why should she expect anything different from Shelley, Head of Mission for Help Sudan, an Irish Non-Governmental Organisation, a charity!

It was over twenty-five hours since Martha had taken an early morning taxi to Dublin airport. She was past being tired. She was at that point that felt something between a drunken stupor and a bad hangover. She needed a shower. She made her way to the shower room and stood transfixed under the warm water. Memories of the day's struggles whirled and crashed through her semi-conscious mind.

Firstly, why on earth did they book her on the red eye from Dublin to London? She had nearly screamed when she discovered that this gave her a five-hour stopover in Heathrow. And then she had to trudge with all her baggage over to another terminal and go through check-in and security all over again. Her frustration and nerves had been further fuelled by an encounter with an overly talkative ground steward at the check-in desk.

"Oh, Khartoum," he had said, as he looked up from her ticket and bent towards her in a conspiratorial gesture.

"What would bring a young lady like you to a place like that? You do know that there is almost full-blown Sharia law there?" He had paused and stared at her over his glasses and whispered, "They'll have you wearing a hijab before you know it!"

"Sure," Martha had mumbled, thinking, *Please shut up or feck off.*

"Yes, and what about the war? You're Irish. Well, it's worse than Northern Ireland from what I hear."

"Okay…thanks." *Oh please, I don't need to hear all this crap from some know-it-all ground steward.*

She was aware of the ongoing war between the north and the south of Sudan, sure wasn't that why Help were there in the first place? The northern Sudanese were largely Arab and Muslim, and the southerners were more Christian and tribal. The southerners wanted to rule themselves but the north was having none of it, not least because the south was where the natural resources were like oil, iron and copper. The south did sound a bit like Northern Ireland. It was where the real trouble and fighting took place, while northern Sudan was reasonably safe like southern Ireland, she supposed. She hoped she was right.

But why hadn't she discussed going to Sudan with her good friends and counsellors, Mrs Connolly and Trish? Warm and lovely Mrs Connolly, who had been guiding and supporting her since her days in boarding school. She would have made sure that Martha had done her research before leaving a good job where she was respected and even liked. Trish, well Trish had expressed concerns about who was going to keep Martha from getting bogged down in the mundane when she could be off having fun.

She hadn't even mentioned her plans to her boyfriend, Patrick, until she had been accepted for the mission and had booked her vaccinations. What did he make of her sudden departure? He hadn't said. She imagined herself telling him about the journey and all that had happened in the airport. If he was relaxed and listening, he would laughingly pull her into his arms and tease her. *So how many tampons do you need for a year?...I think he was taking the proverbial, enjoying your bright red face...Bet he buys his own wife her tampons or whatever...Sure, they hardly let their wives out over there...Better watch yourself that you don't fall for one!* Martha smiled as she thought of this possible scenario.

If he wasn't relaxed and his mind was on work or elsewhere, then he would half-listen and grunt in her direction at what he hoped were appropriate intervals. That seemed an equally likely scenario.

Chapter 2

First Day

Sunlight was streaming through the cracks in the shutters, lighting up the colourless room when Martha opened her eyes. She had been dreaming of work and, in particular, a project that had tested her patience and interpersonal skills to the point where she felt that her face might get stuck in a permanent frown. The contrary client had morphed into Shelley and was screaming accusations of incompetence at her. Waking up, Martha slowly realised where she was, one foot back on the carpeted floor of her office in Dublin and the other stepping fearfully onto the cool hard ground in Khartoum.

She shook her head and looked at her clock. It was ten to eleven in the morning. Back in Dublin it would be just before eight in the morning; Trish would have arrived into Martha's office carrying two cups of coffee, sat down and enquired, "Any news, the more scandalous the better."

Martha recalled her recent response. "I'm heading to Sudan for a year. Leaving in ten days."

Trish's face had changed from smiling, to shock, to puzzlement, to trying to smile until, finally, she had uttered, "Why?"

"Good question, Trish. I'll definitely let you know when I figure it out."

Her standard response to others who asked 'why' was to shrug her shoulders and say, "I've had a good life, it's time I gave something back."

It was a lie.

The next day Trish had, as usual, appeared with two coffees.

"On mature reflection and all that crap, while I will miss you terribly, you go girl and you enjoy every bit of it. You might even use the chance to free yourself from that so-called undertow of yours."

Martha was going to miss Trish. She was a no-bullshit friend who said what she meant, whether you wanted to hear it or not. Martha liked not having to second guess her like she felt she had to with so many other people. She knew that whatever Trish said, it came from the heart. And she was fun and brought out a fun side in Martha that many people probably doubted existed.

Martha gazed at the thin lines of sunshine and remembered how grey and cold everything could be at home in December but how lovely it was too, lighting fires and candles and putting up Christmas glitz. There would be no fires or glitz here. She hadn't given any thought to where she would be sleeping or any basic practicalities like that. Having been told to pack torches and batteries, she had not expected proper electricity.

She got out of bed and opened the shutters to her African world. She faced a blank brick wall, less than ten feet away. She opened the window and stuck her head out. The arid heat hit her face; it was hot and it was only going to get hotter. She should get dressed before the delectable Shelley arrived. She chose a light, long-sleeved summer shirt and matching skirt, conscious of the need to keep her elbows and knees covered. She contemplated the merit of Muslim modesty. With her legs covered to her mid-calf she might be assumed to have a decent pair of long legs but a short skirt would reveal the truth of what she regarded as her knobbly knees. Best to keep them guessing she thought. Still, a burqa would be a step too far! How did they survive in such heavy, dark full-length dresses, especially in the heat?

In the shower room, she stared at herself in the mirror and lifted her hands to touch her cheeks, contemplating her face and where she was. She had given up everything, whatever everything was, the good and the bad. She had landed herself in Khartoum for a year so she had just better just get on with it.

She could hear her family back home making snide comments and joking that her rapid departure was all part of her messed-up youngest child syndrome. She was, after all, the much apologised for fourth child whose mother made no secret of her being a terrible, unplanned accident. The same mother told her that when she first saw her as a new-born baby she had exclaimed, "My goodness, she *is* ugly."

Martha turned quickly away from the mirror, avoiding examining that thought any further. She went back to the bedroom, hung up her towel at the end of the bed and turned her focus to rearranging her few things on the desk and table. It was time to test the Walkman speakers that she had bought in Dublin airport. She pressed play and Fleetwood Mac's "Never going back again" filled the silence.

She was back in boarding school dancing with the girls around the dormitory...

"I love Fleetwood Mac too."

Martha jumped.

"Sorry, I gave you a fright – I'm Siobhán."

The young woman of about Martha's age put out her right hand and shook Martha's warmly. Her smile started in her large blue eyes and lit up her freckled face, over which hung whiffs of hair that had broken away from her wonderful mop of long, light brown waves. The rest of her hair fell down over her shoulders onto a loose flowing, pale green dress.

"Hi, I'm Martha."

"I'm one of the nurses. Shelley sent me to get you and bring you to the office."

"Thank you. I'm the new accountant, replacing Liam."

Martha felt a bit stupid as soon as she said it, of course Siobhán knew what her role was.

"Yes, I know. He said that he was going to get you over before Christmas so he could show you everything." She threw her arms out demonstratively. "Then he headed off on holidays the day before you were due to arrive." She shook her head. "Typical Liam."

Martha shrugged, feeling relief that someone understood her frustration.

"You must be famished, you must come and get *fature*, you know, breakfast, at the office. Abdul Halim always makes it at this time."

"Thank you. I need it." She paused. "Oh Siobhán, everyone's post is here." She indicated the pile of small parcels and envelopes on the table as the mention of food slowly registered, making her realise just how hungry she actually was.

"Oh, great! I love getting post." Siobhán beamed. "But I won't look now…I like to draw out the anticipation…Mam always includes lots of news…and some treats."

The dry heat felt good to Martha when they got outside. Siobhán warned her to enjoy it while she could because in a few months it would be scorching. They walked slowly down the side of the road, the tarmac barely visible under all the sand. They passed more blocks of flats like their own and some single-storey houses set in their own gardens. It had the look of well-faded, post-colonial elegance. Of the few cars on the road, most were very old, bright yellow taxis, hand-painted judging by the visible brush strokes. The rest were large, flashy four-wheel drive pickups – Land Cruisers, Land Rovers or similar – driven by white-faced expats or by dark-skinned drivers with white passengers. These shiny white vehicles were emblazoned with various UN or NGO logos, UNICEF, UNHCR, USAID, OXFAM. Clearly, Martha thought, charity is big business in Sudan.

They walked along in silence at first as Martha observed her new surroundings. They passed men in white *jallabiyahs*, groups of them squatting in a circle and talking animatedly, others just standing around watching the world go by as if that was all that they had to do. Not a woman in sight. *Sudan – "blád as- súdan," land of black people…more like the land of coffee-coloured men!*

"So, what brought you to this strange country of sand and sunshine?"

"Oh…you know." Martha shrugged before giving Siobhán one of her stock answers. "One of the partners where I work is from the same small town in Cork as Monica who started Help. She told him that she urgently needed a volunteer accountant for Sudan and he told her that he didn't think that such an apparent contradiction existed, but he would put a note up on the staff notice board anyway. I rang the number and, before I knew it, I was on my way here! And you?"

"Oh, I was working as a staff nurse in Temple Street Children's Hospital and I was forever complaining to my flatmate that there must be more to life than injections, vomit and ward sisters, particularly ward sisters! She suggested Africa. I was no sooner gone than her boyfriend moved in!"

"My friend Trish, in work, encouraged me to bite the bullet too…But, tell me, what's it actually like here?"

"Strange at first. The language, the people, how they dress, the heat, the military, sand everywhere, how basic everything is…all of those things! But now, after less than three months, it feels normal – I don't even notice the heat most of the time."

"Less injections, vomit and ward sisters so?"

"Exactly. I'm the boss in the clinic. I'm like the ward sister in one of Help's primary health care centres and outreach programs outside Khartoum. Mainly mothers and babies, immunisations, basic healthcare, some male circumcisions. Now, that takes a bit of getting used to!"

"I bet it does." Martha grimaced. She remembered visiting a friend's little brother in the Harcourt Street Hospital after he had a circumcision for a medical reason. A big fuss was made of him and he was in hospital for four whole days recovering from the operation and the anaesthetic.

"Bet it's not been done under a general over here?" she said.

Siobhán laughed. "But at least by being done in our clinics, we know they are using clean blades. To be honest I leave that to Ahmed Mohammed, our local clinic manager. A number of men usually bring their sons to the clinic together for circumcision. The boys arrive excited and…and they often leave for home with bright red blood stains glowing on the front of their white *jallabiyahs*! You know it's almost like they're proclaiming, 'I've been circumcised'. It was weird the first time that I saw it, but to be honest, I don't pay much heed to that now either!"

Martha didn't know what to say so she just nodded.

"I know." Siobhán mirrored Martha's nodding. "It's all a far cry from working in an Irish hospital. But still, I love it."

"I suppose my accounting will be a far cry from working in an Irish office too," Martha responded, nodding again but more slowly.

She wondered if there would be any computers; the thought of doing everything manually horrified her. And how was she going to survive with Sister Shelley as her boss?

They reached the Help's offices, a flat-roofed, single-storey building painted white and green; it may have been a house in a previous existence. In the main office, Siobhan introduced Martha to various members of staff, most of whose names Martha immediately forgot as they were all new to her and she wasn't good with names at the best of times. There were no women in *thobes* or men in *jallabiyahs*, just people in normal western clothes. Martha gathered that the staff, who were predominantly male, were all either from southern Sudan or Ethiopia and all had reasonable English, something for which she was immediately grateful.

They came to two desks on their own at the back of the office and Siobhán pointed at one, almost half of which was taken up with a large PC.

"That's Liam's desk, where you'll be sitting and beside you is Dawit here," Siobhán said. A tall, handsome man with a neat beard sat at the desk beside Liam's, his pen suspended over some accounting books and his other hand resting on the keys of an electric calculator.

"Dawit, this is Martha, the new accountant, you know, to replace Liam. Dawit is from Ethiopia and has excellent English."

"Hi Martha, I'm the bookkeeper." He pointed momentarily at the large, red-covered analysis books before looking down at whatever he was writing.

"Hi Dawit, nice to meet you." Martha put out her hand.

Dawit half-nodded without looking up at her. She withdrew her hand, swallowed hard and took a quiet deep breath before finding her voice again.

"Would it be okay if I came and talked with you later, please? I would really appreciate it if you could explain to me how things work here."

"Yes. Should be alright." Again, he didn't look up and Martha felt a distinct lack of enthusiasm in his tone.

Siobhán took her out through the kitchen to a small backyard where the air was filled with the smell of hot fresh bread. Martha started to salivate and thought she might collapse with hunger. Flat tortilla-like breads were being cooked on a little charcoal stove by an older almost black-skinned man with short salt-and-pepper hair. Siobhán had taken a brown bread roll out from under a cloth in the kitchen and she handed it to Martha.

"Hi Abdul Halim, this is Martha. She's our new Liam. Much better looking though, don't you think?"

Abdul Halim nodded and gave a broad toothless smile. "Hi Martha, nice to meet you," he said, perching bird-like over the breads.

"And you too." Martha walked over to him and they shook hands firmly.

"Any chance of some of your magical coffee?"

Abdul Halim grinned crookedly at Siobhán, got up from the stove and went over to another low stove from which he lifted a small kettle. He filled two mugs and handed one to Martha with a little bow.

"Thank you."

"You're welcome."

Martha liked Abdul Halim immediately. He handed the other mug of coffee to Siobhán and returned to his cooking. They sat down on the chairs in the small yard and Martha ate the crusty bread roll that Siobhán had given her, dipping it into the strong, dark coffee that was like no coffee that she had ever had before; it had a distinctly sweet but spicy flavour, predominantly cardamom. Abdul Halim gave them two flatbreads, fresh from the stove, the colour of brown speckled flour, and deliciously soft and warm.

As they were eating, another white woman walked into the yard with a cup in her hand. She had tight-cropped brown hair and warm hazel eyes, and although she was of solid build she glided along on light feet.

"Ah, another divil for punishment. You must be Martha, you're very welcome." She gave Martha a warm hug.

"This is Molly. She's the one to tell you all you need to know about Help and Sudan," Siobhán said as Molly sat down to join them.

"Well, Martha, what do you want to know?"

"Oh, I know very little about Help or Sudan really. I did ask at the Cork head office but they didn't get around to telling me much more than what injections to get, and where to get them." Martha paused, thinking that came out the wrong way. "I mean where to go to get all the injections…"

"Well, let me give you some background so…First thing is that the south is a war zone with lots of fighting and landmines everywhere, making it increasingly impossible to live, never mind farm there. Between one and two million people have so far been displaced from the south and are now living in pretty dire conditions on the outskirts of Khartoum. The people mainly walk, arriving with nothing but the clothes on their backs and no food in their stomachs. How they manage to trudge that distance – thirteen hundred miles, often carrying their young children on their backs – is beyond me but the resilience of African people has astounded me every time I've come here…By the time they arrive they are weak and often in very poor health. In a nutshell they keep Help and other charities busy. The numbers arriving has

17

slowed but the need for feeding and healthcare remains. Hence, we have primary healthcare centres and outreach programmes in three settlements outside Khartoum, including the one that Siobhán works in." Molly looked over at Siobhán.

"Yep, that's me! Speaking of which, I'd better get to work."

As Siobhán stood up, Martha heard a sonorous call in the distance. It took a while for her ears to tune in to hear the words.

"Allahu Akbar, Allahu Akbar..."

It was a strangely captivating, melodious and soothing sound.

"That is the muezzin calling the people to prayer. God is Greatest. God is Greatest," Molly said.

"Oh, listen, they're calling me," Siobhán joked. "And Ahmed, my driver, will be wondering where I am. Half the people here are called Ahmed or Mohammed, by the way, even both sometimes. He was off getting the tyre repaired and then restocking the ambulance with supplies for the clinic...See you later."

With a flick of her long, wild hair, she was gone.

"She's nice, you'll like her," Molly said.

"Yes, I do already."

Martha glanced after Siobhán, wishing that she could go with her rather than face Dawit.

"So, what do you do here, Molly?"

"Oh, I'm filling a gap really. I'm temporarily running one of the health centres and helping with administration. The Cork office is currently recruiting another nurse and administrator."

"So you're doing the work of two people then?"

"This is nothing." Molly laughed. "When I first came over here five years ago, in 1984, during the three-year drought, we worked eighteen-hour days getting food and water to people and it was horrendous...It was the drought and famine that led Monica to start Help, you know."

"Yes, I heard. It sounds awful," Martha said thinking, slightly guiltily, that 1984 sounded quite exciting.

"Our efforts weren't helped by the civil war which had broken out again in 1983 but we just got on with it. Speaking of which, I'd better go with

Fuad, our local administrator, to the Ministry of Foreign Affairs and sort out a visa for a volunteer who is expected in the New Year. What about you?"

"I think that I'll brave talking to Dawit, though he didn't seem too keen on the idea earlier."

"Ah, Dawit, he doesn't like to answer to anyone but Liam. The rest of us are merely women! You'll be grand."

Chapter 3

Visiting the Projects

Martha was grateful that her upbringing had helped her develop a thick skin which had seen her through some challenging work situations at home in Ireland. She was definitely going to need it to survive in Sudan. She may have thought that her biggest challenges were going to be adjusting to the excessive heat, the ever-present military rule or the strangeness of Islamic culture. But she soon found that trying to do her work efficiently and effectively in the inhospitable work environment of the Help office was most likely to put a grimace firmly back on her face.

Over the first few days, Dawit did his best to keep her away from the records. She persisted with a small measure of charm and a large dollop of doggedness, and gradually got to know her way around the charity's bookkeeping system. She made notes on ways to improve it, to make it easier to produce prompt, reliable reports and to better ensure that all monies were properly accounted for while allowing for the cash-only economy on which Sudanese business survived.

It struck Martha that expats' weekly *volunteer* allowances alone were at least three or four times the average salary paid to local staff employed by Help. In addition to these weekly allowances, expats' in-country rent, household bills, security and transport costs were all paid by the charity. Before each expat arrived in Sudan, Help spent at least a couple of thousand dollars on flights and vaccinations. Over the following weeks, Martha learned there were numerous Sudanese people ready and able to do most of the work that expats were doing. She envisioned little old ladies in Ireland listening to Help's advertisements on the radio: 'Give generously and help the starving in

20

Africa'. Cries of 'Famine in Africa' were slowly replacing the missionary calls she had grown up with; 'Help the black babies' was no longer considered an entirely appropriate refrain. Martha didn't understand what had brought about this shift in mantra; was it the use of the word black? Was it the words 'black babies'? Or was it a shift away from religious missionaries going into Africa focussing on feeding children as a way to spread *The Good Word* and add to their number? Whatever it was she only had the present situation to consider. She imagined poor old ladies, barely surviving on their state pension themselves, going without food at times so that they could make a donation to Help's gallant efforts. How would these people, most of them from Cork, feel if they knew how much of their money went to paying for expats to do jobs that could be done at a fraction of the cost by well-qualified local staff? Martha was not happy; Help was robbing the Irish poor to give an African adventure to white volunteers when the Sudanese masses, struggling to survive, would be best served by their own being given the resources to help them. What was this insistence at having white expats do jobs in Africa that locals could do?

She didn't mention to Dawit the accounting changes that she intended to make as it was clear he would resist them, at least as long as Liam was still lurking in the background. And she certainly didn't dare to voice her thoughts on the use of expats versus locals to her fellow volunteers as they all seemed to be perfectly happy with how things were. Why wouldn't they be? They lived in reasonably comfortable accommodation with all living expenses paid for, which left their volunteer allowances to cover extras or luxuries. On top of that, a Sudanese man came into each flat once a week to change the beds and clean the rooms from top to bottom. They ate out more often than in as they could rarely be bothered to shop, something which Martha soon learned had its own challenges as there wasn't much to be easily found in the thin scattering of shops that existed. She asked Fuad about this and he explained that most goods were sold at street markets or souks and he promised to take her to some. Martha liked Fuad, the local office administrator. He had a warm fatherly way about him, not that Martha could reliably judge having not had the best of experience of fatherly ways.

Liam arrived back a few days before Christmas. When he strutted into the office behind Shelley, the first thing that struck Martha was his size. At most he was five foot six, at least two inches shorter than Martha, and, in her experience, men didn't like women looking down on them, literally or metaphorically. He carried himself with an inflated air of importance with his chest puffed out and his head held high, trying to compensate for his height no doubt, Martha concluded. There was something effeminate about how he walked, hitting the ground with the tips of his toes rather than with the flats of his feet.

When he arrived, Martha was sitting at his desk. She stood up apprehensively to greet him and to vacate the seat for him.

"I was wondering…I mean it would be great if you could talk me through what needs doing," she gently suggested following Shelley's introductions.

"Oh," he said in his high-pitched voice, "I have far too many financial reports to prepare for donors to have time to explain anything."

"Well…" Martha paused, trying not to show her annoyance. "Perhaps I could be of help?"

"Oh no. Thank you, but I'm much better doing it myself. I *know* what I'm doing."

He dismissed her with a wave of a hand. Martha took his dismissal to mean that it would all be beyond her and other mere earthlings who didn't operate in the same elitist hot air bubble as Little Liam and Sister Shelley.

She quietly screamed at such ridiculous shenanigans. She turned towards Shelley without any expectation of support.

"Shelley, perhaps, if you don't mind, I could use the next while to get to know the Help projects on the ground?" Martha said through almost gritted teeth. "I could work wherever I might be made useful."

"Good idea, speak to Molly," Shelley replied as she walked off.

So she spoke to Molly and Siobhán over a cup of Fuad's spicy coffee in the backyard later that day.

"That's a great idea. Liam has never been out to my projects," Siobhán said. "Come with me tomorrow. Ahmed Mohammed, the clinic administrator, has arranged that we assess some new arrivals and then I must visit my TB family and see how they are doing."

"And come with me the next day to the leper settlement. I have to finish a blanket distribution there. It's surprising how cold it can get at night in the desert, you know," Molly said.

"I didn't even know that there was leprosy in Sudan!" Martha exclaimed quietly, feeling, not for the first time, rather naïve.

The next morning, having restocked the large four-wheel drive which Siobhán referred to as 'the ambulance', Ahmed, the driver, drove them out through Khartoum city to Siobhán's clinic. Khartoum city centre was surprisingly high rise relative to Dublin and relative to Martha's expectations, with many new buildings being five or more stories. Khartoum's streetscape was a strange architectural mix of smart, modern buildings – mainly banks – basic low-rise buildings, and older buildings which were more ornate with elaborate stone or brick columns, showing some of Sudan's British colonial past. Some of it reminded her of what she had seen in Zimbabwe the previous year, but others were more Greek in style and she wondered at the Greek influence. But what set Khartoum apart from anywhere Martha had been before were the many minaret towers that rose above the buildings. From these towers, muezzins called the people to pray five times a day. Martha was growing used to hearing the loud calls; she welcomed the sound like a much-needed calming prayer. The Sudanese equivalent of The Angelus in Ireland.

Outside of Khartoum, as they drove into its larger sister city Omdurman, the streetscape became more African in style with its low mud structures, narrow streets and roads that were more sand than tarmac. There were less cars and only the odd old colourful bus. Most people walked and some used a donkey and cart. They passed few shops; business happened at souks or simple stalls set out on the side of the streets. One part of the main souk was given over to the things that you might find in a hardware shop like simple tin stoves, saucepans, buckets, basic tools, etc., many of which appeared second hand. The wares were set neatly on sheets on the ground with the sellers, all men in *jallabiyahs*, squatting on their hunkers chatting amiably to each other as they waited for customers. Like the men that Martha had seen on the side of the street on her first day, they looked as if they could happily sit that way for hours; if there was one thing that the Sudanese seemed to have in abundance, it was time.

On another street there were various food stalls, some selling a limited variety of fresh vegetables and then some fast-food stalls, as Siobhán referred to them, selling goat and spicy chicken cooked on racks over charcoal stoves. With the window rolled down, the air was filled with delicious spicy aromas and Martha craved trying some.

"Siobhán, do you ever eat anything from the fast-food stalls?" she asked hopefully.

"Oh yes, I love to buy my lunch from them, though I always choose the well-done pieces to be safe! They're really delicious."

As they drove on, they heard the call to prayer echoing from one of the towers, *Allahu Akbar, Allahu Akbar.* It seeped through the narrow streets invoking the men to congregate at large earthen pots and scoop water from them. Slowly and reverentially they washed their hands, followed by their face and arms and finished with their feet. They stood momentarily with their heads bowed, then rolled out their prayer mats, knelt down and lowered their heads and upper bodies. Martha, Siobhán and Ahmed watched all of this in silence. The traffic on the street had come to a halt as prayers took place. It was, as Martha had already observed, the Sudanese equivalent of The Angelus but it was more devotedly observed.

As they waited for the prayers to finish, even with all the windows fully down, the vehicle became like an airless sauna. The intense heat aggravated Martha's lumpy mosquito bites and she fought the urge to scratch them. Since the end of her first week, she had averaged eighteen large, angry red bites and that was just counting from below her knees! There were plenty elsewhere too. The repeated sprays of repellent were a waste of time. Insects had always been attracted to her, like bees to sweet flowers, she joked to herself, stopping herself from thinking, like flies to dirt. With all these bites she needed to be careful, malaria was common so she needed to remember to take her anti-malaria tablets every day.

There was general relief in the hot vehicle when the prayers were over and the traffic resumed. Before long, they were driving between small neat rows of clay buildings with metal doors and soon Martha saw the Help flag flying above a large single-storey mud building. Along the side of the building, down the narrow street, was a neat queue of thirty or more women. Some held babies in their arms, and many also had children, mostly girls, sitting quietly at their feet. They were all dressed in old and well-worn colourless clothes. They were thin and looked sad, or maybe resigned. Martha wasn't sure. A well-dressed man wearing a *jallabiyah* and a loose turban was making his way down the queue taking a list of names. Siobhán referred to him as her right-hand man at the clinic, Ahmed Mohammed, and she explained that the queue was made up of the newly arrived refugees from the south.

"I've heard that the government are arming local rebel tribes in the south with guns, even AK47s. It keeps them fighting amongst themselves," Siobhán half whispered.

"United they stand, divided they fall," Martha responded, remembering that that had been a well-known tactic of the British in their colonies.

"Yes, something like that. Eventually they hope to clear the land of local tribes and make way for the oil companies."

Martha was silent as she took in the tragic scene of the thin, listless women and their children, displaced from their homes, queuing for a chance at survival. Words of a favourite Leaving Cert. poem by William Butler Yeats came to her.

What need you, being come to sense,
But fumble in a greasy till
And add the halfpence to the pence
And prayer to shivering prayer, until
You have dried the marrow from the bone;
For men were born to pray and save...

"You never see too many men or even boys among the southern refugees as the southern army, the SPLA, have gathered as many males as possible into military camps. They may be only ten or eleven years old."

Siobhán had unintentionally interrupted Martha's silent recital.

Martha paused before answering. "They are only children."

She shook her head, visualising the little shiny white primary-school children back in Ireland getting dropped at school by their mammies each morning. She couldn't picture these clean boys wielding real machine guns as they faced an enemy, an enemy armed and ready, and prepared to shoot to kill. The ten- and eleven-year-old Sudanese boys wouldn't be any bigger than the Irish boys and a gun would look just as large and out of place in their hands as they lost their innocence ahead of their time.

As the ambulance came to a stop, three women and a man emerged from the Help building. They greeted Siobhán and the driver and started offloading supplies. They were tall and dark skinned and were neatly dressed in clean western clothes, no *thobes*, *jallabiyahs* or turbans. *They must be southerners*, Martha thought.

Martha was introduced to the staff and Siobhán explained that the female staff were nurses who had trained in hospitals in the south but had fled to the north.

"Ahmed Mohammed and Soha – who is our outreach worker – visited the new settlement yesterday and arranged for those who were able to come here today for assessment and vaccinations. We will go with Soha to see the sick and weak at the camp later."

"Come, I'll show you around," said Elizabeth, one of the other nurses, taking Martha gently by the arm. "Siobhán said that you can record our weight and height assessments and vaccinations and then we can give each adult food vouchers according to their family's needs."

Throughout the morning, the women and children were measured and weighed and vaccinated. Martha carefully recorded their statistics and observed how thin, yet elegant, many of them appeared, even in their well-worn clothes. Elizabeth explained that many of them had walked for days, or sometimes weeks, often on empty stomachs.

"Things are very dangerous in southern Sudan. This may be their only chance of survival. They have nothing but the clothes they wear. No food for themselves or their families. Nothing. You must understand, they need food for their journey. Some have sold their older daughters to buy food. They love their daughters as your mother loves you."

Martha looked silently at Elizabeth. What can you say to something like this? A mother's love was not something Martha had ever felt but still she could imagine the pain and torment the Sudanese mothers must experience in choosing how to give each or any of their children a chance of survival.

"If they don't sell their daughters then the family may all die. There is no food, only guns and mines. Hopefully they can buy them back when things get better. Who knows? Now their daughters work for people in the north, working in houses, cleaning, cooking. Perhaps they aren't as lucky and they have to do other work, bad work."

"Bad work?" Martha repeated, hoping that it wasn't what she thought it was.

"Yes, *bad work*. They might get pregnant and then…it isn't that the families don't love their daughters…" Elizabeth was keen to explain. "It's just that if they don't do it then they may all die."

"Cruel, cruel decisions in desperate times." Martha struggled with the thought of these vulnerable women being forced to make such mind-blowing decisions. She wondered how her own mother would cope in such a situation. Martha was the youngest of a son and three daughters, the unloved and most dispensable one in her mother's mind, that much she knew beyond doubt.

"Sadly, many of them can't read or write so there is little real chance that they will be able to make contact with their children again. In Khartoum, the remaining family members have some hope as charities, like Help, will organise feeding programmes to give them the basics like grain and milk powder. They are relatively safe. It's not much but it is all that we can offer," Siobhán whispered to Martha.

With all this new and cruel information floating through her head, Martha felt every bit the green-behind-the-ears blow-in; she sat in the small mud room with its dirt floor and its gathering of these women and children and was in awe of it all. Most of all she was in awe of their warmth and their innate dignity amidst such horror. How could she know or begin to understand what they had faced to get their dwindling families to safety? Many of them had been forced to give up their few cattle and had been burned out of their villages, and all had fled what they saw as certain death or, at best, some form of slavery. People back home wouldn't be able to imagine such horror…how lucky we really are.

After a lunch of spicy chicken from one stall and *Kisra* bread from another, they set off with the driver and Soha to meet the remaining sick and weak refugees from the new camp. They left behind the neatly ordered mud buildings and were soon on the edge of the desert where there were a number of small settlements, each consisting of eight or more dome-shaped hovels made of sticks, rags, plastic and cardboard, surrounded by a ring fence of thorn bushes. Between these settlements lay open dumps where small, almost-naked children with distended stomachs wandered, searching for food or an-

ything of value. Martha had never seen such squalor, such wanton depriva-
tion. The rough sleepers that Martha had visited each week with the Simon
soup-run in Dublin were rich and well-fed by comparison. In Ireland, if you
know where to look and are willing to accept charity, you don't have to go
hungry. In Sudan it was clear that for many refugees, starvation was often not
an option: it was an unassailable harsh reality. *How can this be? How can we
let this happen?* Martha was horrified and angry that the western world, the
EU in particular, maintained food mountains of butter and cereals – all to
keep prices high – while in the developing world, people starved.

They came to the new settlement and got out of the ambulance. A tall
Sudanese gentleman approached them and led them to one of the hovels
where a weak, pregnant woman lay stretched on the remains of an old blanket. Siobhán examined her and suggested that she be brought to the clinic in
the ambulance for observation and, if necessary, moved to the hospital in
Khartoum.

In another hovel a young woman held her child lovingly in her arms and
was slowly and determinedly feeding her a soft white mashed meal, pausing
occasionally to kiss her on her temple or play with her little feet and legs. The
small girl, who must have been about one, had an open cleft palate, creating
a strange void between her nose and her chin, and leaving the dark inside of
her mouth visible. The child's face and eyes laughed spontaneously every time
the mother tickled her little feet and a happy little gurgle came from her
throat. This child would never have been able to suck at her mother's breast
and her survival was a heart-wrenching testament to her mother's love and
patience. What great sacrifices must the mother have made to keep her child
alive? Martha felt tears running down her face and only then did she become
aware that she had been standing for some minutes watching the mother and
child.

"Sorry," she said as she turned briefly away, feeling guilty for staring.

Later that evening, when she was turning the memory over in her head,
she thought that, in the squalor of that tent made of sticks and rubbish, she
had seen something unsettling but heart-stoppingly beautiful. If she was ever
to paint a picture of unconditional love then that vision of the mother and
child would be it. It filled her with a deep yearning, a yearning to be wrapped
in someone's arms, to feel that love and to laugh and gurgle freely. She knew

it was not something she had ever done with her mother; perhaps it was something she would share with a child of her own someday.

Now, in that make-shift tent, Martha watched as Siobhán sat down beside the mother and daughter and gently took the baby in her arms, checking her weight and health. She then assessed the mother and vaccinated them both. With Soha translating, Siobhán told the mother that her child was wonderfully healthy and the mother smiled with pride. Soha gave the mother some food vouchers and explained that Ahmed Mohammed would be back later to give out food.

Ahmed then left Soha and the weak, pregnant refugee at the clinic and headed with Martha and Siobhán to see Siobhán's TB family, as she affectionately referred to them. They drove for about thirty minutes before coming to a settlement of neat but scattered mud buildings. They stopped at a small building, separate to the rest, and Siobhán and Martha got out of the ambulance. The door of the house was flung open immediately and Siobhán was greeted with unfettered excitement and affection by six lively children and their smiling mother. Siobhán and, at the mother's insistence, Martha entered the building's only room which, before the children piled into it, was sparse and neat. Martha took in the simple surroundings: a small narrow bed made from string and branches was along one wall with a neat pile of blankets on it. Cardboard boxes lay tidily underneath. In another corner was a saucepan and a small stove, ingeniously made of opened and bent tin cans. This was the family's home and they were happy in it. Siobhán greeted each child warmly as they quickly lined up for her to listen to their chests and give each of them their dose of antibiotic – one would think it was Santa who had arrived, not a nurse with a syringe.

When Siobhán explained to them that they were all well and required no further treatment, the children were clearly reluctant to say goodbye. At Siobhán's suggestion they arranged themselves on the bed and posed excitedly for a photo. Then, as Siobhán and Martha made to leave, the mother and children put their hands to their hearts and bowed gently to express their gratitude to Siobhán for all her care over the previous weeks. The mother then bent down and reached into a box under the bed and took out two light bulbs. One was covered in neat red crochet and the other green crochet. The mother held them out to Siobhán, insisting that she choose one to acknowledge their thanks to her. Siobhán was embarrassed and put her hand to her heart as she chose the red one, then she smiled and bowed gently. Martha felt tears filling up in her eyes again and she turned away to hide them. She was struck by the beauty and warmth, yet sparseness, of the whole encounter with the family; the mother had given away one of her two prized possessions as a mark of gratitude to Siobhán for her kindness. They were the only things that the mother owned that were not strictly essential to her and her family's survival and so must have been very dear to her. It dawned on Martha later, as she wrote about it in her letter to Patrick, that not a single word of English and only a few simple words of Arabic had been spoken, yet so much had been said and felt.

Chapter 4

The Accident

Molly sent Martha with Fuad to the Ministry of Foreign Affairs to get her visa sorted and to get the required licence to have a camera. Fuad, although born and bred in Khartoum, spoke excellent English and spoke not only Arabic but a number of other languages too. He also was an expert in the intricacies of Sudanese bureaucracy and was the best person to show Martha how the system worked. The visa that Martha had arrived with was not much more than an entry visa and she needed a permit to stay. Though it depended on the mood of the person dealing with it as to how long the visa would be granted for!

Molly warned her that many of the government officials in the Foreign Ministry spoke good English but only understood what suited them. Many of them got their jobs as a sort of thank you to their families for political favours. However, the jobs were poorly paid and Molly had heard of staff arriving at the start of the day, hanging up their jackets on their office chairs, doing a day's work elsewhere, and collecting their jackets at the end of the day.

Fuad explained that they should aim to get there as soon after 10:00 a.m. as possible, after *fature* but before lunch, as you couldn't be sure that you would get someone after that. As Fuad didn't drive, Martha used the opportunity to test her nerves on the Khartoum roads. Unfortunately, she had to take Help's only right-hand drive vehicle, the thought of which made her more than a bit nervous in case she ended up on the wrong side of the road. Molly had laughed when Martha had asked her why they drove on the right in Sudan when it was a former British colony.

"I asked the same question and the only answer I ever got was that when Sudan got its independence, they decided to get rid of everything British. So, the government declared that, as from Monday, all trucks will drive on the right, as from Tuesday all trucks and buses will drive on the right and as from Wednesday, all vehicles will drive on the right."

"Ah, that explains the mad driving here then!" Martha chortled.

"Oh yes, and you wait until Ramadan when people are tired and hungry – it's like bumper cars on the roads."

Fuad was Help's only office employee from northern Sudan. He was older than the other staff and he was one of nature's gentlemen. He was a calm passenger and navigator, and Martha was surprisingly at ease as they made their way through the city. They arrived at a rundown concrete building that served as the offices of the Ministry of Foreign Affairs. It had definitely seen better days and looked as if nothing had been done to it since it was first built some forty years previously. The chairs and desks were in an equally sorry state.

There were long, noisy queues at every desk, or so Martha thought, until Fuad directed her over to a desk with nobody in front of it.

"Separate queue for ladies."

A man with a white shirt sat behind the desk busying himself shuffling paper.

"*Salaam alaykum,*" he said as he looked up and directed Martha and Fuad towards the chairs in front of his desk.

"*Alaykum salaam,*" Martha and Fuad chorused.

Fuad introduced them and the conversation proceeded in English; forms were filled, signed and dated; passport and paperwork were checked and double-checked; Martha's licence to take photographs was issued, permitting her to take photos of just her friends and family, nothing more; records were made in a large book; money was paid; a receipt was given for less than the money paid. Then, without comment, the man picked up the forms and passport and disappeared for twenty minutes.

As they sat waiting Martha considered the date: 24 December 1989. Christmas Eve. It didn't feel like Christmas Eve. Nobody had mentioned it other than when Molly and Martha had planned the meal for Christmas Day. Otherwise it was business as usual in Sudan.

When the man returned, he gave Martha back her passport and told Fuad to come back in a week for the permits.

"I will go back in a week, but always it will be another week and always more Sudanese pounds," Fuad said as they headed towards the car.

"It's a complicated country," Martha responded. "But then again, aren't they all?" she added as she thought of some of the shenanigans back home in Ireland.

Later that afternoon, with the ambulance loaded up with blankets, Martha and Molly headed off with Armad, a Help driver, to the leper settlement out beyond the city. They drove through the narrow sandy streets and on through Khartoum's shanty settlements with their tent-like structures made of sticks, grass, hemp sacks and plastic bags. After that they drove across miles of almost empty desert. How Armad knew where to go was beyond Martha as she couldn't see anything but a sea of sand. She assumed that the leper settlement was out in the middle of nowhere to prevent the spread of the disease.

"I've heard of 'leper colonies' and 'being treated like a leper' but other than that I know nothing about leprosy," Martha said sheepishly.

"You mean is there a risk that you'll catch it and have to live on an island in the middle of nowhere for the rest of your days?" Molly teased.

"Well…you know."

"Don't worry. Leprosy is one of the least infectious diseases. Most people working or living with people with leprosy never get it. More importantly, the people at the settlement have all been treated and are no longer infectious."

"Really? But why then are they still kept out in the middle of the desert?"

"Good old-fashioned superstition, I think. People have leprosy for years before they know it. They basically don't feel pain in their extremities and as a result they lose parts of their arms or legs. And when this happens it is known that they have the disease and they are ostracised."

After a few miles driving across the desert, there appeared a small, orderly village of mud houses which, Molly explained, was where the people with leprosy had been settled over many years. The charity which ran the settlement knew that Help had a store of blankets left over from the time of the famine and had asked them to distribute them. Molly had taken a large batch the previous week but had run out, so she had given out stamped and signed vouchers to those who didn't get one, and those people were to be the first to receive one this week.

As soon as the ambulance pulled up a crowd gathered and an air of excitement prevailed as a disorganised queue formed. Martha had expected to be overwhelmed by the tragedy of the place and its damaged people but was surprised when she found herself enjoying a sort of wordless banter with them. Despite the disorder of the queue, there was no aggression between anyone – no shoving or pushing – and they all seemed to respect one another's space, smiling and laughing easily. Not speaking Arabic proved not to be a problem and Martha handed out the blankets and interacted comfortably with the people. A smile seemed to be sufficient common language; each blanket handed out was met with words of gratitude and a smile. A man missing one hand above the wrist and one leg from just below his knee pointed at a blanket and handed her a tightly folded piece of paper. Martha opened the piece of paper and it had nothing more than a few random scribbles on it. It was not a voucher. Martha handed the slip of paper to Molly who looked at the man with a gentle smile and shook her head.

"*La, la.* No blanket," she said.

Martha felt uncomfortable at not giving this poor man one blanket and observed him to see what his reaction would be. He burst into laughter and beamed at her with a warm, one-tooth smile. Martha instantly relaxed and smiled and laughed too. She was struck by how strangely happy she felt interacting with these wonderful people, people who were visibly damaged by leprosy and were stuck living in the middle of the desert, with no resources of their own. She marvelled at the joy they exuded when they had so little. *Could it be that the more we have, the more miserable we are?* Not for the first time since coming to Sudan, she wondered had we, who had so much, forgotten that all we needed was enough?

By the time they finished the blanket distribution it was getting dark. As she sat in the ambulance she thought to herself that giving out blankets was the perfect thing to do on Christmas Eve. In fact, it was the most Christmas-spirited thing she had ever done on Christmas Eve. She wondered at how messed up Christmas at home had become. All the presents and the more than ample food, not to mention how much was wasted and thrown away at the end of it all. Those leftovers could feed these people for weeks, and how much more grateful they'd be for it too.

Armad drove them back across the desert through the refugee settlements and into a dense maze of narrow streets. Without warning, beside a row of small houses, he stopped the ambulance and got out.

"Good night. Happy Christmas," he said nonchalantly as he handed Molly the keys and disappeared down a narrow side street, long before she had time to respond.

"Well, I guess we'd better find our own way home then," Molly said looking after him. "It's Christmas and Armad is a southern Christian so I suppose he wants to get back to his family."

Molly moved across to the driver's seat and started the vehicle. "The only problem is that I haven't a clue where we are. I don't know this part of Khartoum at all!"

Martha said nothing, biting her lip with fear as they made a number of false starts down endless narrow alleyways between houses. They may have gone down the same alleyways a number of times; they all looked the same in the dark. Finally, they found their way to a main road and from there onto a wider road that Molly thought she recognised. Even on the wider roads it was pitch dark as there were no street lights. Here and there Martha could make out small groups of men, some standing around and some sitting on their hunkers in tight circles. Molly drove tentatively along trying to work out which direction she should take. Martha held her hands tightly on her lap and stared straight ahead. It was getting late. It would be curfew soon. How were they going to find their way home on time?

Bang! Molly's side of the pickup had hit something making them both jump. A half-stumbling child appeared in front of the vehicle. Molly braked. The child ran on across the road and disappeared. Molly stalled the pickup. She tried to restart it but stalled again.

"That was close," she said in a shaky voice, pausing before trying to again restart the vehicle.

In that moment the vehicle was surrounded by a large group of men, some carrying guns, two of which were pointing at them. A man in khakis directed them with the point of his rifle to pull over to the side of the road. Two more men appeared carrying the probably injured child, whom Martha reckoned was no more than eight years old. They were swinging him by his arms and legs. If he had been injured in the accident, he wasn't going to be the better of being dangled like that! Molly was pulled out of the pickup while Martha watched, speechless. Martha instinctively reached for the car keys but one of the men stopped her, hitting the back of her hand on the knuckles with his gun. He then reached in and snatched the keys. Martha gasped and sat back in her seat, watching and listening. There were various exchanges in Arabic between Molly and the man with the rifle, none of which Martha understood other than the mention of police. Rifle-man was clearly in charge. Martha didn't fancy going to a Sudanese police station, she was sure they would have dirty, crammed, communal prisons and you'd be lucky if anyone would ever find out where you were. Molly was struggling to make herself understood but was doing her best with what Arabic she had. Martha was impressed with how assertive she was despite being surrounded now by ten men, four or more of whom were carrying guns, one of which was aimed at her. Molly pointed at the boy still being suspended in mid-air by one arm and one leg.

"*Rooh la bait,*" Molly said repeatedly. Rifle-man finally nodded in agreement.

Five men, including two with guns, piled into the back of the vehicle, dragging the boy in with them. As Molly got back into the driver's seat, she explained that they had agreed to go to the boy's house, *rooh la bait*. Rifle-man squeezed in between Martha and Molly in the front of the pickup, holding his gun pointing upwards between his legs. He directed Molly, relaying directions from the child through a mixture of Arabic, broken English and hand signals. Martha was praying silently but frantically. She regarded herself as an *à la carte* Christian and the God whom she prayed to seemed to work most of the time…at least in desperate situations. Having driven through a warren of houses and other buildings, they finally stopped outside a solid brick house. The door opened immediately. With much shouting and heaving, they all piled out and into the house. They followed the man who opened the door, chatting noisily as they went through a hall with electric lighting and a large freezer, into a well-lit bedroom with two single beds. The child was dumped unceremoniously onto one bed. This was the first 'proper' house she'd visited in Sudan, Martha realised as she stood with her back to the bedroom wall observing everything. *It is not a mud house and it has electricity! These people are rich!*

Men and women appeared from nowhere and crowded into the room, all swarming around the silent, wide-eyed child, and chattering endlessly in noisy Arabic. It reminded Martha of a country wake except that the body was bewildered and still breathing. By some miracle, Molly and Martha had both spotted a large green cross and the word 'Medicin' on a sign on a building across the street and Molly suggested that a doctor be called. Martha pressed her back tight to the bedroom wall, willing herself to disappear. She continued to pray silently and determinedly. After some time, a doctor appeared with a stethoscope around his neck, carrying a small dark bag. He checked the boy from head to toe as Martha, and she imagined Molly too, held their breath. The doctor revealed not a single cut or bruise on the child's sallow skin. Another strange miracle. Martha had never before seen a young boy of his age who hadn't at least a couple of bruises or cuts. It was bizarre and unbelievable – given normal childhood activities – even more so given the thump with which he had hit the vehicle.

The child was declared well. Martha sensed a certain disappointment in the crowd as they started to disperse. She mumbled *Al Hamdillallah* quietly to herself, thinking that was it, sorted, situation over, time to find their way home. But the men who had travelled in the pickup led Molly and Martha back out to it and piled in, guns and all. Over the next half hour, they directed Molly to drive each of them to wherever they wished to be left. Molly could hardly argue with them but she and Martha needed to get home before curfew.

Martha sat in the front passenger seat feeling Rifle-man's leg press tight against her own trembling leg. She clasped her hand around it to try to stop it shaking and moved as tight to the passenger door as possible, turning her head to face out the window. She sensed a certain sexual energy emanating from Rifle-man. It unsettled her. This man couldn't sit in a private car beside a Sudanese woman who wasn't directly related to him but somehow it was okay for him to sit with his leg pressed against her, a *Khawaji*, a white woman.

By the time the last man got out of the pickup, Molly was well and truly lost again and it was 11:20 p.m., twenty minutes after curfew. Martha reckoned they would need The Third Miracle of Khartoum not to land themselves in prison after all. At every turn they expected to come to an army roadblock where they could be stopped, be found not to have a curfew pass and be taken straight to jail. It was a full hour later that they arrived outside their flats. In all that time they did not encounter another man in a uniform and, to their relief, not a single roadblock.

They walked into Molly's flat mystified, hungry and exhausted. Shelley was there helping herself to some food.

"We got delayed because we got lost, a child ran across in front of the pickup," Molly blurted out. "It took forever to sort it all out. We thought that we were going to get arrested for injuring the boy but luckily, he was okay. Then we got lost again and then we thought that we would get arrested anyway because we'd missed curfew."

"Sure, we heard two hours ago that curfew is lifted for Christmas Eve. There's a party at Famine Action. Siobhán and the others have gone already and I'm off now. You guys can follow," Shelley said as she walked out the door.

Shelley may as well have said, *Who cares, not my problem. Feck off. Get over it.*

Martha went from relieved to furious. Relieved to be home but furious that Shelley, Head of Mission, didn't give a rat's arse about them and their terrifying ordeal. In Martha's head she told Shelley exactly what she thought of her and what she said wasn't pretty. If Shelley thought that Martha was going to put on her glad rags and head to an effing party to wear an insincere smile, then Shelley could go and take a flying jump.

"Well!" Molly looked from the door that Shelley had exited to Martha.

"Well nothing. I am not going anywhere. Thank you," Martha said emphatically, trying to temper her tone as she spoke, lest Molly think that she was cross with her.

"Me neither. I'm wrecked. Let's break into the Christmas goodies so. We deserve it."

They dug into some Christmas cake, crisps and chocolate, accompanied by a welcome cup of tea.

"You can't beat a cup of Irish tea, especially at times like this," Molly said, and that was the last reference she made to the trials of the evening they'd had.

Martha soon nodded off on the couch and was woken by Molly who suggested she might like to head to bed. They said their good nights, forgetting it was Christmas and Martha made her way to the peace of her own flat next door.

Martha moved about her flat with tear-filled eyes as wave after wave of loneliness washed over her. She wouldn't let herself cry alone and with no hope of comfort. She longed to talk to one of her friends, Mrs Connolly or Trish especially. She would have loved Patrick's counsel, and yearned for a long hug reassuring her that all would be well. She needed to hear any familiar sympathetic voice, even down a telephone line would have helped. But the only way to call home was from the Acropole Hotel which wasn't going to be possible at that hour on Christmas morning. She had spoken to Patrick from there once, briefly, to let him know that she had arrived safely. He had said that he was fine, busy of course, no news. A tall dark horse was her boyfriend and a man of few words.

She lay down on her bed to sleep, certain that exhaustion would get the better of her, but an hour later her mind was still churning. What if they had been imprisoned? How would anyone have known where they were? What if curfew hadn't been lifted? She got out of bed and took out the long letter she had been writing to Patrick, a bit each day so that he would know what she was experiencing. She had told him in her first letter that she had decided, instead of keeping a diary, she would write to him and when she got home the letters would be there for her as her diary. She had already sent the first with an aid worker going home for Christmas. She had filled him in on all her trials and tribulations, from the airport dollars and tampons incident to her concerns about foreign exchange. Now, she sat down and wrote four dense pages of her usual scrawl. Her hand could hardly keep up with her mind as the words poured onto the page and tears flowed down her face. She wrote about the sheer squalor that the refugees lived in; how little the people had, yet how they managed to smile; how grateful they were for the small things; how much she had enjoyed the people in the leprosy village. She smiled as she remembered it. She wrote about getting lost; the horror of the accident with the little boy; getting lost again; the fear of being arrested and imprisoned for breaching curfew; the fear that nobody would know where they were. She didn't stop until she had written a good rant about how Shelley didn't fecking care what had happened to them and was only interested in getting to a bloody party. Her sense of gloom lifted slightly. She reminded herself that she was okay, she had enough, in fact she had plenty. She would probably never be truly cold or hungry; she had always taken that for granted until she came to Sudan. When she finished writing, she closed her eyes and imagined Patrick staying over at his family's house on Christmas Eve, as he always did, being fussed and clucked over by his doting mother. *Are you alright, dear? Would you like another drink? Did you have enough to eat?* Sure, he wouldn't be thinking of her feeling lonely, lying on a narrow bed in a dreary room in Khartoum...And why should he be?

Chapter 5

Christmas Day

The trials of the previous day, combined with waking up in the soulless flat, gave Martha the feeling of a bad hangover without the drink. Not a Christmas decoration in sight and hot sunshine coming through the bedroom window. Hardly Christmas at all.

Could be worse, she thought, determined by power of mind to drag herself out of her manky mood. After yesterday's blanket distribution, who was she to complain? Cup of tea, toast and raspberry jam for breakfast. That will more than do. Thank you Siobhán's mam for the jam and thank you Abdul Halim for the sack of flour and yeast. Amazing how quickly one adjusts one's standards. Abdul Halim had been delighted to get Martha a sack of flour and some yeast to make bread but he hadn't seen any need to mention the little white maggots in the flour. Martha had spotted them only because they were alive and wiggling. Fortunately, she had managed to find a sieve at the back of one of the kitchen cupboards. She had sieved out the creatures and thrown them out of her bedroom window, wishing them well in the heat. The day before Christmas Eve she had made her second batch of bread and it had turned out quite well. The girls loved it. Martha felt reasonably confident making a batch of dough on Christmas morning as she had promised to have two fresh loaves for Christmas dinner. She cleared enough space on the narrow kitchen counter, sprinkled out some flour and turned the stiff dough out onto it. The mixing, kneading and folding were all gently therapeutic. Not for the first time in her life, she would knead and punch herself into a better frame of mind. Risen dough always put a smile on her face. It looked at her and said,

"You must have done something right!" She left the dough in the warm spare bedroom to prove while she prepared to eat her Christmas breakfast alone.

She toasted some of the older bread under the small grill, brewed some tea in a saucepan and laid a place for herself at the desk in her room. The flat had no dining area or dining table, only a low garden table surrounded by the dirty, dull garden furniture that served as the sitting-room suite. Martha sat down with her tea and toast and got engrossed in her book, *Veil, The Secret Wars of the CIA*. It was the second book that she had read by Woodward and Bernstein, and it was another gripping eye-opener on how the world is really run. It struck her how naïve and innocent she had been about the workings of the world and how various governments, especially the American government, secretly pull strings around the world. Their power stretched from Cuba to Iraq, to Israel and beyond. It made her wonder what ulterior motives were at play when charities such as USAID are established in countries like Sudan.

Martha checked on the bread, smiled at its pouty face, punched it down and then split it between two oiled baking tins. She put it in the oven and prayed that the gas cylinder would last as long as was needed. Then she went for a welcome shower.

As she was taking the bread out of the oven, there was a tap on the small hatch that connected her kitchen to the kitchen in Molly and Siobhán's flat. She put the bread down on the top of the cooker and opened the hatch.

Molly's head appeared. "Oh, it smells good."

Martha inhaled the yeasty bread herself and nodded with a smile. "Let it cool a bit and I'll give you some shortly."

"That would be lovely. My Christmas treat."

"And well deserved…and may I ask, what's the plan for the day?"

"Well, Áine and Judy arrived up from the west last night. You didn't get to meet them because they had gone out with Siobhán before we got back. Anyway, they are keen to go to the pool, have a swim and all that. Then we will come back and cook dinner at our leisure. How does all that sound?"

"Grand. Nothing like a bit of exercise, so that we can eat, drink and be merry, guilt free," Martha said with a smile that surprised her.

"Ah, before you get too excited about having an easy-going Christmas dinner, you should know that the bold Shelley has asked a number of extras, so those chickens and vegetables will have to stretch a long way."

"Forewarned is…what time are you planning on going to the pool?" *Fucking Shelley*, Martha thought.

"Soonish, I'll call for you."

An hour later, Molly, Siobhán, Áine and Judy called for Martha and they headed off to the Sudan Club. Molly insisted that Martha did the driving: she said that after yesterday's experience she needed a break. Siobhán asked what happened and Molly gave them an edited version of events.

"Wow," said Siobhán, "scary stuff. I know why you need a breather from driving all right. Wish I could help but I've never even sat behind the wheel of a car!"

They were not long at the Sudan Club before Martha, Áine and Judy jumped into the water. They had the pool to themselves and Martha swam up and down at speed in her duck-like way, her head above water, perched on her well-stretched neck. As she swam, she glanced at Molly and Siobhán, splayed out on sunbeds, chatting and laughing without a care in the world. She smiled as she thought to herself how friendly and welcoming they had been to her, and at how indulgent it seemed to be to spend Christmas day in glorious sunshine by the pool. She would be fooling herself if she said that she missed the hard work that was expected of her on Christmas Day at home and the general *bah humbug* atmosphere that prevailed there, despite the abundance of Christmas decorations that festooned their house for all the neighbours to see. Every Christmas for as long as she could remember she had been the one doing all the work: preparing the food; laying the table; cooking the food; cleaning up after the food. Occasionally, her father gave her a sneaky hand with the washing but her mother just stood around looking glamorous until too much Christmas drink got the better of her. Her siblings took their lead from their mother and treated Martha like the resident skivvy. Martha had never actually sat down to eat a Christmas dinner. Yes, she thought, even with the heat and the lack of decorations, there was a better chance of some proper Christmas cheer for her in Sudan than back home in Sligo. She loved that the Muslim security guard at the entrance, and the various waiters, had greeted them all warmly with "Happy Christmas!" Maybe she would learn when the Muslim festivals were and give them the appropriate greetings then.

She continued swimming up and down, mostly oblivious to the others around her. Patrick would be at home in bed in his mother's house with a few more hours to go before it would be time to get up and have a home-cooked breakfast. At some stage, either today or tomorrow, he would open the present she had left him. It was a set of four colourful fine bone china espresso coffee cups and saucers. He had bought himself a rare posh coffee maker and was really becoming quite a coffee connoisseur. She presumed that he had already opened the cheerful Christmas card that she had left but, then again, he might not have.

Before she left, he had given her three albums for her Walkman: Verdi's *Rigoletto*, a lively production of which they had enjoyed at The Gaiety Theatre; Bruce Springsteen's "Born in the USA", another favourite; and of course, U2's "The Joshua Tree". Patrick had never missed a U2 concert in Ireland and owned all their albums. He hadn't wrapped the tapes, arguing that they would only get opened by airport security anyway. He hadn't thought of a card either. The Bruce Springsteen and U2 albums brought fond memories of two great concerts for Martha. It was a good selection and each album was, in its own familiar way, uplifting and comforting. She thought of the poignancy of the songs on the Joshua Tree with a smile, "Where the Streets have No Name", "I Still Haven't Found What I'm Looking For", and "With or Without You". A good question, she thought. *With or without you, Patrick? I just don't know.*

Her thoughts were interrupted when Siobhán threw a ball into the pool and jumped in beside her.

"You staying here for the whole day?"

"Uh, Sorry, I was lost in my own world."

"Cheapest and the best place to go, Mam always says."

"Yes, yes it certainly is," Martha said, knowing that she had often been very glad to escape to her own little world.

Siobhán grabbed the ball and called Áine and Judy. "Come on d-o-n-k-e-y. Here, catch," she said as she threw the ball hard at Judy.

They continued playing and with some dubious throws from Siobhán, Judy was at 'e', when Molly let out a quiet whistle to attract their attention and pointed at her watch.

"Cooking time."

Siobhán threw the ball straight at Judy's head and it bounced off her forehead and out of the pool. Judy laughed.

"I'll get you," she said splashing water in Siobhán's direction.

"Judy is a donkey. Judy is a donkey," teased Siobhán as she climbed out of the pool laughing.

When they arrived back at the flats, there was no sign of Shelley or Liam. Catherine, who had also arrived the previous evening from the west and had stayed in their three-bedroom flat, said they hadn't yet appeared from their bedrooms.

The girls set about organising dinner. Molly took charge of arranging tables and chairs gathering them from around the three flats. Siobhán decorated the table with napkins and crackers that Martha had brought over from Head Office, along with gravy, cranberry sauce and plum pudding, all of which had been ordered by Molly. As the Sudanese chickens were tough as leather, Molly had boiled the three of them the previous night. Martha set about drying them and covering them with some salt, pepper and oil before finishing them in the hot oven. She parboiled the potatoes that Áine and Judy had peeled earlier and then dried them and tossed them in oil and seasoning and put them to roast in the oven in her flat. Between them they prepared some carrots, onions and some okra or ladies' fingers and cooked them on the gas hob.

Siobhán expressed delight that Abdul Halim had managed to get some mangoes and melons for them to have as starters and when these were arranged on plates around the table, it started to look quite colourful.

Eventually, Liam and Shelley appeared. Shelley walked in looking neat and immaculately presented, as always, but gone was Sister Shelley and by contrast Martha saw before her Sexy Shelley. She wore a low-cut sleeveless fitted short dress that showed off her large breasts, slim legs and beautiful figure and her hair was worn in a loose elegant bun. There was a touch of Audrey Hepburn in *Breakfast at Tiffany's* about the new Shelley. If Martha had been a man, she thought that she wouldn't have been able to resist a wolf whistle! Little Liam, in his pink shirt and smelling strongly of sweet after-shave, followed behind her like a willing lap dog, clearly in awe of his mistress. He produced eight bottles of Ethiopian gin, acquired through a contact of Dawit's, and Shelley produced a dozen bottles of tonic water that she had got on a credit card at Khartoum duty-free, a government-run shop that only accepted hard currency.

At around 6 p.m., others arrived and Molly briefed Martha in little asides in the kitchen as to who was who. There was Susannah, an English woman who was a lifelong expat with a British agency. *Her husband played off-side with another expat and was surprised when Susannah found this unacceptable; weren't they expats? Of course, he played off-side.* Then there was Shane and Elaine, a miserable Irish couple working in salaried positions in Dutch NGOs. Molly thought their families had probably encouraged them to leave Ireland and take their misery elsewhere. Lucky for Ireland, unlucky for Sudan. Christian and Hugo, a couple of French doctors working for Médicins Sans Frontieres. *Decent lads, genuine, either might make a good catch.* Lastly there was Stefan, an Austrian pilot who worked for a privately run company that flew small planes around Sudan, providing their services to both the government and to NGOs. *A bit sexy don't you think? I'm very fond of him and he's a bit of craic, he'd be a fine catch.* Martha discreetly peered out of the kitchen at Stefan and agreed that he was pretty hunky. He was tall, broad-shouldered and athletic with untidy wavy brown hair but it was his warm brown eyes and easy smile that Martha thought made him particularly attractive. *Wouldn't kick him out of bed for eating crisps,* she thought. It wasn't that she fancied him as such, she had Patrick at home of course. But Trish always said, "Just because you're on a diet, doesn't mean that you can't look at the menu!"

The atmosphere was cheerful and lively, and Martha and Molly were quite relaxed as they finished cooking and served to the increasingly noisy crew, who seemed to demolish the food as soon as it hit the table.

After dessert Martha found herself sitting beside Stefan. She was telling him about the accident with the boy and her other adventures of the previous day. She'd had a few gin and tonics, her first alcohol in a month, and, disturbingly, she found his large brown eyes very distracting as they gave her their undivided attention. He listened sympathetically, not seeming to mind when she repeated herself! She got on a roll and was about to blurt out her thoughts on Shelley's reaction to their late return but, spotting the said Sexy Shelley across the table, she stopped herself. Stefan then started to tell her a story of a fellow pilot getting stopped at a curfew checkpoint without a curfew pass. He was telling her that the guy had been pulled from his truck by a young pup in a uniform with a gun too big for him, when Shelley pulled up a chair between them. She turned her back on Martha, flung her now released long auburn hair over her shoulder, and hit Martha in the face with it. She then leaned in towards Stefan and put her hand on his knee, leaving it to linger there.

"So how are things in the flying world, Stefan?" she said loudly, in that plummy accent of hers.

With Shelley's biggest assets looming large in front of his eyes, Stefan looked as if he didn't know where to turn. He coughed and moved his chair back a bit and, as Martha turned to talk to Molly and Siobhán, she thought she saw him glance around to her, seeking her to rescue him.

Chapter 6

Post-Christmas

Molly was determined that Martha should get to know her way around the workings and idiosyncrasies of Sudanese bureaucracy before Molly herself had to head back to Ireland, so as decreed by Molly, Martha was dispatched, mainly with Fuad, her great saviour as Martha thought of him, to various government departments and ministries.

On one particular day Martha was using the general office computer to type up a letter, with Fuad's guidance. They were seeking to have a vehicle, needed by Help's team in the west, released by customs from Port Sudan where it had been stuck in limbo for months. The fear was that by the time the official paperwork was finalised, the vehicle would no longer be in Port Sudan but would have disappeared, having been commandeered for army or other use, as appeared to have happened to various agencies' vehicles over recent years.

As she was typing the letter there had been one of the many power cuts and there was a delay in getting the generator going. Finally, Martha heard through the open doorway to the yard a few loud coughs and a bang and the generator's engine chugged noisily into life, filling the office with the pungent smell of dirty oil as it spewed out thick smoke. Martha restarted the computer and went back to the letter. The computer was set to save every fifteen minutes in expectation of the power cuts but that was frustrating in itself as the slow computer meant that saving took a couple of minutes each time and so continuously interrupted the flow of Martha's work.

"Oh, the trials of Sudanese life, more feckin' paperwork and power cuts…" she sighed.

"Indeed! The bureaucracy in this country could drive you demented if you let it!" Molly responded.

"Don't I know?"

"Giving out won't get anything done, Martha," Shelley stated as she whizzed through the main office to go out the front door. "You'll have to adjust your expectations, as we all did."

"I'm doing my best," Martha mumbled defensively, mainly to herself, but within earshot of Molly.

"Don't worry. I know the feeling. The best advice that I was given when I came here is, if you have ten things on your list that you expect to get done in a day, and you get one done, be grateful. Follow the Sudanese IBM policy: *Inshallah, Bukhara, Mumbkin*. If it be the will of God, Tomorrow, Maybe!" Molly said smiling and putting an arm around Martha's shoulders.

"Thanks, Molly. You're right. That's probably just the advice I needed to hear. Slow down and you'll get there faster!" Martha said, putting her letter into an envelope for delivery in the hope of finally getting the clearance certificate for the vehicle. She didn't expect it would be another month before Fuad's and her efforts finally paid off and Siobhán's driver, Ahmed, would take a bus to Port Sudan to collect the pickup which, miraculously, was still there and in one piece. By the time it arrived in Khartoum, Martha was more in tune with the Sudanese IBM policy and she ran her hand along the side of the shiny new vehicle with a sense of victory against the odds.

The vehicle clearance was one in a long line of approvals and other red tape issues. Regular permissions had to be obtained to get diesel supplies for the Help vehicles. Then there were the Entry Visas that had to be chased for the new engineer for western Sudan, for the administrator and nurse who were coming to replace Molly and for a qualified mechanic who was seen as needed to keep existing vehicles safely on the road. The bureaucracy was endless and each authorisation or visa took many trips to various offices to get a piece of paper here, to bring it somewhere else, to get a stamp there...During their years of rule, when it came to tedious bureaucracy, the British had taught the Sudanese well.

As with Martha's experience on her first visit to the Foreign Ministry, it was normally more expedient for Molly or Martha, being white and women, to accompany Fuad to government offices and join the women's queues, which were always short or non-existent. Plus, Martha reckoned the Sudanese civil servants enjoyed seeing the white women, the *Khawaji,* sweat for their paperwork. Not to mention liking the few extra Sudanese pounds here or there.

New Year's Eve arrived and curfew was lifted until 3:00 a.m. A party was declared at the English charity Food for All, and all the Help volunteers went, including Martha and Molly. It was an easy affair with food, music and dancing. Molly used the opportunity to introduce Martha to her financial counterpart in Food for All, Jeremy, in case she wanted some help or guidance in dealing with the Sudanese government or with the funding agencies.

"Very pleased to meet you," Jeremy said, giving Martha a firm and long handshake.

"Good to meet you too," Martha said, gently releasing her hand and looking away from his uncomfortable, prolonged gaze.

"Sorry! Yes, Molly said that maybe…perhaps I could help you with some of the wonderful particulars of the Sudanese financial ways. I would be more than happy to be of assistance to you, anytime," Jeremy said, looking slightly dazed as his eyes moved up from her bare ankles, pausing at her waist and stopping to gaze into her eyes.

"Thank you. That would be great. I appreciate it," Martha said before turning to slowly walk away.

"Please, Martha, call over to my office anytime."

"I will definitely do that. Thank you."

Molly teased Martha later about how businesslike she was when chatting to Jeremy. It seemed perfectly clear to her that Jeremy was making a pass at Martha.

"Come over to my office anytime you like, Martha, I'll be jolly happy to help, any way I can," Molly teased, fluttering her eyelids. Siobhán laughed as Martha protested and went bright red.

On New Year's morning Martha got up before curfew was lifted and drove Judy, Áine and Catherine to the airport to get a flight to Wadi Dabor in western Sudan. They passed through the checkpoint with their curfew pass barely being glanced at.

Not alone was Sudan's main airline joked about amongst the expats for its perceived lack of attention to maintenance, but Judy told Martha that the Fokker 50 planes were commonly referred to as vomit comets.

"A flight in a Fokker in this climate is often like a roller-coaster ride; it's as if it rides up on a pocket of hot air, hits colder air and drops down in one fell swoop, leaving your stomach hanging somewhere in the middle…then the puking starts. And you know how contagious that is!"

For all these reasons, Judy, Áine and Catherine were not looking forward to their flight and wished it over, but first they had to face the usual queues and chaos at the airport. It was a couple of hours before they were called to board and Martha could go back to the office knowing that the plane had actually taken off.

Martha was back at the airport a week later collecting Simon, the new engineer for the hospital in the west. A tall, thin young man walked out of arrivals wearing large glasses and an intense expression. On the brief journey from the airport to the flat he sat jittering his knee up and down and asked endless questions about Help in Sudan and then, more specifically, about the operations in the west.

"Simon, I'm afraid to say that, as yet, I have virtually no knowledge of operations in the west as, unfortunately, neither Liam nor Shelley have told me anything about the projects. All I know is that Help is renovating a hospital and has two health clinics there but that is the extent of it. Sorry." She was being defensive thinking she should of course have asked Judy, Áine or Catherine about the projects, but because they were all in Christmas mode at the time of their visit, she hadn't felt right about asking them. The west sounded like a tough station, and they deserved their break.

"I'll ask Liam or Shelley about it so," Simon said.

"Please do. And I hope you'll have more luck than I did!" Martha said remembering the last time she asked Shelley about the west. *When you need to know, Martha, I will tell you. In the meantime, patience is a virtue!*

At the office, Liam continued to bury himself preparing reports for the funding agencies, and throughout the coming weeks he consistently refused Martha's offers of help, or to even allow her any involvement so that she might get to know her way around the books and records and learn what reports were required.

"I'm going to the bank now. Are you coming?" he said – apparently to her – one day without any warning.

Martha looked behind her to see if he was actually addressing her. "Sure," she answered, following him out the office door.

"Well, I'll be finishing up here soon so you'd better start to get to know a few people, don't you think?" he said as he trotted along.

"Absolutely," Martha said, thinking about fecking time. "How often do you go to the bank so?"

"Oh, about once a fortnight or more, mostly to draw out money to pay the endless cash expenses and wages."

Liam drove like a lunatic, overtaking other vehicles on short stretches of road, throwing the vehicle around corners and speeding up to the rear of vehicles in front. He always chose to drive the Land Rover whenever possible. Behind its large steering wheel, he was a boy who had borrowed his father's car and it took all the strength of his puny arms to turn the heavy vehicle. Martha considered his driving and his choice of vehicle all part of his small-man syndrome. Trish would have been a bit crueller and said that a small man driving a big car is compensating for what he hasn't got between his legs. Either way, Martha was relieved when he finally pulled up outside the modern five-storey building. She followed him up to the first floor where there were a number of bank clerks behind desks, in front of which were long, slow-moving queues of men in lose turbans and white *jallabiyahs*. As they headed across the room to join a queue, the bank manager, another Ahmed Mohammed, spotted Liam and Martha and ushered them over to him, and then through a door into his immaculate, bright, air-conditioned office.

"Ahmed Mohammed, and you must be the new finance person. Good to meet you," he said holding out his hand.

"Martha Hyland," Martha responded, shaking his hand with a smile. "Pleased to meet you too."

After some small talk, Ahmed offered them some coffee and an elegant lady in a smart suit appeared and served them spicy Sudanese coffee and sweet biscuits. Being in the bank was like being dropped into a bit of modern Europe, with the exceptions of the queues of *jallabiyahed* and turbaned men, and the mountains of paper money that seemed to be involved in the most mundane transactions.

Ahmed brought the thirty thousand Sudanese pounds into his office with the help of the elegant lady, who was not introduced. It took two runs each as they presented the money piled high on four trays. You would be a long time robbing some decent money from a Sudanese bank, Martha thought, given the sheer volume of it.

The money which only equated to six thousand, six hundred and sixty-six dollars, was piled into Liam's large holdall. At the enforced exchange rate, Help was being cleaned out by the government. The true international market rate, if it was possible to establish it, given the unstable political environment, was possibly ten to fifteen times the government rate but despite this, the IMF had failed to get the Sudanese government to shift from its miserable fixed rate. What remained more sickening to Martha was that the fixed exchange rate was effectively providing an excessive amount of dollars to the government which, in turn, gave them hard currency to finance the continuing war with the south. Martha's dilemma from when she arrived in Sudan remained: the aid agencies were needed in Sudan largely because of the war in the south; the war in the south meant that millions of people from there had been displaced because of fear of bombings, because they couldn't farm because of landmines, because women – their husbands and sons, by choice or otherwise, gone to war – couldn't see how they had any chance of surviving unless they trudged with their children some thirteen hundred miles to the refugee settlements in Khartoum. Between them, the aid agencies brought millions of dollars into Sudan to improve the economic and health situation but significantly to keep the people in these settlements alive; the dollar amount brought in could be many times less if it was exchanged at a proper floating rate; the difference between the two rates of exchange, Martha argued, helped to finance the war. Was it the aid agencies, by default, therefore, who financed the war and kept the country in upheaval and themselves in business?

Looking at the size of the holdall with the thirty thousand Sudanese dollars in it hanging on Liam's puny shoulders, Martha almost offered to carry it into the office for him. There Dawit made up the wages for the forty odd local staff at head office and the health centres. He also made up the weekly expat volunteer allowances. With the exchange rate dilemma still sitting heavily on her, Martha wondered how he and the other staff felt about the expat allowances being three or four times the local staff average wages.

Chapter 7

After Christmas Post

Before Christmas Martha had sent home her first long, rambling letter to Patrick and some much shorter letters to her friends and her mother. After Christmas, she had sent Patrick another long letter with another expat going home. Most of the second letter had been written on Christmas Eve night when Martha was particularly tired and emotional following the traumatic escapade of getting lost and then nearly arrested after knocking down the little boy. Before she sent it, she realised that she'd been more expressive and emotional in it than she ever had been when she was face to face with Patrick. She'd nearly ripped up the offending pages, thinking Patrick wouldn't want to hear all that stuff.

A week into the New Year, post arrived for the Help volunteers with two Irish UNHCR staff returning from home leave.

Four envelopes arrived for Martha, her first post in Sudan. The main envelope contained a bundle of letters from the office.

Philip, her immediate boss, wrote:

Not much news here. The Basil Fawlty project [as Martha used to refer to the hotel project that she had been working on] *finished up in early December and many of your recommendations are being implemented. We have negotiated an additional fee payment in six months' time assuming that your recommendations pay the anticipated dividends. I will be earmarking a portion of it as a bonus for you when you come back next year.*

Matilda Jane [his pet name for his secretary, Jane] *has announced that she is getting married the summer after next to Marvellous Martin. She said to tell you that you had better be home for the wedding to say a few words or I might*

feel tempted to make a speech and give away a few of her best-kept secrets that
everyone except Martin already knows.

Hope you are keeping well and not finding the heat, the sand and the lack of
technology too much.

Martha had a few light laughs reading Philip's letter and she realised that
she had caught her habit of giving pet names to people from him. He was a
good soul. And a great boss.

Trish (Patricia) wrote a long and newsy letter.

"You won't believe the goings-on at the Christmas party...Áine got a bit pissed
and went and sat on Ian's knee. Ian was clearly uncomfortable even though we
all know that he has been mad about her for forever. She started to tell him, at
the top of her voice, that she had been in love with him for months (none of us
knew that!). She had decided to have a few drinks so that she would finally be
brave enough to tell him straight to his face! With that, she then fell clean off his
knee, or he dropped her with shock, I'm not sure which, even though I was sitting
at the table witnessing the whole thing! I nearly broke my sides laughing but I
really tried to hide it and so I let out a big loud snort – you know the sort! Ian
turned and gave me, what was by his standards, a filthy look and immediately
bent down and picked Áine up off the floor and carried her, like a gallant prince,
out the restaurant door. It was hilarious. Páidí, the sneaky git, who had been
watching all along, had to hold me back from going after them. I told him that
he spoilt my fun so he better dance with me there and then to make up for it. "My
pleasure," he said and I can tell you it was my pleasure too 'cos I made him dance
up close and personal to "Yes sir I can boogie"! And, as they say, the rest is history!
Except it's not just history. We are still boogying. Now, Sunshine, what do you
make of that...Jeeze, I really miss you and wish you were here. Páidí sends his
love too..."

Well, well, thought Martha, *Páidí and Patricia, that's brilliant. I'm sorry to*
miss that. She felt a heart-wrenching pang of homesickness but swallowed
hard and read the rest of Trish's newsy letter. She wanted to write straight
back to her. Trish always made her smile.

The other letters from friends and colleagues were short and added nothing much in terms of news. They pretty much showed that office life went
on much the same without her. There was the odd quibble that the manager

who had taken over from her wasn't as nice or efficient and other niceties like that. Martha allowed herself to feel a bit chuffed.

After the office letters, Martha turned her attention, with trepidation, to the envelope with her name written clearly in her brother's heavy handwriting. For a brief moment she dared to hope that it would be a letter of reconciliation, a change of heart sparked by her sudden departure for Africa.

Martha,

Have you any idea how difficult it is for us to cope with Mother since you skedaddled off to Africa? We are all having to take it in turns to visit her and even at times cook her meals. As you well know Jennifer and I have our own family and work commitments and of course, Robyn's career is at a crucially busy stage for her. Margaret is also up to her tonsils. How selfish and mean-spirited can you be to run off to Africa and leave us in the lurch? We all agree that we don't know what you got from all that therapy. It certainly wasn't a sense of duty but more likely selfishness.

You knew that our little family was heading off to Renvale House for a much-needed quiet Christmas and you couldn't even wait until after that. No, you had to go when it suited that bloody charity. Well I'll have you know that we got no peace in Renvale House because Mother was hardly off the phone to the place the whole time that we were there. We were sorry that we hadn't brought her with us. It might have been less stressful.

Robyn and Mathew went up to Sligo for Christmas Day and took her out to The Sligo Park for Christmas dinner but she said that she would have preferred to have Christmas at home as she has always done. She had expected you to be there to cook it.

Robyn, Margaret and I have been talking by phone this week and we all decided that you should come home as soon as possible and take care of Mother. You are the one with the least commitments and therefore the most available. It is not as though there is much to keep you in Sudan.

Please let me know by return when you intend to come home.

Your brother,

Jim

Martha's hands shook as she read the letter. Sweat poured down her back. Her chest tightened. She physically shrank as she pulled her knees up to her chest and rocked in her chair.

"No, no," she said in a loud whisper forcing herself to sit up straight and lower her feet to the floor. *I am not going back. I deserve a life too. I do.*

For the last three years, since their father died, she alone had gone home once a month, cleaned the house and cooked the meals. She had worked morning to night to leave everything sorted for their mother, not just her mother, *their* mother. All the time, not one of them lifted a finger. She had not been greeted with a welcome hug or waved goodbye with a warm thank you. In between times, since her mother's stroke two years ago, carers looked in on her each day. Her siblings had swanned in briefly every few months. But weren't they great? They worked so hard, they had wonderful children who kept them oh so busy, what with the football, the swimming, the ballet and the drama…They had such demanding jobs and big mortgages…In between cleaning and cooking, that is what Martha had listened to all weekend, every weekend that she went home. Home? How could she call it home? Home is where the heart is.

Oh, the carers were supposed to cook and do a bit of cleaning too, but nothing they did was good enough for Mrs Hyland. She had flat-out refused to eat anything but biscuits and cake for a week when Martha took ill and hadn't made it down to restock the freezer.

There were times on those weekends that Martha had wanted to scream, *I've got a demanding career too! I've got a life. Actually, I've even got a boyfriend, son of a High Court Judge, doing very well in one of the leading law firms himself, fast track to partner, they say. Thank you very much. Right up your snobby street, Mother. Wouldn't you love to tell the neighbours that your daughter is going out with a High Court Judge's son?*

But Martha didn't say any of this to her mother or her siblings. What was the point?

She had tried. She had gone to counselling and, emboldened by the counsellor, had tried talking to each of her siblings and her mother in turn.

Jim had sneered at her, "Poor Martha, always the victim. That's one hell of a distorted version of what happened. Did they put you on anti-depressants? God, you'll drive us all to them. Do you think I've time for this stuff?"

Martha then approached Robyn and she responded in Robyn fashion. "Oh, I'm sorry that you feel that way. Sure, we were only kids. I don't remember much of it. I am sure that we were all treated the same. Maybe you should, you know, put the past behind you."

By the time Martha spoke to Margaret she said pretty much what Jim had said but adding, "Build a bridge and get over it, Martha. For God's sake, we all have problems. I am so busy at work trying to pay the mortgage that I've no time to think about the past, never mind analyse it."

Her Mother's response was predictable. "After all I did for you...Didn't we send you to boarding school? We gave you everything you ever needed. Have you any idea of the childhood I had? You think you had it tough..."

Maybe her mother had a point. She had let her go to boarding school where she had been free to get on with her studies and work out a career path for herself with the help of the school Career Guidance Counsellor and part-time Boarding House Mistress, Mrs Connolly.

Mrs Connolly was on duty when, a few months after starting boarding school, Martha got into a fight with another boarder. She didn't remember what it was about, but she did remember that the other girl, Mary, had raised her fists and said provocatively, "Okay then, do you want to fight?" and then issued a few jabs in Martha's direction. Martha stared briefly at her before throwing a decisive right punch. To her horror Mary fell to the ground and stretched out in front of her. Martha stood looking at Mary, thinking, *That's it, I'll be kicked out of here before I can count to ten.* But Mary stood up, nodded at her and walked away. A watching boarding prefect had reported the incident. Mrs Connolly had found Martha and asked her if she would like to come down and talk to her in the quiet sick bay room after study. She sat Martha down opposite her and calmly asked her what had happened. She waited silently for Martha's answers, nodding encouragingly. In talking to Mrs Connolly Martha slowly realised why she had reacted the way that she had. Boarding school was her escape from her brother's and sisters' jabs. She needed that escape.

"I know that I shouldn't have hit Mary. I'm really very sorry," Martha said between sobs. "Will...will I be expelled?"

"No, Martha, I think that this one incident doesn't need to go any further. I don't think that you're likely to become the school boxer or bully or anything. Do you?"

Martha half-smiled and shook her head.

Mrs Connolly said perhaps they would make time to have little chats now and again; sometimes these chats were prompted by some incident or other but more often than not, Mrs Connolly called Martha into sick bay, "Just to see how you are and how things are going."

It was Mrs Connolly whom Martha had told, years later, about her recurrent nightmares. One was that she was in her mother's kitchen trying to clean it while everyone in the family kept coming in and deliberately spilling something on the counter or the floor, or anywhere, and so she couldn't get the job done. Another was that the family had all gone to Bundoran on a picnic for the day and Martha was left to pick up the picnic things from the beach and bring them to the car. When she got there, she saw the family in the car driving off, waving and smiling at her as they went. She woke up each time to the sound of her mother, sisters and brother cackling at her.

Mrs Connolly's response was, "Always ask yourself, what is the worst thing that can happen, then remember, Martha, that given everything you have faced in life already, you can probably face it. Love yourself and believe in yourself."

Martha had the idea that she would like to work with people when she finished school and, with Mrs Connolly in her role as the school's Career Guidance Counsellor, she had researched various careers including teaching, occupational therapy and psychology. She decided she would like to study psychology on the basis that it would allow her to develop one of her favourite pastimes, people watching and trying to work out what made them behave the way they did. When the time came to apply to university, she had to tell her mother her plans as she needed the CAO application fee.

"You become a psychologist? Don't make me laugh. If you became a psychologist there would be a marked increase in the number of suicides!" her mother sneered, rolling her eyes to heaven.

"What makes you think that we will pay for you to go to university? Haven't we already forked out for you to go to boarding school? Well, we won't be forking out for university too…" she ranted.

It was like a slap in the face and Martha stood momentarily in shock. When she felt the tears well up, she ran out of the room and out of the house, into a corner of the back garden where she broke into uncontrollable, but barely audible, sobs. For years she had tried not to cry at all when her mother or siblings inflicted some physical or emotional stinging pain, but she seemed pre-programmed to cry and could not stop herself; the best she ever managed was the ability to cry almost silently.

Eventually she calmed herself as she always did, and the involuntary heaving turned to hiccups. Boarding school had been her saviour. Her mother continuously reminded her of her good fortune, as if Martha's school fees had somehow deprived her mother of another new car, another holiday abroad or various designer outfits that she might otherwise have bought.

Martha had seen no point in talking to her father. He was always kind to her when he was around, but his life had revolved around work, rugby and golf. He had rarely been at home as there was plenty of drinking and socialising thrown into the work and sports mix, sometimes with her mother, sometimes not. Her mother had thrived as Queen Socialite, married to the local bank manager and sometime Golf Club Captain.

Mrs Connolly didn't seem entirely surprised when Martha said that, after talking to her mother, she had changed her mind about studying psychology. Martha kept her head down and looked at her hands as she said that university wasn't really for her, and it would be better to go straight to work and earn money.

For a few moments, Mrs Connolly simply sat at her desk and looked at Martha, bowing her head slowly as she processed Martha's words. As Martha watched she felt the colour rising high in her hot cheeks.

"Well I suppose we'd better see what other possibilities may exist for your talents," Mrs Connolly said kindly after what seemed like a long pause.

She then looked over Martha's school reports and noted that she shone in a number of areas but particularly business and accounting. Perhaps, she suggested, Martha should consider accountancy. They made a hit list of about fifteen medium-sized firms that took direct entries and Martha applied to each of them. Mrs Connolly then gave Martha a number of increasingly gruelling practice interviews, followed by two with parents from the school who worked as accountants. She had gradually started to get her nerves under control and had learnt how to sell herself at an interview as if she was not only competent, but also a confident young woman.

In the end, she was offered no less than eight traineeships. *Thank goodness for Mrs Connolly, where would I be without her?* Martha thought. *I can't believe I didn't talk to her before I thought of heading off here.*

Martha had enjoyed rapid promotion at her firm, at times even ahead of those who had come in at the same time as her with business degrees under their belts. She was willing and able to get on with whatever challenges were put her way.

Martha reread the letter from her brother. How little they knew her and would ever know her. There was no point in trying. She systematically ripped the letter up into tiny pieces wishing for its author and its sentiments to disappear out of her life, preferably forever.

Then a wave of guilt hit her.

With Martha away, her mother would not be getting the home-cooked meals that she was used to. The others were unlikely to visit too often and anything could happen. It would be Martha's fault if her mother deteriorated further through neglect. What should she do? She didn't want to go back. The thought of it made her feel like a small mouse who had been trapped in a tiny cage. One minute she had been on a treadmill, then the cage door had opened and she escaped. Now the door was open again and she was looking in at the same treadmill. She checked herself, aware of the danger of being drawn back to the familiarity of the treadmill, away from the perils of the wider world. She resolved to face the new perils.

She turned to the letter from Mrs Connolly, whom she had written to before Christmas. They had become firm friends after Martha had left school and were no longer restricted by the school guidance counsellor/housemistress–student relationship. Martha had filled Mrs Connolly in fully on her home situation and it was Mrs Connolly who had encouraged her to seek help to empower her to move on. Easier said than done. But some progress had been made. Mrs Connolly's letter was full of concern and encouragement, followed by paragraphs filled with delight at the successes and amusing misdemeanours of her four grandchildren.

...Going away from friends and family will at times be lonely but there is no better place to find your true self than away from people who think that they know you...Settling into the challenging world of Sudan will take time and effort and, based on what you said in your letter, the Sudanese and Sudan will be the least of it. But no better person than you to rise to the challenge. Think how brilliantly you got on at work. Embrace the time away. Feel free to be your beautiful self...I anticipate hearing more tales of your many adventures, perhaps I'll even include some of them in my grandchildren's story time. They keep asking for you and say that you are their favourite babysitter...

The letter lightened Martha's dark mood.

She held the last remaining envelope, from Patrick, and uncertain of its content, she decided that she couldn't face another possible disappointment. She picked up her togs and towel and headed off for a swim, alone.

A couple of nights later she opened the envelope. Inside were two letters.

Dear Martha,
You won't believe it but a few days before Christmas I was at the best gig ever. It was David Byrne of Talking Heads and it was amazing. It was even better than the Bruce Springsteen concert we went to last summer. What a showman, the best. And of course, I love his lyrics too. He did some of the old Talking Heads numbers and his own recent stuff. You'd have loved it too.
Got your long letter. Thanks.
I stayed at Mother's for Christmas Eve and night. All the usual suspects were there, including Maria and Julie and their partners. Mother and the girls cooked a lovely dinner and I must admit spoiled me a bit..."

There followed a commentary on some new albums that he had bought and who he had been out with over Christmas. Mrs McCarthy, being a true Irish Mammy, worshipped the ground Patrick walked on and his two sisters played second fiddle by comparison. They were expected to help with the cooking and cleaning while Patrick was expected to sit and be waited on like Lord Muck! Patrick's mother had taken a conspicuous dislike to Martha.

"Oh, you are from Sligo. I think I was there once...oh, you didn't go to university...Patrick's last girlfriend, Emer, lovely girl, she did law, you know..."

All these comments were made with her rabbit nose twitching upwards as if Martha was a bad smell under it. She wished Patrick would give his mother a good dose of truth about the lovely Emer, how she was a bit fond of the drink and didn't always hold it well and that, on more than one occasion, she had played off-side. Patrick had only found this out when, one day when she was supposed to be away with work, he had called to her place to collect some of his things. To his tremendous horror, he had found her in bed recovering from an abortion she'd had in England. She had left him in no doubt that the baby wasn't his. He had been distraught. How could she be sure the baby wasn't his? How could she have had unprotected sex with various other men when he had been faithful to her all the time? She had laughed at him, laughed at his stupidity, called him a boy. And now that Martha thought about it again, she was surprised that Patrick had told her about the Emer situation at all. He had opened up late one night when he stumbled into her place after an office party. He needs to learn how to talk more, she thought. *But still, lovely Emer my eye; tragic drunken Emer more like.*

Patrick's letter made no mention of his kindly, quiet, unassuming, hen-pecked father, who Martha decided she would definitely ask after in her next letter.

Off to a U2 gig on New Year's Eve, should be good.
Bye for now
Love
Patrick
PS. Wrote this letter before New Year but missed getting it to the Help office to get it to you.

The second letter was in a similar vein.

Dear Martha,
The U2 gig on New Year's, would you believe, was even better than the David Byrne concert. Con and I had a great night. When the lights went down, just before midnight, we didn't know what was coming next but it was the tremendous sound like the ringing of bells, followed by their own version of a bit of Auld Lang Syne and then Bono broke into "Where the streets have no name",

then "I will follow" and then "I still haven't found what I'm looking for" which
was followed by a long list of great songs.
Needless to say that U2 all seemed quickly to be in the dim and distant past as
soon as I got back to work yesterday as it was straight back to the grindstone. No
rest for the wicked. Working flat out.
Not much else to report,
Love
Patrick

Martha read the two rather brief letters a second time in case she had missed anything. But she hadn't. Patrick hadn't once referred to her except by name after "Dear" and in reference to the Bruce concert. He hadn't once said that he missed her or even asked how she was, nor referred to anything in her first or second long letters. There she was pouring out her heart and soul to him and all she got was the best feckin' gig ever...and then an even better gig. Her first reaction was feck him, he can feck off with his bloody gigs. But after a couple of days she decided that she was being too hard on him. She was forgetting that he was still in Dublin with its gentle climate and familiar work environment where he could have no real concept of what it was like in scorching hot Sudan with its variable electricity and other limitations. And he was probably too busy to read her letters properly, never mind write her more extensive ones.

Chapter 8

School and Orphanage

In mid-January, Molly asked Martha if she would be brave enough to face another trip with her to the outskirts of Khartoum, this time to visit a school at a large established refugee settlement. It would be more fun than a blanket distribution, Molly promised, as they had shoe boxes filled with pencils, notebooks, crayons and colouring books from children in primary schools in Ireland to distribute. Despite everything, Martha could honestly say that she had enjoyed the blanket distribution so she was keen to visit a school.

The school, with its well-qualified southern Sudanese teacher, was considered a significant addition for the refugees. It went some way to making up for the education they might have received if they had not been displaced from their homes in the war-ridden south.

They arrived at a single-storey mud building with a metal door and wooden shutters. They had barely pulled up outside when the door was opened by a tall, smartly dressed man.

"Welcome, welcome. Good to see you again, Molly," he said with a smile that spread across his narrow face.

"This is John Paul," Molly said as she shook his hand warmly and introduced him to Martha.

Martha shook his hand and stared at his handsome face with its striking tribal imprints on each cheek.

John Paul held her gaze and smiled. Molly explained that they had boxes for his students. He turned and called into the classroom and three tall boys quickly appeared to help bring the boxes from the pickup to the teacher's desk at the front of the classroom. The students stood up from their bench-like, mud seats as they entered. John Paul counted up the boxes and, when he was happy there was more than enough for each of the forty-eight children in his class, he got them to line up around the room to receive them. Martha loved how they could hardly contain themselves with excitement and each time John Paul calmed them down it was just a few seconds before there were more whoops of joy and clapping as another child opened a box. Finally, when the last student had received his, John Paul got the children to sing a simple song in a southern dialect for Molly and Martha to enjoy. They sang with great gusto and such was their enthusiasm that Martha expected the tin roof to lift off the cramped room. She felt as thrilled as she had ever been about the possibility of the tin roof lifting off; she was sure she could burst from the pleasure of the shared joy.

They eventually and reluctantly left the school, taking with them some of the children's excitement and leaving Martha on a high for the first part of the journey back towards the office. But as they neared the office, she fell quiet.

"Penny for your thoughts?" Molly asked.

"Well," said Martha, "I was thinking that I love going out meeting people and getting a taste of Sudan, why we are here and all that. And, after Liam is gone, I could find myself submerged in boring old figures with precious little interaction with the real world!"

"I have a funny feeling that won't happen. The reason that Liam is so busy now is because he did very little accounting up until recently and pretty much left Dawit to run the show."

"Really? So, what did he do?"

"He made grandiose appearances in the office from time to time and at fundraiser meetings etc., but none of us have a clue what he was up to most of the time. Off doing shady deals buying Ethiopian gin maybe!"

"Yeah. He told me that when he left it would be my job to buy the gin and exchange the dollars!" Martha half laughed.

"In the meantime, tomorrow, I have to visit an orphanage to deliver vaccines and other things that the agency who run it have requested, why not come with me?"

After *fature* the next day, they loaded up the ambulance with vaccines, drips and other medical supplies and headed to the orphanage. Molly pulled up on the side of a narrow street in front of a metal gate with some small Arabic writing, which, it turned out, was all that indicated that this was the orphanage. They entered through the unlocked gate into an open courtyard surrounded by low-lying, painted buildings. There was no obvious sign of life as they made their way over to the nurses' office, knocked on the door and entered. There were no nurses in the office but, on a desk by the wall, were two small babies lying perfectly still on their sides on small plastic mattresses. They had intravenous drips in their thin arms, which were visible above the thin blankets that covered them.

"The nurses' office doubles as the Intensive Care Unit," Molly whispered.

"Intensive care?" Martha whispered back as Molly gently touched the little babies on the forehead to assure herself that they were still alive.

"These poor little mites probably have AIDS and their chances of survival are slim to none. Though, I'm fairly certain they don't test for AIDS in Sudan," Molly said quietly while gently stroking one of the little baby's arms and bowing her head mournfully. "To do so would be to admit that sex outside marriage occurs."

She straightened herself up, shaking her head as if disbelieving her own words. She headed out the door with Martha following. They walked along the covered walkway through an open door into the next room. Twelve or more cots lined the walls, most of which had two babies lying quietly on bare plastic mattresses, wearing nothing more than plain, short-sleeved, well-worn T-shirts and triangles of green cloth tied around their waists and bottoms. Over at a sink in front of a window, stood a tall, slim man with his back to them washing out a number of these pieces of green cloth. He turned as they entered.

"*Salaam alaykum.*"

"*Alaykum Salaam,*" Molly and Martha chorused.

"Martha, this is Abdel, a nurse and manager. He's been here for the last few years since he came to Sudan from Ethiopia...we know each other from the last time I was here."

As Molly and Abdel talked, Martha contemplated the room with its more than twenty babies. It felt strange and it was a while before it dawned on her why. None of the babies were crying or making any keening sounds. Though, the near silence was weirdly expectant. In the middle of the room were two large Sudanese ladies, sitting on chairs, each bottle feeding a baby. There was no pausing to burp the babies, no smiles or tickles. When one baby had finished its bottle, another was picked up from a cot. If the green triangle of cloth was wet or dirty, it was taken off and thrown in a bucket and the baby's bare bottom was put under the tap and washed and a new triangle tied on. The baby was then fed and returned to its cot and the process began again with the next. It was all very different to the litany of tasks and accoutrements required to look after the babies whom Martha knew: sterilisation, hand washing, bum wiping, disposable nappy on, hand washing, clean clothes, bottle, bib, feeding, burping, more feeding, more hand washing... *The Grand Invasion of a Baby*, Martha jokingly referred to it.

Abdel suggested that Martha help feed the babies. He pulled up an extra chair and, before she had time to feel awkward, he handed her a small bald-headed little boy who was perhaps six months old.

"Kamil," Abdel said. Martha smiled down at Kamil and was automatically drawn to tickle his long, narrow feet. His over-sized brown eyes lit up and he smiled back and even gurgled. Martha washed and changed him, took a bottle from the side table and sat down to feed him. As she fed Kamil, she wondered at the incredibly silent babies around her. Perhaps they had made noise when they were first born, but it hadn't gotten them any extra attention or affection, so they stopped. Martha's mother had told her that she screamed horribly non-stop for the first year of her life and that nobody, especially her mother, had ever wanted to mind her. If she had kept it up that long, then it must have got her something, something more than the eggshells that her siblings said they had fed her to see what might happen. Nothing much had happened. She was still here. Perhaps, she considered as she stroked Kamil's arm gently, her babyhood had been better than she had previously thought.

Having fed Kamil, Martha moved on to a curly haired little girl with a big smile, Nedal.

"Oh, I could run away with you," Martha said quietly, not realising that Abdel was standing beside her.

"She is already adopted. She is going to her new home this week."

"Do you know that Nedal, you're going to a new home soon?" Martha said with an air of surprise.

Martha looked up from Nedal to Abdel. "Do many get adopted?"

Abdel looked around him and noted that the Sudanese ladies had left the room. He took advantage of their absence to explain.

"Not too many, I'm afraid. We do not know the stories of most of the babies. They come to us having been left in different places, behind bins or amongst piles of rubbish. Some come into this world due to rape and the girls hide their pregnancy by binding themselves. The babies are often born very small. Sometimes the girls may not know they are pregnant and the babies are born unexpectedly and their mothers may either hide them or leave them outside a hospital or somewhere that they might or might not be found. Some of them are born to southern Sudanese girls working for northern Sudanese families. You know?"

Martha nodded solemnly.

"Either way these babies are considered unclean by many Muslims so they won't adopt them. Still, thankfully, some do. Some adopt them and bring them home as their own or a relative's child or something like that."

"So sad. The poor wee innocent mites. And to think that there are so many couples back home dying to adopt a baby."

"Yes, but it is almost impossible for foreigners to adopt here in Sudan. I think that you have to be Sudanese and/or Muslim."

Martha fed four more babies and then Molly appeared and took her to another room containing twelve large cots. In some there were toddlers standing up or sitting down quietly watching an activity that was happening in the middle of the room. On the floor there were seven toddlers dressed in simple old T-shirts and similar cloth triangles as the babies in the baby room but these were in off-white. The children were either lying down or toddling or crawling around the floor. Two Sudanese women sat on chairs near the door talking to each other. There was none of the playful energy in the room that you saw on the Pampers' advertisements back home.

Apart from one soft ball lying under a cot, there were no toys visible. Martha felt drawn to sit down on the floor amongst the children and play with them, but she wondered how the women would react. Abdel, who had followed them into the room, seemed to read her dilemma and got down on his knees and reached for the ball from under the cot and threw it straight to her. She caught it with an uncertain smile and sat down on the floor. The toddlers all looked at her. One edged his way over towards her, keeping his eyes firmly fixed on her face. Martha smiled and rolled the ball over to him. He smiled back and watched the ball roll past him over towards another little child who looked at it and then at Martha. Martha moved over towards him on her knees and gently used his hand to roll the ball towards the other boy who stared curiously over at Martha. She smiled and nodded encouragement and he carefully rolled the ball back to her. Another toddler moved towards Martha and bumped his chest to her shoulder as if to say play with me too. Martha rolled the ball to him next. Within a few minutes all but one of the toddlers on the floor were joining in, watching the ball rolling and rolling it when it came their way. There were smiles and small surges of laughter. One little girl on the floor sat sucking her thumb and watched the others play and the children in the cots stood or sat and watched too. At times Martha sat and watched as the children played but they never let her stay out of the game for long. She yearned to hug them all and if the Sudanese women had not been sitting there watching her, she might have grabbed them all into a big hug, or hugged each one in turn, or both. The thought thrilled her.

"I think we have found you a job," Molly said, smiling at Martha.

"Could do worse." Martha laughed.

"Well, we are always glad of help," Abdel said. "Anytime, just arrive."

"I might do that," Martha said, nodding thoughtfully.

Molly had to head off but Martha chose to stay on at the orphanage.

After helping the toddlers to feed themselves, at Abdel's suggestion, Martha moved on to a room with six older children, ranging in age from about four to twelve. The room was supervised by a large Sudanese woman who was sitting in the middle of the floor surrounded by four of the children, one of whom had her arms around her neck as she snuggled up to it. By contrast with the women in the other rooms, the woman's presence was a ray of sunshine that lit up the children and energised them.

"*Salaam alaykum*," she greeted Martha warmly.

"*Alaykum Salaam*. Nice to meet you. I'm Martha." Martha put her right hand to her heart.

"Lamya," the woman replied, also putting her hand to her heart.

Martha turned to look down at a thin girl who was pulling at her skirt. The girl, who Martha guessed was about ten, had been running around the room in a slightly frantic way while staring long and hard at her feet, as if they were unpredictable and separate to her and a source of deep fascination. She peered up at Martha with dark penetrating eyes and put up her arms to be picked up.

"Ghaliya," Lamya said pointing at the girl.

"*Salaam alaykum*, Ghaliya," Martha said as she picked up the surprisingly light girl who snuggled into her momentarily and then reached up and touched Martha's neck and then her bare lower arms, staring intently at Martha all the time, exploring her white face and skin. Martha smiled and touched Ghaliya's arms. Ghaliya snuggled into Martha again for a couple of minutes but then she abruptly pulled away, hit Martha smack across her face, broke out of her arms and ran into a corner of the room. Martha was stunned and had to bite hard on her lower lip to stop herself from bursting into tears. It was not so much the sting of the slap that hurt, it was that it had knocked her out of the loved feeling that she had been having since feeding the babies and playing ball with the toddlers.

"*Malesh, malesh,*" Lamya said.

"It's okay. I'm fine," Martha said rubbing her face as a rather scared and almost possessed looking Ghaliya crouched in the corner.

"It's okay, Ghaliya, it's okay," Martha said becoming aware of another child's hand pulling at her skirt. She looked down to see a gorgeous, curly haired boy smiling up at her with deep, imploring dark eyes. He put up his arms for Martha to pick him up but as Martha did so, Ghaliya dived across the room and ran hard at both of them. Martha wobbled a bit but managed to hold the boy and stay standing.

Lamya was surprisingly quick to get to her feet and grabbed Ghaliya in a tight bear hug.

"Emir, Emir," the little boy said prodding his chest and then hugging Martha tight.

Martha carried him out into the hot sunshine where she had spotted another rather sad-looking old ball earlier. She put him down and picked up the ball and threw it gently to him. Even though the throw was less than ten feet, he struggled to catch it and, when he did, he laughed with delight. They stayed out there until Molly arrived back to collect Martha. They played ball some of the time but mostly Emir just wanted to be walked around the yard in Martha's arms, which she was more than willing to do, grateful for the touching affection. He stared up at her and ran the fingers of both hands down her face and then peered hard at them as if expecting the white of Martha's skin to have wiped off onto his fingers. Martha copied him and ran her fingers down his face and looked at them. He laughed. Then she ran her fingers down each of his arms, tickling him gently. She inspected her fingers and shook her head with a smile; he laughed heartedly and then did the same to her arms checking his fingers carefully with a laughing smile. They repeated this game a number of times, ending each time with Emir throwing his arms around Martha's neck and snuggling his face into her chest. It gave Martha a wonderful glow from her head to her toes and she realised that she'd had no physical intimacy since saying goodbye to Patrick the night before she had taken a taxi to Dublin airport to start her journey to Khartoum. Babysitting Mrs Connolly's grandchildren, Martha had emotionally and physically embraced and savoured the joy of children hugging her as if she was the best cuddly toy ever, but with Emir, she felt something more, something deeper. Emir needed her love and affection and perhaps she needed his too; neither of them could assume to find love and affection elsewhere. When she said goodbye to him that day she knew she would be back, and before she left the orphanage that evening, she assured Abdel that she would aim to visit once a week, if possible. She silently promised this to herself.

She joined Molly and Siobhán in the flat for food later and then drove over to the Sudan Club for a quiet swim, as had become a regular habit.

The pool was sheltered by some generous planting, and an expansive lawn separated it from the humdrum of the Club's low-key night-time activities. It soothed her mind and body to be alone with only her thoughts for company and the water embracing and comforting her. As she swam quietly under the starry sky, she felt at peace with herself and with the world in a way that she had never felt before. Her mind drifted happily to all she had enjoyed that afternoon. She imagined many other afternoons there, playing with Emir and other children, and maybe...hopefully witnessing the women there playing more with the children after seeing the fun that she had with them and their happy faces.

Her thoughts floated back to her own childhood. She remembered the rare occasions when she made an objection to how her mother treated her, like when her siblings had made a mess of the kitchen that she had cleaned.

"Just clean it, Martha. Stop making a fuss about it. For goodness sake."

"But they should do it. They dirtied it."

The back of her mother's hand would come out of nowhere and strike her ear leaving it roaring red, hot and stinging.

"I've obviously been too soft on you, for far too long, if you still think that you can answer me back."

Perhaps ignoring me all together would have been a more effective means of silencing me, Martha thought. *Now I have abandoned her and left her to her carers and the unreliable support of her other children. Should I be at home to look after her? Or do I belong here with these little unloved children?*

She was still contemplating this dilemma as she headed back to her flat.

She was no sooner there, making a cup of tea before she sat down to write letters, when she heard a knock on the door. She went over and opened it to find Stefan standing there, holding two bottles of Pepsi.

"I thought that you might be thirsty," he said with a grin, clanking the bottles.

"Oh, I was going to…That would be great, thanks. I was making tea but Pepsi is definitely better for this heat."

"We never got to finish that conversation we were having about the joys of curfew…"

Chapter 9

A Driving Lesson

"So where are you sneaking off to now?" Siobhán asked Martha teasingly after dinner later that week.

Martha hesitated, knowing what the consequences of telling her would be.

"I'm going for a swim at the Club."

"Can you swim this late? Can I come too? Pretty please."

"Okay. But even you will have to be quiet. We're not supposed to swim after sunset. So far, the staff pass no remarks and I pretend that I don't know the rule! Okay?"

"You know what holds me back from getting out and doing things is that I'm always relying on other people to bring me. I need to learn to drive so I can do more things for myself," Siobhán whispered as they swam.

"Did you ever drive a tractor on your farm, or anything?"

"Never. Nothing. What do you think? Will you teach me?"

Martha could think of lots of good reasons why this was a bad idea…it could be the end of their friendship, for one.

"Okay. I'll teach you."

Martha then relayed to Siobhán her own protracted learning to drive experience. She had started with a boyfriend teaching her but broke up with him before she had finished. She then got some lessons but took ill the night before her first test, after which the GP had as good as called her a fool for attempting to work, never mind do a driving test, with such a severe kidney infection. The calamity that was her first test was further compounded by having to borrow Patrick's car, which she had never driven before, as the one she was supposed to be using had broken down. She was just getting to know Patrick at that stage and they hadn't even had a first date as such but he had very kindly offered his car. He had even taken time off work to drive it around to her and talk her through the basics. But despite his and her best efforts, she had failed her first test fair and square.

For the second test, Martha had felt that she could not have driven better but she saw the tester mark an 'X' as she reversed safely and neatly around a corner and again as she did an equally good three-point turn.

"The fecker had his own predetermined fail rates, and I was on the wrong side of them! Feck him!"

"So how did you finally get your feckin' test then?"

On the third attempt, Martha remembered, it had been a busy, sweltering Friday afternoon in Dublin and the traffic was mostly at a standstill. Sweat poured down from her hairline and her nerves and frustration were no doubt written clearly on her face when, out of the blue, a friendly voice had said, "Don't worry, the traffic is not your fault." Was that really the tester that had spoken? Based on her previous experiences, she had thought that driver-testers were not fully human. She had eventually, after struggling through more heavy traffic, driven the tester back to his office and he had passed her with a smile!

"I was so relieved that I told my friends that the only other test I ever intended to take after that was a pregnancy test!"

"Well with all that well-honed driving experience," Siobhán said laughing, "you're just the person to teach me and so how about it now?"

"Not quite what I planned but...okay. Ten more lengths, alone, and you're on."

Martha took her out to an open space on the outskirts of Khartoum, telling Siobhán that they would avoid the "mad balls" roundabout that vehicles went around in both directions. It was crazy – vehicles mostly only narrowly avoided collision, though there were some crashes, especially, she had been told, during the chaos of Ramadan.

"To drive around that roundabout you need real balls!"

"Bad enough having to look at nothing but balls on the other roundabouts," Siobhán said. "Isn't Muslim law a bit mad all the same? You know, the way they can't paint, or include in any art, any living thing, so every sculpture here is just…well, balls!"

"Yes, very limiting! I can't imagine what their art galleries look like! But I've always been curious about how our commandments came to be rewritten. Being a 'good' protestant, before making my confirmation, I had to learn by heart the old-fashioned commandments for my religious exams. I remember the second one was something like, *'Thou shall not make for thyself any graven images or the likeness of anything that is in heaven above, or in the earth beneath, or in the waters under the earth. Thou shall not bow down to them, nor worship them, for I am the Lord, thy God. I am a jealous God…*etc. etc. Maybe Mohammed took our original commandments as the inspiration for his…"

Siobhán hadn't said anything while Martha had been speaking and had looked at her with curiosity as she spoke and drove. Martha suddenly became aware of this and paused.

"Sorry, I went off on one again."

"You're something else!" Siobhán laughed.

The open space was beside one of the many large settlements that surrounded the city. These sorts of settlements, like the one Martha had previously visited with Siobhán, housed, if you could call it housing, more than a million internally displaced people escaping the long and brutal war in southern Sudan. The settlement, like so many others, looked like a glorified dump. She struggled to imagine that entire families lived in these miserable hovels which were hot in the summer and relatively cold in winter. What few scraps were considered actual rubbish made up a dump of sorts beside the settlement, which also served as the communal toilet for those living in the hovels. Little was wasted. Certainly not food. Martha had seen, on one occasion, empty tins converted into a toy car and a toy bicycle, both with moving wheels. These had seemed like an extravagance relative to the refugees' usual way of turning tins into something functional, like kitchen utensils. This way of life meant there was a limited amount of rubbish in the dump compared to what got thrown out at home. *Something we could learn from, perhaps?* Wild dogs were not going to find many pickings here.

Martha stopped the Land Cruiser in the open space at the side of the little dump as darkness was falling.

"First things first, key in the ignition, right? Okay, these are the pedals. Left foot, clutch," Martha said putting her left foot on the clutch. "Middle, brake. Right pedal, accelerator." Martha moved her right foot from the brake to the accelerator.

"You use your right foot for the brake and the accelerator – it wouldn't make much sense to try braking and accelerating at the same time, would it?" Martha said with a smile. "Okay, so which is which?"

"Clutch, brake and accelerator," Siobhán said as Martha again moved her feet from pedal to pedal.

"Excellent."

"Now with my foot on the clutch, fully down, I'm going to put the Land Cruiser into neutral. See it is right in the middle and when the gears are in neutral, you can wiggle the gear stick, like so."

"You try it now. Okay?"

Siobhán nodded and wiggled the gear stick.

Martha spent the next few minutes talking Siobhán through the basics of driving, demonstrating as she went.

"Okay? You got all that?"

Siobhán nodded uncertainly and Martha went through it all again.

"Now your turn." Martha turned off the engine, got out of the Land Cruiser and Siobhán slid over to the driver's seat as Martha got into the passenger seat.

"Oh dear," sighed Siobhán. "This is going to be fun! Clutch, brake, accelerator, neutral and first," she said as she moved her feet and hands across them. "Fasten seat belts. Ready for take-off?"

"Aye aye, Captain."

"In neutral, check, key in ignition, check, foot on clutch, foot on brake, turn key." She turned the key. A horrible grating sound came from the engine.

"What the feck? What did I do wrong?"

"Don't worry, everybody does that. You just overturned the key and didn't release it. Turn off the ignition and start again."

Siobhán repeated her actions this time releasing the key on time. "Okay, what now? Oh, I know release handbrake, clutch down, into first gear. Press accelerator. Release clutch," she said releasing the handbrake and moving her feet as she spoke, while all the time looking down at her feet.

"Oh shit," they chorused as the car lurched forward and stalled.

"Thank God for seatbelts!" Martha laughed.

"I thought we were going to take off all together. It's not as easy as it looks!"

Martha smiled.

"You're very patient. Thank you," Siobhán said.

The lesson continued and, before Siobhán knew it, she was driving comfortably around the patch of desert going from stopping to first and then to second gear. It wasn't without its little mishaps. At one stage, as Siobhán turned the car towards the dump – smiling to herself with a certain sense of achievement – the headlights caught in their full glare two Sudanese women quietly relieving themselves. Siobhán was so startled that she swerved the car around, narrowly missing a small heap of rubbish from which emerged the whites of two little eyes staring straight at her as the owner of the eyes rose from squatting position and then raced off. Siobhán immediately stalled the car.

"Well, that's me done for the night…" she said, as she made to get out of the driver's seat.

Martha grabbed her back.

"Oh no, you can't end on that note." Martha laughed. "Learning to drive in Sudan has its own unique challenges! Two more startings and stoppings and then we're off."

Siobhán reluctantly started up twice more, thinking all was fine with the world again.

"Oh shit. Oh shit."

"What? What now?" asked Siobhán.

"It's quarter to eleven. Move over or we will be late for curfew and after what happened to Stefan's mate…I don't fancy a night or two in a cell in Souq Libya."

Stefan had told Martha about Khartoum's large police station in the Souq Libya area, with its packed prison cells where people were sent for all sorts of crimes and misdemeanours, some never to be seen again.

Martha sped off throwing up a spray of sand behind them. They raced back to the main road, past the many and varied balls, including the mad balls – commonly referred to as Bashir's balls by the expats. They made it past the checkpoint near their block of flats just as the security team, in their miscellany of army combats and carrying the usual array of ancient guns, were setting it up.

"I'll do, mammy," Siobhán said as she poured Martha a cup of tea later. "I think you deserve it."

She sat down on the couch beside Martha and turned and looked at her with the same curiosity that she had earlier.

"You're so different to my first impression. I thought you were sort of superior or standoffish. But you're not. It's more like you're uncomfortable until you get to know people." Siobhán paused momentarily as Martha stared into her tea, only glancing in Siobhán's direction momentarily with a quizzical smile.

"In the office, you're all business-like, you know professional and confident. But if someone new walks into the flat or somewhere, you'll go silent or even politely make an excuse and leave…"

Martha wondered what Siobhán was leading to. She left her to continue.

"What I'm trying to say is you're great to have the patience to teach me how to drive. We, as in Molly and I, think that once we got to know you, you're fun and kind and considerate and all that."

Martha said nothing as she waited for a sting in the tail.

"Why did I start that? Will you feckin' say something?"

"Sorry. Thank you," Martha said, still processing that there was no sting at the end in what Siobhán had to say. She smiled. "I guess I'm a slow burner. At least that's what Trish, back home, says. She kindly says that I'm worth the wait! I hope so. You and Molly have made me so welcome and helped me adjust to the people and the place. And I'm really grateful. But in truth I'm not good at these…these sort of conversations."

"Me neither. So, moving rapidly on, tell me, what happened to Stefan's friend? Did he end up in a cell in Souq Libya or something?"

"Well, on Christmas Day, I told him the extended version of Molly's and my little escapade on Christmas Eve and he was starting to tell me about his mate's near miss when Sister Sexy Shelley interrupted him, the way only Shelley can."

"Ah! I know exactly what Shelley is like. Sister Sexy Shelley, that's bang on. I love it!"

"Well, the other night he called around to me for a chat and a Pepsi and there was just the two of us, so we got talking…"

"Go on. I'll want all the gories later – sure we all know that he has the hots for you!"

"Will you feck off! He couldn't be interested in me. Moving rapidly on again…his friend, Andrew, left Stefan's house one night with plenty of time to get home before curfew. But on the way he met a curfew roadblock. Three guns were pointed at him and he was scared shitless. He didn't know what was going on so he radioed one of the other pilots, to tell him where he was. Well your man answered the radio with a yawn and said 'Okay. Fine. Good night,' and went straight off the air. A lot of use he was, Stefan said. The army guys made Andrew get out of the Land Cruiser and stand with his arms on the bonnet and his legs spread eagle. Next thing he feels the barrel of a young army fellow's gun dig into the back of his neck, shaking like this," Martha said as she reached behind Siobhán and stuck her index finger firmly into the back of Siobhán's neck.

"Ouch."

"Sorry, but you get the point!"

In response Siobhán smacked her on the arm with a smile and then nodded to tell her to continue.

"All Andrew could think was that the guy was so bloody nervous, he was going to shoot his head off…accidently! Eventually, one of the older guys told Andrew to get back in the Land Cruiser and the young fellow got in with him and made him drive, at gunpoint, to Souq Libya police station. He was sure that he was going to be thrown in a cell. But, when they got there, the guy in charge started screaming at the young fellow and pointing at the clock on the wall. They all looked at the clock and it said five to eleven. Your man told Andrew that he could go home and he followed him in his police truck himself to get him through the checkpoints."

"So, Stefan's friend nearly got his head shot off or thrown into a cell because those guys on the checkpoint got the time wrong?"

"Exactly. Imagine what they might do to us if we were *actually* late."

Chapter 10

Máire

At the start of February, Liam announced that he was leaving. He declared that everything was in order and that all the reports had been done and submitted to the relevant funding agencies and final payments were due. Some of the agencies were awaiting budgets for the coming year before the first tranche of the current year's funding would be released.

Martha tried to tie him down to specifics. What reports had been submitted? To whom? What funds were owing? What budgets were required? When were they due?

Liam swept his fairy hand in the direction of the filing cabinet beside his desk, soon to be Martha's desk. "The files are all there."

Could there be a more frustrating gobshite to take over from? Martha thought.

"Okay, thanks. I'll check before you go so. In case I've any questions."

Martha spent that afternoon and evening going through the files and listing questions that she wanted to ask him. The next day he was unavailable other than to drag her to the offices of UNICEF, USAID and UNHCR, all of which funded Help projects. He introduced her to Help's project funding contacts at each of these offices in a cursory and dismissive manner and actively excluded her from any subsequent conversations. Martha was both furious and mortified. At the meeting in UNICEF she was introduced to Robert Smith, responsible for primary healthcare, and Máire O'Reilly, his next in line.

"Máire, Máire O'Reilly," Martha quietly gasped as she recognised her neighbour from home.

"Martha Hyland. Gosh it's been years since I saw you," she said, looking at Martha intently. "How are you? How have you been?"

"Fine. Just fine."

"How good to see you."

"And you too," Martha responded, meeting and holding her gaze.

"Well," said Robert, "Liam, I believe has given us the financials for last year for the Health Centre so we only need you to give us the budget for this year and then we are sorted and we can start the usual process of approval, etc. Is that right Liam?"

"Perfect, Robert. We're all set. There is very little left for Martha to do."

"Great, great. And what about you, back on time for the Triple Crown and all that? Could be our year. God, we need the rugby after the cricket disaster."

"Ah, the cricket. A blip in a long series of wins. Don't see Australia repeating that performance."

The conversation continued in that vein, with both men talking loudly across the table. Full of their own importance, Martha thought. Neither of them looked the sporty types: Liam looked too delicate and Robert had the physique of a large couch potato. Martha hardly listened as they boomed on.

She couldn't believe that Máire was there, sitting opposite her. It must have been well over ten years since she had last seen her. Máire had gone off to UCD to study languages when Martha was finishing primary school and Martha had only seen her a few times after that. Mrs O'Reilly had told everyone she met that Máire was top of her class. She was going places. Whenever Martha was down home and bumped into Mrs O'Reilly, they would stop for a long chat providing none of Martha's other family members were about, which was most of the time. Mrs O'Reilly would ask Martha how she was getting on and tell her where Máire was and how well she was doing. She was rising through the ranks of UNICEF, virtually running the place, according to Mrs O'Reilly, who enjoyed visiting Máire every couple of years wherever she might be posted. Martha suspected that Máire would be mortified to hear the glowing way that her mother talked about her. Martha, however, was happy to listen because, going back to her less than easy childhood, she had a soft spot for Máire and an even bigger one for her kind mother. It was strange to be sitting across from her in a foreign country, all those years later.

Martha felt the urge to reach across the table and say, *Thank you, Máire, thank you to you and your Mother for caring, thank you both for your kindnesses to me, it mattered. It still matters.*

It would have been a weird thing to do and after all the years, Máire might have wondered what on earth she was referring to. Martha was still thinking these thoughts when she realised that everyone was standing up and the meeting was over.

Robert and Liam shook hands and walked out the door. Martha stood up and Máire took Martha's hand in a both of hers.

"It is so good to see you, and looking so well, too. We will meet again soon, I hope."

"I am glad to say that we will see each other soon one way or another. It seems that I've a budget to produce for you!"

Less than a week later, Martha was standing slightly to the side of a small crowd of expats, waiting for what was known as the Hash run to start. She was hopping from foot to foot self-consciously, feeling like a stray who had wandered into the wrong pack. She had never done a paper chase and she had no idea what to expect.

"Hi Martha. I didn't know that you did the Hash."

Martha turned around to see Máire and smiled.

"My first time, I bumped into Angie and she suggested it." Martha pulled her shorts down on her hips to make sure they covered her knees.

"Do these look long enough?"

"They're grand. Gosh it totally threw me to see you at the meeting the other day. You look so different."

"It's been a while. You look different too. I remembered you being taller!" Martha laughed. "That's probably because I was shorter and chubbier myself!" She remembered how she used to hate everyone sticking their fingers in her tummy and saying, "Look at your puppy fat."

"Oh, I remember you well until you were about eleven or twelve and for a bit after I started in university. Then I left Ireland and went off chasing this career. Our families were such close neighbours and good friends for years. We used to go on picnics together and all...but then...oh, eh...we didn't…because…" Máire paused as if she feared that she was about to say the wrong thing.

"Oh, there" – she nodded in the direction of a man who was raising a big battered horn – "the horn is about to be blown; we are about to start. Talk to you later."

Máire, Martha and the rest of the small crowd took off on the paper chase, stopping and starting at each junction or paper marking, deciding to go one way or the other, turning back on false turns and trying a different route. On and on, with lots of hoots and general comradery, they ran through the low-lying desert scrub, often colliding with each other as they stopped to consider the next marking or when they hit a dead-end.

Angie, who was a well-travelled expat, had suggested the Hash, the Hash House Harriers, to Martha as a way of getting a bit of exercise and maybe meeting new people. Angie had explained that the Hash was originally set up by British expats in Malaysia for that purpose and also to help them get over their hangovers after what was often a hard weekend's drinking. It was held on a Monday, even in Khartoum where Friday was the one full day of the Sudanese weekend. It ran at various locations around the outskirts of the city, the location being determined by whoever was setting the run that week. As part of the Hash tradition the run was always followed by Down Downs where there was drink, food and a sing song. The alcohol ban in Sudan didn't seem to get in the way of expat drinking, so long as you knew where to get it.

As Martha ran, she remembered Máire being there for her at various times when she was growing up, making a point of including her when she was being left out or giving her a sweet from her pocket when her siblings had shared theirs but skipped Martha. Mrs O'Reilly was the same. She often gave Martha a lift to or from primary school on a wet day, miraculously appearing at the right moment, picking her up at the side of the main road and dropping her off at school or near home, just far enough away from Martha's house for them not to be seen. She somehow would have a biscuit or a piece of fruit "leftover" for Martha. Martha wondered how Máire's mother would happen to be there so often at the right time when her own children were older than her and were either at boarding school or had flown the nest. Now, all those years later, it struck Martha that, for it to have happened as often as it did, Mrs O'Reilly must have for some reason planned it that way.

It was hot, very hot. Martha had never run in such heat before. Lost in her own thoughts, she didn't give the paper chase much consideration. She followed the crowd. She stopped when they came to a scattering of paper, a few people would break off and some would go left, some would go right and some would go straight on. She waited to see which group didn't return and followed the posse to the words "on, on." It was a disjointed way of running but, in the heat, Martha was glad of the stoppages. In between, her mind wandered back to Máire and her mother. Why had their families fallen out? Martha couldn't remember and wasn't sure that she had ever known.

She finished the Hash, crossing the finishing line in the middle of a noisy bunch. Purple faced, pouring sweat, and gasping for a drink, she saw Máire up ahead of her. She wanted to go over to her but Máire was talking to friends whom Martha didn't know, so she headed back to her own pickup. Before she got there, she was cornered by Angie and a few other people whom she had met at the Sudan Club.

"Come on, Martha, you can't be sneaking off after your first Hash. On, on to the Down Downs!" Angie said. "Malcolm, I'll go with Martha to show her the way, so I'll see you there. You know Paul laid that rather tedious trail today so it's at his place this week, okay?"

Malcom gave her the thumbs up and she waved at him while turning to Martha. "Do you know Paul's house?"

"No, but I have a feeling that I am about to!" Martha tried to smile at the prospect.

If the Hash run was supposed to be a cure for a hangover, then the Down Downs seemed to be where you got another one. The drink flowed and before Martha knew it, she got pulled into a large, open circle of people singing and moving in what they probably thought was synchronization. She felt distinctly uncomfortable – singing silly songs and making even sillier gestures with a bunch of adults was not her thing. If men, and even a few women, wanted to act like lewd immature misogynists then Martha's attitude was, *let them, but don't expect me to join in.* She stood awkwardly at the edge of the circle thinking here we go again. It all reminded her of the drunken eejits in the teams that used to visit the local rugby club: the players frequently acted like big silly boys with an immature fascination for toilet humour. They too had liked to sing lewd songs and had often been liberal with their hands, as

Martha and some of the other girls her age discovered when they had to serve them a post-match meal. Surely, this lot were old enough to know better. But they didn't. The group of mainly men launched into – with enthusiastic vigour in both voice and gesture – "Swing low sweet chariots, coming to carry me home…" with the emphasis firmly on the word "coming" as they made a lose fist and reached for their crotches. Martha kept her hands by her sides and didn't join in in the singing. She couldn't bring herself to participate even though some other women, whom she knew, were fully into it. She wanted to leave but she felt it would be too obvious if she was to go immediately. *Here I am again*, she thought, *stuck in the middle of a crowd with that familiar feeling of not quite fitting in*. Eventually, she could bear it no longer and made the excuse of needing a bathroom and slipped away.

She stood with her head down at the start of the following week's Hash. She was trying to avoid being cornered again by Angie, when Máire appeared unexpectedly beside her.

"How did you find your first Hash?"

"Well, I enjoyed the run, it was a bit of fun, but…" Martha hesitated. "The Down Downs, I suppose they are not my sort of thing."

"A sort of post-match drunken brawl, if you ask me. Not for me either." Máire laughed.

Chapter 11

Reports and Exchange

Within a week of announcing that he was leaving and introducing Martha to the funding agencies, Liam left without answering a single one of Martha's questions. She spent hours going through the records trying to work out what needed to be done to secure monies due. At times she had to get in touch with the agencies directly to establish what financial information they were still looking for and what exactly was outstanding.

Dawit improved only slightly after Liam left and, at first, Martha trod carefully with him. She was getting very frustrated trying to keep him sweet and dragging information from him. Then it dawned on her that she had a significant say in whether he kept his job or not. There were plenty of possibilities to employ other equally well-qualified, or even better qualified, bookkeepers. When he was being particularly unhelpful one day and he was staring at the paperwork on his desk, as if he was too busy engrossed in the records to listen to her, she put her hand gently on his shoulder and he peered up at her in surprise.

"You know, Dawit, if you are not happy to work with me, that's fine. You can feel free to leave. I have received some CVs from other English-speaking bookkeepers and, if you like, I will employ one of them instead. Some of them seem really keen to get work here. I met one…"

"What, no, it's fine. I'm fine. I'll get you that information now."

It was a significant turning point in their working relationship. It wasn't that Dawit was suddenly fawning over Martha to do work for her but at least he started producing the information she requested promptly and with a better attitude. In those few sentences, Martha felt that she had tipped the balance of power more in her favour.

Working with Dawit, Molly and Siobhán and with the financial reports from the previous year as prepared by Liam, Martha managed to prepare budgets for the current year for the projects based in Khartoum. These she submitted to the funding agencies. There were also some financial reports and budgets needed for projects in western Sudan but, with only poor radio contact with the volunteers over there, she realised that she really needed to visit them. As it happened, Shelley was planning a field trip there late the following month and, to Martha's surprise, she agreed that Martha should travel with her.

In between times, a number of the agencies got in contact with Martha about the financial reports that Liam had submitted. Some of them could not tie in the reports with the supporting documentation that he had provided. They returned the reports and the boxes of receipt books to the Help office and Martha and Dawit spent hours trying to work out how Liam had calculated his figures.

"Dawit, we would be a lot quicker in the long run if I set up a spreadsheet and we record all the receipts by month under the various project headings. We could then generate the reports on the spreadsheets directly in accordance with each agency's relevant formats. Have you any computer experience?"

"Yes, yes. Back home I did much work on a computer."

"Great. We got a donation of two second-hand computers so you can have one of them and I have Liam's old one."

Over the next few weeks Martha set up the spreadsheets and showed Dawit how to input the data from the receipts. Together they produced revised reports which could be tied directly into the receipts as required by the agencies. It was all a tedious and time-consuming exercise but it was worth it as the revised reports meant that the last tranche of funding due for the previous year's projects could be released to Help.

The added advantage of setting up the spreadsheets was that they provided templates for recording the current year's receipts and generating the necessary reports automatically in a straightforward and timely manner. This also meant that expenditure could be monitored against budget by project on an ongoing basis with relative ease. Dawit was delighted to switch from a purely manual bookkeeping system to a more computerised one and, despite the flickering and uncertain electricity, he surprisingly quickly had all the current year records up on the new spreadsheet system. Though, he wasn't so keen on the in-built checks and reconciliations that Martha had included in the spreadsheets, as these had never been included in the manual system. It made everyone a bit more careful about recording money as they spent it, getting receipts and keeping track of the cash. It didn't make Martha top of the popularity stakes but, then again, that wasn't her job.

When Martha introduced a system to keep track of medical and other supplies, Siobhán and Molly were quick to start slagging her.

"Hey Martha, I forgot to tell you I took three paperclips yesterday. Dawit said that you noticed you were short a few last night," said Siobhán.

"Yeah," said Molly, "I hear that you had poor Dawit crawling around the floor looking for them!"

Martha sighed and shrugged her shoulders, barely managing a small laugh at their repeated joke.

Once Martha had prepared the budgets and financial reports, she set about doing something about the dreaded foreign exchange situation. Before Liam had left, he had introduced her to an elegant, middle-aged Sudanese woman and in front of Martha, in her own dreary flat, he had exchanged ten thousand dollars at ten times the government rate. As part of the transaction Liam filled out a docket in a receipt book writing out his name, the woman's name, the amount exchanged and the amount received. The woman signed the docket and was given the top copy and a carbon copy was left in the safe under Martha's bed along with another ten thousand dollars to be exchanged at a later date. Until Liam left, Martha tried not to think too much about the evidence of illegal foreign exchange dealings sitting in her bedroom but she couldn't stop worrying that the dealings with the woman were some sort of set-up. She half expected the Sudanese police to turn up and open the safe and seek to arrest her and Liam.

Within a couple of weeks of the foreign exchange deal in Martha's flat, news hit the expat community that a middle-aged Sudanese woman had been arrested in Khartoum carrying a couple of thousand undeclared dollars. She was imprisoned without trial and the talk amongst the expats was that any trial would be postponed indefinitely as the Sudanese government wouldn't want a trial to reach the international media and highlight the discrepancy between the government-enforced exchange rate and a true market rate. Martha understood that given the political and economic instability of Sudan, it would be impossible to accurately estimate what a true market rate might be. But it would certainly be closer to the rate that the Sudanese woman had offered Help than the government rate. If it didn't take a genius to work out that the difference between the two rates played a significant role in financing the very war that rendered Sudan politically and economically unstable and caused the displacement of so many southern refugees, then why hadn't the geniuses in the IMF done something about it? The ridiculously low rate also helped keep the government in power and in the lifestyle to which they had become accustomed. If the woman's arrest was not already publicly known, then the matter could have been dealt with quietly and quickly. But Martha thought that the Sudanese were probably not as likely to deal with women as expediently as they might deal with men in these situations. International media coverage of the case, if there had been coverage, might have put pressure on the IMF to force Sudan to address the situation and on the UN and other agencies to reconsider how they funded projects in Sudan. The government might have then been pressurised to operate a genuine foreign exchange regime. *Inshallah, Bukhara, Mumbkin!*

In the meantime, some poor woman was lying in certain squalor in a Sudanese jail, not knowing what would become of her. A part of Martha feared that she would find herself in a similar position.

She didn't tell Máire or Molly, or even speak to anyone in Sudan about the money sitting in the safe under her bed. She considered moving the heavy safe into another room, as far away from her as possible, but the weight of it made that impossible without significant help. She lay awake in bed on more than one night wondering how to resolve the problem. In the middle of one night, she gave into her sleeplessness and resumed a letter to Patrick telling him the position she found herself in and expressing the fear that she would find herself in a Sudanese prison. She wrote it all down in her school Irish in case, for some reason, the letter got into the wrong hands. It was probably a silly fear as she hadn't heard of letters being confiscated or stopped as they made their way home, but she felt that the issue was too terrifyingly serious to take any further chances.

She set up a meeting with Jeremy, her counterpart in Food for All, to see what solution, if any, could be found to improve how Help brought money into Sudan.

"You're telling me that you guys are expected to bring in large amounts of US dollars and hide them on your bodies when you come through the airport and not declare them?"

"Yes. Exactly! And when I brought them in, believe it or not, I was almost oblivious of the serious extent of the potential implications," Martha said.

"And then you exchange them on the black market! Have they no idea in Ireland of the implications? I mean you could be thrown into prison never to be seen again…"

"Well, I know…"

"I've never heard of a single other volunteer being asked to do such a crazy and dangerous thing. You must have been terrified."

"Jeremy, you don't need to remind me. I'm going to put a stop to it, I hope. Right now, I'm looking for some alternative solutions."

"Okay, for starters you've got to spend as little as possible in country and try and pay in dollars outside of Sudan for all big items."

"Fair enough. I'm doing some of that already."

"Secondly, all expat salaries are tax free and can be brought into the country at twelve point five Sudanese pounds to the dollar as opposed to four point five."

"Okay? Go on…"

"Well then what you do is you add up all your expat costs, rent, electricity, food, travel, Sudan Club expenses, etc. and allocate them as salary to each expat. Then these plus the expat volunteer allowances become the value of gross salaries each month that you can bring in at the twelve point five rate."

"That sounds good. Thank you," Martha said seeing the potential for bringing considerable costs in under this heading.

"I wonder why Liam never did it before…"

"I wonder a lot of things about Liam," Martha replied. "Thank you for your guidance. It's very helpful."

"I am very glad to be of assistance, Martha, anytime. Maybe we should meet up for an ice cream or something soon? You know, meet up outside of work."

"Thank you, Jeremy. That sounds good. I will be in touch soon." Martha looked at her watch. "I've taken up enough of your time today already. I really better get going."

Remembering Molly teasing her about Jeremy making a pass at her at the New Year's Eve party and at another party since, Martha smiled to herself as she drove home from the meeting. If Siobhán or Molly had been flies on the wall, they would have teased her for wearing her confident, all-business, professional mask, while poor Jeremy was falling over himself offering her a snack or a cold drink. She told Molly that she felt guilty because she had said that she would be in touch soon and had run out the door before a date could be set, safe in the knowledge that he wouldn't be able to phone her to follow up on the offer.

"Poor Jeremy," Molly said, "he doesn't know that there's a queue."

"Very funny!" Martha said.

Martha set Jeremy's two suggestions in train with immediate effect and advised head office by fax of the new system. She also miraculously managed to get through by phone to the head office manager. It had taken her only ten attempts to get a line and she was so surprised when someone answered and said, "Help head office" that she nearly hung up. It was the first time she had succeeded in calling anyone from the office phone and to her further surprise the manager took her call. Martha advised her that given the very real threat of prison, no volunteers should in future be expected to bring in undeclared dollars. She tried to stress the dangers involved but she wasn't convinced that the manager was taking her seriously from her cushy office in civilised Ireland! She tried a different tack. She told the manager that she understood why Help brought some money in the way they did but it was small money in the scheme of Help's in-country expenditure and that the new, safer ways that she proposed could do much to avoid the punitive exchange rates. There was silence on the other end of the phone and Martha could have sworn that she heard the manager's fingers drumming on the desk. She took the hint and said that the line was bad so she'd better hang up.

Later, she managed to get in touch, through Dawit, with the Sudanese woman that Liam had exchanged dollars with and was relieved to confirm for herself that she was not the woman who had been arrested. The woman agreed to exchange the remaining ten thousand dollars for Sudanese pounds but at a lower rate than previously to reflect the increased risk since the arrest of the other woman. No record was made by Martha of the deal and after the meeting she set about burning all the foreign exchange receipts with Liam's and the Sudanese woman's name on them in her kitchen sink. As she watched the flames eat their way through the evidence, sending flutters of black ash into the air, she hoped and prayed that it would be the end of the matter.

Within less than two weeks, the big wig from Help Head Office, Monica McCarthy, decided to visit Sudan. She was a tall fat woman in her mid to late sixties, maybe less, maybe more. Martha found it hard to tell with overweight people. The French say that women over forty have to choose between their face and their figure. Monica had chosen to neglect both with equal distain. She had long straggly, dirty, pale grey hair which hung across her forehead and down her back to her large bottom, spread like a thick build-up of cob-webs across her back. It gave her a wicked witch appearance when combined with the black rings around her deeply set eyes. Martha doubted that they made brooms big enough to carry her. She was rude and demanding and, despite money being continuously in short supply in the charity, she didn't give Martha more than three minutes of her time to discuss the financial or exchange situation. With Monica's thick Cork accent, Martha struggled to understand the few words that she did say to her. Throughout her stay Sister Shelley and Monica swanned around Khartoum dragging her large body through the scorching heat, leaving a trail of sweat and the aftertaste of Monica's bad manners behind them.

Martha watched the two of them at a party one night as they talked to a middle-aged senior UNHCR administrator who had a proper English public-school demeanour and accent. Monica was looking straight into the man's face and Shelley was looking up, stretching herself as tall as possible appearing like a child desperately trying to be included in an adult conversation. Monica was almost shouting and the administrator was continuously backing away. While Martha couldn't hear all of what was being said, she couldn't believe some of the expletives coming from Monica as she ranted on about the problems in Sudan. The administrator every so often succeeded in getting a few words in but he rarely got beyond "indeed" or "do you think" or "what a shambles". The expats, especially those in the funding agencies, who met Monica at meetings or socially, were talking about how obnoxious she was for a long time after she had left. Martha found herself apologising for her and politely blaming her size and the heat for her bad behaviour.

In the week after Monica had returned to Ireland a senior army officer, in full decorated uniform, called to the Help offices and spoke to Fuad. Fuad glanced over at Martha as he spoke and, despite the air conditioning being on beside her, fear-induced sweat poured down Martha's face and back. She couldn't concentrate on her work while the officer was there and was relieved but apprehensive when he left and Fuad came over to talk to her. The officer had informed Fuad that Martha was to go into the Ministry of Security first thing on the following Wednesday morning and meet someone whom Fuad described as being only one step down from the minister himself.

"I understand that they want to ask you about foreign exchange."

Martha's heart stopped. What if they had arrested the Sudanese woman that Martha had dealt with? What if she had told them everything? What if it had all been a set-up? What if they knew about the safe under her bed? At least she'd got rid of some of the evidence – but could they have the top copies of the receipts and, in Liam's absence, hold her to blame? Could they arrest her and put her in jail?

From then until the meeting Martha barely slept or ate; her stomach was in a tight knot, varying between a feeling of constipation and a need to run to the toilet. She managed to keep herself just about sane by going for a nightly swim alone at the club.

On Wednesday morning she drove in silence over to the Ministry's offices, parked and walked with Fuad to the senior official's secretary's office. Martha didn't dare share her fears with Fuad in case she gave him information that could implicate him in some way if he was questioned too. They gave their names and details and were told to take a seat under a closed window outside the officer's office door. They sat in the sweltering heat and waited. Three hours later they were still sitting, sweltering and waiting. The heat, as always, irritated Martha's many mosquito bites and the longer they sat there, the more she scratched them, two of them to the point of bleeding leaving blood trickling down the calves of both her legs. Eventually, at Fuad's enquiry, the secretary said that the officer would be with them soon. Two hours later, by which time Martha thought that she would collapse from dehydration, the door opened and they were summoned into an inner office. They were told to sit down opposite a uniformed man behind the desk. No introductions were made. The tall, upright man asked Martha one question after the other: Who was it who visited Help last week? Where did Monica travel to? Why was Monica seen at Omdurman on the Tuesday? Did she have permits to travel outside Khartoum? He then listed off various places that Monica had visited, including times and dates. Who was the French person with her at such and such a place? Did she have a permit for her camera? Did she have a special permit to take the photos and videos she had taken?

As Martha knew virtually nothing about Monica's movements and had in total only spent probably two hours in the same room as her, never mind only a few minutes talking to her, she answered all the questions honestly with, "I don't know."

There was a small part of her wanting to scream, *Ask me something I do know. Ask me about foreign exchange, like you said you would.* But another voice in her head told her, *Just answer the questions that are asked and hope and pray that they don't get onto more dangerous stuff.* One thing was clear and that was that the ministry had made it their business to know Monica's every move while she was in Sudan, and now they were letting Martha know that they knew. Were they marking her cards that they might know everything about her too, including about the foreign exchange? Were they saving these questions until the end? Was this their way of saying, *We are onto you guys in Help, watch out?*

After an hour and a half of endless questions, all of which were about Monica, the uniformed man stood up and, with a nod of his head, dismissed them. They walked down the corridors, out into the heat and back to the pickup with a weary sense of relief, not daring to utter a word.

Martha sat in the hot pickup, wiggling from side to side on her bottom, lifting one bum cheek at a time, trying desperately not to burn herself on the scorching seat.

"Well, it seems that I'm not getting jail this time…but what do you make of all that?"

"Well," said Fuad, "that wasn't the major I was expecting, that was someone given the job of letting you know that they know almost everything about Help. What they don't know they can, and will, find out."

"How?"

"They have their ways. They have people everywhere and they especially put pressure on people like the Ethiopians working in Help's office. They bring them in for questioning continuously, threaten them with losing their jobs, or worse again their refugee status: which means deportation."

"Gosh! But we have mostly Ethiopians working for us in the office! I always found that strange actually. We are after all in Sudan, trying to work with the Sudanese."

"It might be time to employ more northern Sudanese. I am the only one, you know! It will appear less suspicious and, if Help are up to anything…" He paused and looked at Martha. "Stop it. Stop it now or they will find out and they will put a stop to it, as they see fit."

Martha sighed. "Fuad, do you think that you could repeat those last few sentences to Shelley please?"

During her long swim that night, Martha turned the pressures of the last few weeks over in her head. She longed to discuss it with someone who might understand. Patrick, as a lawyer, was an obvious choice. Normally he would give her a good hearing and sensible advice on such matters. But his third letter to her was no more encouraging than his two previous ones. She wondered if he had moved on without her and if she should move on too. If he had moved on then he probably wouldn't tell her as much. She'd be left to work it out for herself reading between the lines of his ever shorter and less frequent letters. Communication on emotional matters was not Patrick's forte and normally only happened when he had a few drinks more than his normal two or three. Martha felt tired and alone swimming under the unspoilt night sky which lent a sparkle of magic to her swim. She thought of Stefan, who had become a regular visitor to her flat over the previous weeks. She would see him the day after next when six of them were due to spend the best part of the day on Crocodile Island. He had assured her there were no crocodiles – the island's name came from its shape.

Chapter 12

Crocodile Island

The beauty salon in The Meridien Hotel was the only place that Martha knew where *Khawaji,* white women, got to mix freely and comfortably with Sudanese women. It was an intimate, girly place and not somewhere that Martha would normally go. With Siobhán's encouragement she had made a previous visit there and had immersed herself in the relaxed banter with the women. She had gone with the sole intention of getting a half-leg wax. But, under good-natured pressure, from no less than four Sudanese women, she also had her right foot and ankle painted with delicate henna designs. The same women had also tried to persuade her to have a full leg and arm wax, declaring, through contagious giggles and rubbing of her arms, that the short light hair on them was *ma kwas*, not good.

The evening before the trip to Crocodile Island, Martha and Siobhán again enjoyed the relaxed banter but this time Martha was adamant that a half-leg wax would be plenty in preparation for the day with Stefan, Michael, Angie and Malcolm. Anything more she thought would seem flirtatious and imply that she was interested in Stefan. She told Siobhán very clearly that this was not the case and that she and Stefan were just friends who 'got' each other. She had joked that this was because they both came from dysfunctional families, who didn't understand them. Stefan understood her because he had struggled so much with his family, in particular with his father, whom he had a long and difficult history of clashing with. And apart from anything else, Stefan was way out of her league. Siobhán had punched her on the arm and said, "Look at you girl, why you think that he is out of your league is beyond me!"

Siobhán was again teasing Martha about possible romance blooming for her on the Nile when Stefan and his friend and fellow pilot, Michael, collected them after breakfast the next day. Martha smiled to herself when she saw how Siobhán and Michael's eyes lingered that moment longer than necessary when they greeted each other. As Siobhán got into the car beside her, she uttered, "Touché, babe, touché!" Siobhán laughed and they chatted like a pair of twittering teenagers in the back of the pickup as they made their way to the other side of Khartoum to meet Angie and Malcolm on the banks of the Blue Nile.

Michael had managed to borrow a large, rigid inflatable boat, a RIB, with a surprisingly good engine from a French charity who had brought it to Khartoum as transport during the floods of 1988. Driving around the dry sandy streets of Khartoum it was hard to imagine that, only a few years previously, boats had been the required mode of transport. The RIB no longer had any real purpose for the charity and so they were happy to lend it out to others who could supply their own fuel, which was always in scarce supply and was subject to the wonders of Sudanese bureaucracy. As pilots, this was not a problem for Michael or Stefan.

"Not so blue, more brown, I'd say," commented Siobhán, as they set off on the murky waters of the Blue Nile and around the island.

"Are we really going to swim in that?"

"Hasn't killed anyone yet, as far as I know!" Stefan replied laughing.

They pulled up on a long, flat sandy beach which was quiet apart from a few Sudanese families. The sun was already scorching and they put aside any doubts about the water and all ran in for a welcome swim. They kept their T-shirts on over their togs in deference to Sudanese modesty and the increasing imposition of Sharia law. There was much splashing and messing and nothing would do Stefan and Michael but to race each other. Stefan won comfortably, cheered on by Martha, who was still feeling the relief of having survived her visit to the ministry the previous day, and Michael was noticeably pleased when Siobhán cheered him on. They allowed the sun to dry them off and then enjoyed a mixed picnic of Scotch eggs from the Sudan Club, bread that Martha had made, and cucumber, nuts and mangoes, all washed down with precious bottles of Pepsi.

"You never see Coca Cola here, do you?" Martha commented, holding up a well-scratched old Pepsi bottle in her hand.

"No, I think Pepsi has the market sewn up, not that it can be that big a market given the scarcity of bottles," Michael commented.

"And, it may seem cheap to us, but it would be a bit pricey for the average Sudanese," Stefan added.

"And even if they had the money, they would have to get their hands on some empty bottles too. No bottles, no Pepsi. Great way to control the market," Martha said.

The conversation continued in the same light vein as they finished their lunch, after which Michael uncovered what he had been hiding in the bottom of the boat.

"Water skis! I know now why you insisted on bringing the life jacket even though we only had one! Well done," Stefan said, slapping Michael on the back.

It was decided that Stefan was probably the most experienced skier so he would go first and then he and Michael would swop over. They both got up and skiing quickly and were up for each other's antics. They swerved the boat this way and that and drove it straight over its own swash, trying to bump the skier off, with mixed success. Stefan had the edge over Michael, having the fitter, more athletic body against Michael's slightly overweight one. Next went Malcolm with Michael manning the boat. He was much kinder in his driving with Malcolm than he had been with Stefan but he couldn't resist a few fast turns which quickly sent Malcolm flying. He was kinder again when Siobhán gave it a go but it still took her a few attempts to get up and skiing, partly because she was laughing so much.

"Don't know why I'm laughing, it's my turn next," Martha mumbled.

"It will be no bother to you. You've good strong arms and legs from all that swimming, running and squash!" Stefan assured her as he wagged his finger at Michael, warning him to go easy on her.

Martha somehow landed face first on her first attempt but came up laughing and trying to cough up all the water that she had swallowed. She surprised herself on the second attempt getting up for a long stretch only to fall on the fourth turn. Her third attempt was better again and longer lasting. Feeling satisfied, she happily retired to join the others relaxing on the beach and

Stefan and Michael packed away the skis; Angie had declined to give them a go.

They were still the only expats on the beach and, apart from them, there were now only two Sudanese families. As Michael and Stefan were sorting out the boat and the rest of them sat or stretched out on towels, Malcolm spotted a Sudanese engineer whom he knew through work, less than a couple of hundred yards from them, relaxing by the water with his family. He went over to talk to him. Martha sat on the beach observing the family. She was fascinated by the men fully dressed in their long *jallabiyahs,* and the women in their *thobes,* both walking up to their waists into the water. Then something strange seemed to happen. One of the young men who was standing on his own in the water suddenly disappeared under. She stared hard at where he had stood but he didn't reappear. She thought her eyes had deceived her. She was about to scream but before she could open her mouth, she heard loud cries from his sister who was standing to above her knees in the water with their mother. The mother broke into a loud wail which rose up into a wave of sorrow before falling into a low and prolonged keening. The sister ran to where her father and Malcolm stood and Malcolm rushed into the water to where the young man had been standing.

Martha ran over to Michael and Stefan and explained what she had seen. They pulled the boat back into the water and went searching in the surrounding area, moving downstream of where the young man had been. The father stood still on the beach, staring at the water where his son had stood moments before. A Sudanese man from the other family joined him and talked calmly to him. The other man's wife joined the keening mother, taking her in a tight embrace around her waist and sitting her down beside her daughter who was already sitting on the sand keening quietly. Eventually, Malcolm, Michael and Stefan returned having not found the boy. Siobhán, Angie and Martha had packed everything up to be ready to depart, not knowing what else to do, and trying their best to keep busy to cover up their sense of shock and uselessness. They loaded everything into the RIB and then made their way back across the river. The sound of the mother and daughter's keening followed them, and they uttered very little on the way back, speaking only when needed. After subdued goodbyes, Malcolm and Angie headed off in their small four-by-four and the rest of them headed off in Michael's Land Cruiser with the boat on tow.

Martha had a dark feeling of déjà vu. In her early twenties, she had been walking by the coast in Galway near a local yacht club where she had been sailing. She had paused to look across the sea at the huge red ball of sun, hovering above the horizon promising more sunshine the next day. The surreal beauty of it and its promises always made her smile. She had wondered happily at the twinkling colourful light reflecting on the almost calm expansive sea, the reflection larger than the sun itself. In the red and orange water she spotted a kayaker and she yearned to swop places with him. As she walked on along the path, it struck her that the kayaker was out in the middle of the bay, wearing not even a T-shirt, never mind a life jacket. Living near the sea, it had been drilled into all her friends and family to never go sailing, windsurfing or kayaking without a life jacket. She looked out to sea again and saw the kayak upturned and bobbing on the water and no sign of the kayaker. From Martha's vantage point, nobody on the beach seemed to be aware of what was unfolding. Martha rushed along the path to the club where she met some members rigging their sailing boat. She urgently explained what had happened and the men immediately launched the club's RIB and went around the peninsula into the bay to where Martha had seen the kayak. Martha went into the club house and told the bartender what she had witnessed and he told some other members who went out and launched their own boats. The broken-hearted misery of the Sudanese family on Crocodile Island that day mirrored the heartbreak of the Galway family that awful night. The boats had stayed out searching without any luck until darkness forced them to return to shore. They resumed their search at first light and found the young man's body in shallow water.

As they drove back to the flat to drop Martha and Siobhán off, this memory loomed large and dark in Martha's head and, despite herself, she told the others the story. It felt deeply disconcerting to be present at the scene of another certain drowning of a young man and yet again, to be able to do nothing about it. *What part have I in these tragedies? What should I have done that I did not do? Was I too slow to react, in not just one drowning, but two?*

Siobhán, who was sitting in the back of the Land Cruiser beside Martha, squeezed her arm. "That is so horrible, my gosh."

"It feels very weird and wrong, and so very sad," Martha said, shaking her head and clenching one hand in the other on her lap.

"Sad and shocking. Tell you what, why don't you come in for tea and biscuits after a quick shower when we get back."

"I will, thanks," Martha replied, fidgeting pensively with the zip of her backpack.

"Sure I need some help eating the latest stash of homemade biscuits and treats that Mam sent me. Her latest attempt to fatten me up…as if I need it!" Siobhán said putting her arm across Martha's shoulders and giving her a sideways hug. "I think Mam is scared that I will become one of the people starving in Africa!" Siobhán added, trying to lighten the situation and lessen Martha's unease, which Martha silently appreciated.

They pulled up outside Siobhán and Martha's small block of flats and the girls got out and said their goodbyes with some quick gentle hugs from Michael and Stefan; Sudan wasn't a place where you saw or engaged in conspicuous affection out on the open street. Michael and Stefan had to go to the other side of the city to return the boat. Siobhán and Martha each headed for their separate flats, and as Martha got to her door, she realised that Stefan was behind her.

"I wanted to see that you are okay. You know, that was a bit of a shock for us all, but particularly you."

Martha nodded.

"Do you need me to come back later or anything?"

Martha would have loved that, but instead said, "No, I'm fine really. Honest. I promised Siobhán that I'd hang out with her."

"Okay then. I'll see you later in the week. I don't know my schedule yet."

He moved to embrace her as she turned to put her key in the door, though he was forced to change his mind when her backpack smacked him firmly in the face. She felt like a complete idiot but could only barely manage to mumble, "Sorry." He gave her a kiss on the cheek and left. Martha ran her fingers down her cheek, surprised by the sensual tingling sensation that she felt. She smiled briefly before dismissing it as nothing more than a nice, friendly gesture.

Chapter 13

Conversation

Máire had been one of the first people in the funding agencies to contact Martha about some problems with matching the financial reports to the supporting documentation. She was apologetic and keen to acknowledge that the problem seemed to be the lack of a clear audit trail rather than anything untoward. They had a meeting at UNICEF's offices and, when they had finished discussing business, the conversation turned to their hometown of Sligo and people they both knew. Neither Martha nor Máire mentioned Martha's own family but Máire brought Martha up to date on the travels, marriages and births in her own.

"We live near each other in Khartoum too. If you are keeping up the Hash, we could share the drive. If you like?"

"Sounds good. I've managed to get lost a few times already trying to find my way to the start of the runs and you know Khartoum so well."

"I should do. This is my second posting here. I'll pick you up at your flat this Monday at four thirty so?"

It became their habit for Máire to drive them both to and from the Hash run. She explained that she was a nervous passenger but a reasonably comfortable driver. After the run, they normally went straight to the Sudan Club for a shower and a swim, followed by dinner. They also discovered that they both played squash and they often made use of the court at the Club, trying to play early or late in the day to avoid the worst of the heat.

Máire wasn't just warm and engaging, she was also a mine of information. She told Martha some of the recent history of Sudan and introduced her to places in Khartoum that Martha otherwise might not have heard of. Early one Friday morning, they headed off on an outing to Tuti Island, an island that was only three-square miles and was at the confluence of the Blue and the White Nile, after which they became the Nile.

Máire parked beside the beautiful old Grand Hotel which sat, in all its former dusty colonial glory, overlooking the Blue Nile, and they strolled across the road to the ferry. As they stood waiting, Máire told Martha that when the Sudanese government banned alcohol, almost overnight a few years previously, hotels and clubs had to quickly get rid of their supplies. The Grand Hotel had a large stock of miniature spirit bottles and rather than empty each one out individually they had brought a few loads of the bottles down the slipway and dumped them straight into the Nile, expecting them to be quickly washed down river. But they got caught in the silt. People standing in the water, waiting for the ferry or paddling, soon discovered various small unmarked bottles underfoot and they weren't slow to find a market for them, labels or no labels!

Martha laughed and was sorry there wasn't still a supply of such half-decent liquor. Although the Ethiopian gin wasn't too bad, the local drink of Araqi, made from fermented dates or sometimes potatoes, was as raw as paint thinner, even with a generous helping of Pepsi. Máire said she never touched the stuff as the smell alone could knock you out, just like the poitín at home.

They crowded onto the small flat boat with about thirty Sudanese people. There wasn't any room for possible sharia law restrictions of separating men and women, and the boat bumped slowly along with everyone remaining standing, packed in like skittles at a bowling alley; tight enough to provide mutual support. It wasn't long before they reached the island and as soon as they disembarked, Martha stopped and stood in awe at its lush green landscape. It was a stark contrast to the dry, sandy streets of Khartoum. It reminded her of home: Ireland, the emerald isle thanks to plenty of rain. Martha hadn't seen or felt a drop of rain since she had landed in Sudan and she wondered aloud what it took for Tuti Island to be so green.

"As far back as the 1940s, the islanders got together and built an elaborate irrigation system that has served them well to this day," Máire explained. "This island is the fruit and vegetable basket of Khartoum and, you'd probably never think it now, but Sudan was once known as the breadbasket of East Africa!"

They walked around the island, stopping to eat a small snack of bread and fruit they had brought with them. Martha loved the small grassy fields which were interspersed with citrus groves and neat plantings of fruit and vegetables, including cucumbers, beans, tomatoes, okra and lettuce. It felt like being dropped into another country. There was no traffic, just a generous sprinkling of locals, moving slowly about their business, helped by quiet donkeys. There was one small settlement and in some of the fields were square grass huts. Martha and Máire took a leisurely joyful walk, taking in most of the island, finishing as the full heat of the day drove them back to the ferry. It amazed Martha how good it had felt to see such rich greenery after months of being starved of it. The sensation left her giddy.

At Máire's suggestion, they made their way to The Grand Hotel to sit on the veranda and watch the river roll past as they drank a tall fresh fruit drink. The sense of past opulence oozed around them as they relaxed on dark old-fashioned wicker chairs on the spacious veranda of the Victorian hotel.

"Máire, can't you just imagine the English women in colonial times, dressed in their loose, drop-waisted dresses and cute hats and all their finery, holding their long cigarette holders as they demanded drinks from beautiful waiters dressed in starched white uniforms," Martha said, doing a twirl in her own long, loose skirt and pretending to smoke an imaginary cigarette.

Máire laughed.

"I can just see them flirting with uniformed British officers or more excitingly some Indiana Jones type adventurer! Can't you?" Martha added.

"Oh, there were plenty of British Officers and I gather even a few European adventurers too. There was a French adventurer and an Italian adventurer of sorts, who sought out the pyramids of Meroé, just one hundred and twenty-five miles north of Khartoum," Máire said.

"Pyramids in Sudan? Really? Are they still there?"

"Oh yes, very much so and I believe that they are worth a visit. Although the same men left them a bit damaged after they went looking for treasure there."

"That's great. We should try to visit them."

"No thank you! There is no proper road, only rough desert terrain. You wouldn't get me travelling on that in a million years, too dangerous."

Perhaps it was the relaxed mood of their outing that had reminded Máire of some past trip, but to Martha's surprise she told her that some years previously, during her time in Zambia, she had met a wonderful outgoing Italian man. They had spent most weekends on one outing or another, mainly on safari but sometimes walking or kayaking. They had good times together during her two-year contract there; they had even managed to maintain a happy relationship for another few years when they were both posted by UNICEF to different countries. For years they had snatched long and short reunions whenever time allowed.

"It actually wasn't the miles between us that caused us to split up. We could have solved that. Sadly, it was that we both wanted different things. He wanted to settle down and have children. I wanted to stay travelling. I don't think that I'm remotely cut out to have children, much and all as I love them – as long as I know that I can hand them back!"

"Still, it would have been good to have your own fellow adventurer."

"Maybe." Máire half shrugged.

"Any regrets?"

"On balance, no, and I've asked myself that many times. Sometimes it's lonely and I'd like a man in my life but then I think that a relationship might cramp my very particular style. I guess that I like being my own person, making up my own mind – the odd fling does me most of the time!"

"Fair enough, each to their own. I think, on balance, I'd like to settle down and have kids. But who knows whether Mr Right will come along? Based on recent correspondence, or lack thereof, I doubt somehow that Patrick is my fellow adventurer-in-waiting! Mind you, I'm not sure that he is overly adventurous either!"

Following a second drink, they decided to head to the Sudan Club for a swim. After the swim, feeling suitably cooled down, they got warmed up again playing a game of squash on the club's court.

Máire already knew a little bit about Patrick and, with her having confided in Martha about her past lover, Martha felt emboldened to share her situation. As they sat by the now-deserted pool, she told Máire how, instead of keeping a diary, she had been writing long and intense letters to Patrick, documenting the trials and challenges of her time in Sudan and the newness of it all. She explained that she had written about how she felt about different things, like how terrified she was when the little boy had hit off the pickup with a loud bang on Christmas Eve and they had nearly been arrested. She missed Patrick at times like that and at other times, but she wasn't sure if she missed him specifically for himself or just that he might be someone to tell her experiences to. She missed their long walks together and perhaps the odd nice dinner out too. So far, he had written her three quite short letters and it appeared that the gigs he was going to and the music he was listening to was getting better and better and he didn't seem to have time to write to her, never mind miss her!

After Martha's long rant, Máire paused and considered the situation.

"In my not overly extensive experience, some men, not least Irish men, are not very good at expressing themselves, and might need a more direct approach. Perhaps, just perhaps, it might be worth calling him?"

"I was thinking that, but what might I say?"

"I don't know really but maybe try saying it like you said it to me. Maybe tell him that you are confused by his letters and see what he says, ask him straight out if he misses you."

"I might," Martha said, though she wasn't overly optimistic. With the time difference and curfew and the fact that the only phone that she could use was at the Acropole Hotel, it wasn't going to be easy to catch Patrick at home at the right time.

"I really don't know why I'm here trying to give you advice. I mean not alone have I relatively limited experience with long-term relationships, but I also think that I've been socially awkward all my life," Máire said as she stared at the water in the pool.

"I never think of you as socially awkward! Sure, you wouldn't be where you are now in UNICEF if you were."

"Ah, that's different. It's at a more personal level that I feel awkward. You know, sometimes there are things that I want to say but I don't know how to say them. I don't even know if I should say them. I think that maybe somebody needs to hear something but then maybe they don't. Then I think maybe it will spoil our relationship," Máire said as she turned and looked at Martha. "Maybe I shouldn't rock the boat, leave well enough alone and all that…"

"I know that feeling too, I'm always having those conversations with myself but it sounds as if you have something particular on your mind."

"I could have…" Máire replied, turning to stare again at the pool.

Silence fell between them and Martha realised that her time spent in Sudan had gradually made her more aware of how she felt about herself and how her past had played a big part in her feelings of not being good enough. Not in a work sense, but as Máire had referred to about herself, at a personal level. Siobhán had alluded to some of this in her comments a few weeks previously. Martha realised that she had probably needed to escape the judging eyes of family and the familiar to find out who she really was and if she could be liked or even loved for being herself. Trish and Mrs Connolly had both told her that she needed to start by believing in herself and that she had a lot to believe in. They were rare conversations for Martha to have. Now here was Máire sitting beside her, maybe giving her an opening for another big conversation. One she felt that she needed to have. Outside of conversations with Mrs Connolly and Trish and recently Stefan, Martha rarely spoke about her family and a big part of her wanted to talk to Máire about them. She trusted Máire. She felt that she wouldn't be judgemental. Talking to her might even help her clarify her thoughts on her family and her past. Máire had known her past. Máire had known her family.

Her thoughts were interrupted as Angie arrived to join them. She greeted them both warmly and then turned to Martha. "I haven't seen you since that horrendous incident at Crocodile Island," she said quietly. "Did you hear that they found Jamil's body a few days later further down river?"

"No, I didn't. It was awful. What happened to him?" Martha felt a lump form in her throat.

"They don't know really but they think he may have been shocked by an electric eel and that caused him to drown. Would you believe it? The poor family and to think that we were only just out of the water ourselves."

"How horrible for them," Martha said. "There but for the grace of God, whichever God that might be, go any one of us."

"So true," Angie responded.

Chapter 14

Ramadan

Ramadan started at the end of March with the appearance of the new moon and it would end with the first crescent of the next new moon in late April. Martha expected the atmosphere in the city to change but she thought that Molly had been exaggerating when she'd said the roads became like a bumper car carousel.

After the first week of Ramadan Martha started to feel the already slow-moving city become even more sluggish and, on her weekly cycle to the orphanage, she witnessed a number of accidents and more near misses. The cars appeared to just wander into each other, at not much more than the speed of bumper cars; as a result, little damage was done. The general response of the drivers could be summed up in that wonderful Arabic word, "*Malesh*", which seemed to mean something between "so what" and "sorry" or both at the same time.

In her trips to the various government ministries to follow up on permits or organise travel passes for Shelley and her to go to Wadi Dabor, she noticed the service to be even slower than usual, which meant that it was at a virtual halt.

The basic fasting rule was that every sane, healthy Muslim who had reached puberty and was not travelling must fast from sunrise to sunset. Menstruating women, or women bleeding post childbirth, should not fast but should make up the days at a different time; Martha wondered what the rule was for breastfeeding women. Anyone she knew who had breastfed had found good sleep and regular food essential. A communal meal was had pre-dawn and no food was consumed again until after sunset when normally another long and leisurely meal was taken with neighbours and friends. With daytime temperatures at times reaching forty degrees, Martha couldn't believe that this fasting included no drink or worse. Some of the Sudanese took fasting to the extreme, and during the day they continuously hawked and spat, rather than swallow their own saliva. It was clear from what she witnessed, some of the Sudanese were drunk from dehydration and lack of sleep – they slurred their words; they bumped into things; they didn't walk, they staggered.

Towards the end of Ramadan, Martha and Shelley were due to fly to Wadi Dabor to visit the Help projects there. Ahmed arrived before dawn to collect them and bring them to the airport for their early morning flight. When they got to the airport, Martha found out that Shelley had booked them to fly on a small charter plane which would be shared with another agency. She wondered what the extra cost might be, relative to a scheduled flight.

The airport was heaving with expectant travellers, queuing in various directions: men in white *jallabiyahs* and lose turbans; a few women dressed in either black burqas or the more common Sudanese *thobes*; everyone squashed into the chaos of the small space designated for internal flights.

Gradually, they made their way to the top of their queue and presented their tickets and travel passes. It wasn't just their luggage, which included numerous boxes of medical supplies, that was weighed but Shelley and Martha too. This was to determine who would sit where in order to balance the small plane.

Having checked in, they were asked to stand to one side, beside four other expats also waiting to take the flight. Martha took in the overweight man who was due to travel with them and decided that it would need two people bigger than herself and Shelley sitting across from him for the plane to not lean to one side. Their fellow passengers were about to introduce themselves; the large man's hand was extended towards Martha but was suddenly withdrawn. She saw him look over her shoulder and she became conscious of a heaving movement taking place behind her. She turned to see that the airport was slowly but surely being cleared, everyone being ushered out the main door by army personnel, calmly and without explanation. No fire alarms blared. No smoke was visible. There was no smell of burning. Martha wondered if it was a bomb scare; the orderly evacuation of the airport building reminded her of being evacuated from shops in Dublin whenever there was a plausible bomb scare. The passengers slowly made their way out into the sunshine with no sense of urgency just as shoppers evacuated shops in Ireland, except without the sunshine. While they were being weighed and their paperwork checked, another hot day had dawned in Khartoum.

Without comment or question, Martha followed Shelley in her saunter back to the car park. She remained perplexed as to why the airport was being emptied without any explanation: if it was a bomb, she hoped that whoever planted it could be relied upon to give adequate warning. Shelley seemed to take it all in her stride, just like regular shoppers in Dublin took bomb scares in theirs.

Fortunately, past experience had taught Shelley to tell drivers to wait until their plane had taken off before leaving, so Ahmed was still sitting in the Help pickup where they had parked when they arrived at the airport. He passed no comment when they reappeared and Shelley asked him to take them back to their flats. It was still early and when they got there everyone else was asleep. Limited normal conversation was exchanged as they sat in Martha's flat and ate bread and drank tea, and she wondered at how she and Shelley just took the little hiccup at the airport as part of normal Sudanese life. She remembered Molly's expression, I.B.M., *Inshallah, Bukhara, Mumbkin*. If it be the will of God, Tomorrow, Maybe! *It seems that I'm adjusting to Sudanese ways,* she thought.

"Probably a coup attempt," Shelley suggested calmly, as if it was an everyday occurrence and not headline material.

"Oh, so the Sudanese have coup attempts and the Irish drink tea! I think I'm more comfortable with tea drinking," Martha said, unintentionally voicing her thoughts.

Shelley smiled and agreed – it was the nearest thing to a friendly chat they'd had since Martha's arrival so she decided to use the opportunity to raise some of her concerns about funding.

"I met with Jeremy from Food for All the other week and we were discussing how we could improve the currency situation for Help. We know now that we have to stop bringing in undeclared dollars so I'm exploring other ways to save Help money. Jeremy suggested—"

"Martha, if I think that we need to consult other organisations about how we do business in Sudan then I'll be sure to let you know. In the meantime, please do not discuss our business elsewhere. Okay?"

"But we have to do something and I needed to find out what else might work…" Martha struggled not to raise her voice.

"Well, that's all I have to say on the matter. Right!" Shelley said as she stood up quickly and walked out the door of Martha's flat.

Over the course of the morning, news that there had been a coup attempt, which had started at the airport, filtered through. Some said that that was where the leaders had gone wrong. They should have taken over the main Khartoum radio station first and generated ground swell support that way. The word went around that twenty-eight officers and many others had been arrested as the coup attempt had been quickly suppressed by military loyal to President Omar al-Bashir. Within a few days, there were unconfirmed reports that the officers were executed by firing squad after a summary court martial, less than twenty-four hours after the coup had even started. It was also said that two hundred others had been arrested and imprisoned, probably tortured, and that the officers' bodies had been buried unceremoniously, immediately after the execution. If this was the case then it was contrary to Sharia law, which called for the bathing and shrouding of bodies, followed by prayer.

While Martha had been struck by how ordinary their encounter at the airport had felt, the rumours brought home to her the extremes of the country in which she was living. It demonstrated, in no uncertain terms, that there was no limit to how far President al-Bashir would go to put down any dissent against his rule. It seemed that Sharia law could be readily invoked when it suited the powerful and dismissed when it didn't.

"A bit like Christians and the ten commandments, don't you think? Like whatever happened to 'Thou shall not kill'? Or to 'Remember to keep holy the Sabbath day…in it thou shall do no work…'" Martha commented.

"Oh, she's off. Here comes one of her pet rants again," Siobhán teased.

"I don't think religion is the problem, it's what the men in power do with it and it does seem to be men. Therein lies some of the problem – too many men in power," Molly responded.

A heavy discussion followed on power and religion and the absence of 'proper' women in power. It seemed that the few women who made it to the top became more manly than the men they were competing with and worse still, they never seemed to do much to bring more women up with them, but that clearly wasn't the issue in Sudan, because women didn't get to rise anywhere.

The officers' bodies were no sooner buried than the end of Ramadan came and went and with it the Feast of Eid a-Fitr. Khartoum seemed to slip back to normality almost immediately. Perhaps the government's reaction to the coup attempt had led to a 'heads down and be seen to get on with life response'. A sort of 'the coup had nothing to do with me' reaction. Martha found herself wondering did that just happen? *Was there really a coup attempt, right here where I live now?* And has life reverted back to the old normal as if someone had brushed a fresh layer of sand over it all and bingo: normality resumed? And like the little bottles of alcohol, would the bodies turn up eventually from under the pile of sand on a beach in Khartoum where they were rumoured to be buried? Would the Ramadan coup be quickly forgotten and al-Bashir get to continue along the path of destroying any shred of democracy that might still exist in Sudan?

A few days later Martha's feeling of voyaging in another world was further enhanced when she was shopping in the government duty-free shop. She had put some shampoo and soap in her trolley and was turning at the end of an aisle, when she crashed trolleys with someone she never expected, nor would ever have wanted, to meet.

"*Malesh*," she uttered as she peered at him. He barged on past her as she stood open-mouthed. *Feck, that's Gaddafi's son!* She knew that Sudan and Libya were close friends and neighbours but she didn't expect to bump into the notorious Libyan leader's son, a man whose distinctive facial features and mop of hair made him the image of his father, just a younger, fresher version. The full military attire further confirmed for her who he was, if she'd had any doubt.

Chapter 15

Haboob

Early one evening after the coup attempt, Martha found herself sitting at her desk, about to write to Patrick and tell him all that had happened and how bizarre and unsettling it all was. But with the pen in her hand, she stopped and thought about what she was doing. Was she fooling herself, pretending that she still had a relationship with him? How could they expect to be remotely tuned into each other with all the distance between them in both miles and experience? She felt tired after the heat of the day, as she often did after work, so she turned on the almost useless air conditioning unit, lay down on her bed, closed her eyes and nodded off. When she opened her eyes, the bedroom was in total darkness. For a moment she thought she must have fallen asleep for hours and night-time had fallen, but she felt certain it had only been twenty minutes or so.

Something very strange was happening.

She got up, turned on the bedroom light and went over to her window. She stared out at a strange, deep darkness. She turned off the air-conditioning and listened. The loud noise of a whirling, whipping wind filled the silence. It was a sound of cinematic proportions, in stereo. A storm was raging, like none she had ever witnessed before. As she stared out into the darkness, she realised that the air was filled with sand, it was all that she could see in the space between her window and the building next door, an unending storm cloud of sand, pinging off her window panes. It felt disconcerting, almost apocalyptic; she wanted to run into the flat next door and find out what was going on but, as she went to her door, she remembered Molly and Siobhán were out and had promised to call for her when they got back.

She half-ran to the front door of the building. She opened it but could only see a few feet in front of her. The full stinging blast of sand hit her face and arms. The cars outside were buried up to their bonnets. She stood momentarily feeling as if she had been dropped into an exaggerated movie set with the realness of it stinging her skin and piercing her eyes. She backed away and closed the door against it and made her way back into the hallway. As she turned, out of the corner of her eye, she saw Mohammed, the security guard, sitting on the stairs. She hadn't thought about him and was relieved to see that he was not in his exposed tiny sentry hut outside the building, where he usually sat, ate and slept.

"*Ma kwas, haboob*," he said shaking his head.

"*Haboob?*"

"*Na'am – Aaya, haboob*," he replied nodding.

"*Ma kwas.*" Martha nodded in agreement, not good at all.

She returned to her bedroom and sat back down at her desk. Nobody had told her about haboobs or sandstorms or whatever it was that was going on. Were they dangerous? Would Siobhán and Molly be safe? Would it blow over soon? Would they get stuck in the sand? She decided to distract herself while waiting for them and to try again to write to Patrick. She picked up her pen and stared at the page, wrote a few words and stopped. Her heart wasn't in it. The realisation came to her that, in writing long diary type letters to him, she had wanted to draw him into her Sudanese world. She contemplated how she couldn't realistically expect to succeed when she could hardly get her own head around it, and she was living in it.

Worse, she was frustrated that none of his letters showed any response to her ramblings on her many and varied experiences in Sudan. How, if he had read her letters at all, could he express literally no comments? She considered that his head and heart were still firmly in Ireland and that this meant she was no longer part of his life or interests – if she ever had really been, now that she thought about it. *Well now he certainly has moved on. And so should I. And I can't deny that I am increasingly finding it hard to think of Stefan as just a friend. Maybe it's that he's here and Patrick is not? No, it's more than that.* She felt her face redden. *Oh, help. I must bite the bullet and make the phone call that I have been putting off for too long. God, where are Siobhán and Molly? Bring them home safely.*

Maybe not making it to Wadi Dabor earlier in the week was destiny. She had no excuse to postpone the call any longer. She would have the ideal opportunity to ring Patrick at noon Sudanese time on Saturday, two days later. That should be 9:00 a.m. his time which would catch him before he would leave the house. He was a man of habit. Saturday mornings meant a leisurely breakfast with a pile of newspapers bought from the shop around the corner, followed by a trip to the supermarket for his weekly shop at about 10:30 a.m. Having worked this much out, she tried to practice the conversation. But the vision of Siobhán and Molly caught in the sandstorm kept interrupting her thoughts. She decided to have a shower to wash the sand out of her hair, leaving the bathroom door open so she would hear them if they called. She was dried and dressed before there was a knock on her door.

"Wow, that was mad," Siobhán said as she came in. "Bloody mental country this. Did you see it?"

"I got a right feckin' fright too. Where were you?"

"We had called into Mags from UNHCR for a cuppa, when bam, all hell broke loose. My first haboob! It was bloody terrifying."

"I thought the world was going to end!" Martha said and meaning it.

Having had to use saucepans to dig their land cruiser out from the sand, Siobhán was tired. The roads were worse than they were in Ireland after a few inches of snow, Molly said. They decided to stay in and make do with whatever was left in their fridges. Martha managed make up a sort of vegetable curry and a rice dish.

On Saturday morning, Martha went to ring Patrick from the Acropole Hotel. The hotel had been in existence since the 1950s and was owned and run by a Greek family, thus explaining its Greek style. Two years previously, both it and the Sudan Club had been targeted in a terrorist assault and had suffered bomb damage. Seven or eight people had been killed. She didn't know why the attack had happened but thought it was probably some sort of anti-foreigner attack, as the Acropole and the Sudan Club were the main places that journalists and expats hung out.

She made her way up the stairs to the reception area and booked the call. When the receptionist succeeded in getting through, she called Martha into the small, cluttered office and left her in privacy.

"You caught me before I went out the door," Patrick said by way of greeting.

"Oh," said Martha, feeling thrown. "You're early."

"Well it's after ten here so not really."

"I thought there was a three-hour time difference."

"There was but it's summertime here now so the clocks have changed. Anyway, more importantly, how are you?"

"Fine, fine. Interesting place, obviously! Coup attempt this week, who knows what next week. What about you?"

Martha caught herself killing time, avoiding what she wanted to say while knowing that the telephone connection could be lost at any time.

"Work is very busy of course. Not much to report really. Apart from that the country has gone soccer crazy – Ireland has great expectations for the world cup, you know – and I'm managing to fit in the odd match and the odd gig here and there, in between work and more work…Not many gigs in Sudan, I'd say."

"No. No gigs here. How are all your family?"

"Fine, ticking along. They were asking for you."

"Oh, give them my regards."

"I will."

"Patrick, there is something I need to say. I don't know how to say it. I don't think…I think…Well, I don't think that it can work out with me over here and you over there and all that."

"Oh…Martha, what do you mean by that exactly?"

"Well, I think, perhaps that we should, you know…take a break or something."

"Oh, I see. I suppose…perhaps, if you think so…"

"I've been thinking, well, you know, maybe it is what we both need?"

"If you've thought about it then I suppose that's it so."

"I don't know. Maybe let's see how things work out as the year passes. Who knows what will happen in the long run?" Martha said. She wanted him to say that he missed her, say that she's right, say that she's wrong, say that he cares. Say something, for goodness sake! But he didn't.

"Okay. Bye then. Take care."

And he hung up before she could even say goodbye.

Chapter 16

Wadi Dabor

Ten days after the coup attempt, Shelley and Martha took a Khartoum Air scheduled flight to Wadi Dabor, a town situated in the area of western Sudan known as Darfur. The Fokker 50 certainly lived up to its reputation as a vomit comet. Despite chewing endlessly on gum that she had acquired especially for the journey, the roller-coaster plane ride had Martha permanently one more hard-swallowed retch from throwing up. She was not alone. A number of other unfortunate passengers were sitting, heads down, chests heaving, poised with their sick bags at the ready. The plane was stuck in an endlessly recurring pattern of rising into the cloudless sky, settling there momentarily, before plummeting steeply and falling into a deep, invisible valley. In trying to distract herself from the nausea, thoughts of the one hundred and something listed faults that Stefan told her the plane had floated into her head. Perhaps, the feeling of nausea might end prematurely in one massive plummet to the ground. Stefan had told her that Khartoum Air was commonly known as *Insha'Allah Air* – its safety depended on the will of God and not on good maintenance! He regretted telling her.

"*Al Hamdillallah*," Martha exclaimed out loud, thanking God as the Fokker landed in Wadi Dabor with a gentle thud. The airfield was little more than a flat strip of desert with a small building in the middle of it. The plane came to a stop a hundred yards short of the shed-like structure. The passengers ploddingly disembarked and made their way to it forming a messy queue. Permits and passports and other documentation were checked at least twice. Through a window, Martha saw an old tractor pulling a trailer precariously loaded with some of the luggage from the flight. The bags and boxes, including the medical supplies that Shelley and she had brought, were taken to near the building and deposited onto the ground outside. The passengers whose paperwork had been checked made their way back out the door to collect their luggage. The boxes and bags were many times more than Martha and Shelley could manage and they wondered how they might transport them. As they stood contemplating, a Land Cruiser appeared from around the building with the Help logo on it. Judy, whom Martha had met at Christmas, was sitting in the passenger seat, smiling and waving.

"*Al Hamdillallah*," Martha said again.

Judy jumped out of the Land Cruiser and greeted Martha with a warm hug. She turned to greet Shelley but she was already giving instructions to the driver on what was to be loaded onto the vehicle. Shelley then sat in the front seat beside the driver and Martha and Judy happily jumped into the back and sat on the bench-like seat.

It was Martha's first glimpse of rural Sudan. From a distance the land had appeared like a desert with an unexpected scattering of greenery, but up close she realised the land was a sort of reddish-brown soil rather than sand. The resulting trees, bushes and shrubs were nothing as majestic as the incredible neem trees that lined one of the main avenues in Khartoum; it was all more as nature, rather than man, had meant it to be.

"It's so different from Khartoum," Martha commented enthusiastically. "Greener than most of Khartoum, except Tuti Island, which is almost pure green."

Tall grass fencing created small compounds of four or more tukuls, round grass huts that housed entire families. Inside the fences and out, there were children playing, sitting, talking, carrying water and generally running around. There were plenty of women too, walking tall in their colourful *thobes*, carrying children on their hips or backs and water or piles of sticks on their heads, all done with perfect balance, as African women can and do. Women were also noticeably more visible at the market stalls that lined some of the streets than they were in Khartoum. They sat in front of, or opposite, rows of low white open-fronted buildings which served as simple shops or workshops. Like the shops in Khartoum each seemed to specialise in a limited selection of goods: cloth in one, sewing machines in another and so on. The stall holders, both men and women, sat under low-slung scrappy awnings set on wobbly sticks. They were selling mainly fresh produce, sugarcane, carrots, okra, onions and other crops that Martha didn't recognise. As in Omdurman and Souq Libya in Khartoum, important-looking men strode through the town sitting tall on donkeys that looked too small to carry them. Despite their presence, Martha got the feeling that Wadi Dabor was a more relaxed place to live than Khartoum, where men totally dominated and everything was done under the continuous watchful eye of the military.

At the centre of Wadi Dabor was a large red-brick mosque, easily three stories in height, crowned with a large blue dome and surrounded by an elaborate brick wall. The extravagance of the mosque stood in tremendous opulence against the simplicity of the low-lying buildings of the town.

The Land Cruiser stopped at a metal gate set in an eight-foot-high mud wall. Everyone climbed out and the gate was opened by Áine, whom Martha had also met over Christmas. Áine, like Judy, greeted Martha with a warm hug and Shelley grunted hello as she gave orders to the driver on offloading everything.

They made their way in through the gate which opened into a small, simple yard surrounded by basic square clay buildings. Each building was a separate room opening directly onto the courtyard, with three buildings serving as bedrooms and one as a kitchen-communal space. A small diesel generator provided some power but Judy explained that they mainly relied on candlelight and cooked on two open wood-burning stoves.

Judy introduced Shelley and Martha to Jamil who was sitting on his hunkers cooking Kisra, the brown flat bread that Abdul Halim cooked. On the other stove was a stew simmering in an open pan. Its welcome, spicy aroma filled the air and reminded Martha that it had been a long time since they had eaten – she often thought that she must have been a dog in her last life, given how governed by food she was.

Fortunately for Martha, Simon, another Help volunteer based in Wadi Dabor, arrived promptly and Judy announced that it was time for dinner. Simon was an engineer who had arrived a few months earlier and had stayed with Martha in the spare room of her flat in Khartoum for a couple of nights before his transfer to Wadi Dabor. She'd found him very intense and serious despite being not much older than her. He was taller than her and had been at least as thin. Now he was even thinner and his heavy glasses looked cartoonish on his narrow face. He wasn't sporty but was very active in that he never sat still and after a short while in his company, Martha usually found herself feeling like an overwound spring that could do something unexpected at any minute. It only took a few hours with him before she felt exhausted.

Simon shifted from foot to foot as he greeted Martha and Shelley with a formal limp handshake. His job was to oversee and manage the completion of the renovation of the hospital and clinic in Wadi Dabor. Before Help had taken on the project the hospital had been left unused and lying derelict, lacking a proper roof, running water or electricity. Simon had assumed responsibility from a retired engineer who had been on an eighteen-month contract and who, in turn, had taken over from an earlier volunteer engineer. The project was at last nearing completion. The last tranche of the funding would not be sanctioned by the funding agency until they had received a full costing of the completion, supported by an engineer's report on the work done to date and to be done. When Martha had eventually found out the funding agency's requirements, she had briefed Simon and had offered him the spare computer that had been donated to use if it suited him. Now, he had no sooner shook her hand, before he launched straight into an update on progress and, without stopping for breath, asked her when she would like to go through everything with him. Martha let out an involuntary sigh and after a deep breath, she suggested that they should talk the next morning. It was agreed that she would visit the hospital with him and the clinic with Judy the next day and then she would go through the reports and financials with both of them.

Áine, when she could get a word in, explained that she was in Wadi Dabor to sort out medical supplies for the clinic that she ran with Catherine, another nurse who had been in Khartoum for Christmas. Their clinic was many miles away across the desert near the Chad border.

The chat continued over dinner and afterwards until Judy declared that she was fit for nothing more than bed.

"Hope it's okay guys, but, Shelley, you're sharing my room, and Martha, you're sharing with Áine. I think Jamil has left us each some fresh water in the rooms for washing and help yourselves to a cup of water from the filtered tank over beside the kitchen for your teeth."

Martha followed Áine to her bedroom with its mesh door opening to the courtyard and a small glass-free window with mosquito netting pulled over the gap. Inside the mud hut there was an old chest of drawers, a large suitcase and, under mosquito nets, were two low wooden beds with thin mattresses. The mattresses were covered in well worn, off-white sheets that Martha thought may have had colour previously. There was a small equally off-white pillow on each bed too. In the corner, was a plastic basin and a bar of soap sitting on a low shelf with a covered bucket of water underneath.

"I think I'll just brave the latrine again before I wash," Martha said to Áine as she went into the courtyard.

The latrine was a small corrugated structure with a short door facing away from the yard. Martha was relieved that it had a raised, wooden bench-like seat with a hole the shape and size of a toilet seat and a lid. There was even a simple chain-pull flushing mechanism that some previous volunteer engineer had set up. The general rule, Áine told her, was, "If it's yellow, let it mellow. If it's brown, flush it down." Simple. Water wasn't always plentiful and after every couple of flushes the little tank above the toilet had to be filled by bucket from a water tank in the courtyard.

Well, thought Martha, as she sat on the seat, *I've done well so far and I sure hope that, if I'm going to get the inevitable dose of the runs, it's not going to be here.*

She slept soundly through the night on the small bed, waking to the sound of Áine moving around at about 7:00 a.m. Áine opened the door to the courtyard and a blast of unusually fresh air come across the room.

"Well, good morning, Martha."

"Good morning, Áine."

"Good morning indeed. God has been good and sent us some rain during the night," Áine said, before she inhaled deeply.

"Yes, yes. Wow, my first sniff of rain in five months. It smells wonderful."

As Martha and Simon walked over to the hospital later that morning, she felt like an excited child oohing and aahing at how clean, bright and green everything was, gleaming and glistening in the hot sunshine. Not only had the rain given everywhere a good wash, but a generous spread of new green growth had sprouted up overnight.

"It's as if the plants were asleep under the soil, waiting to be woken up by the rain, then they shook themselves off, popped up and said 'here we are, look at us,'" Martha said enthusiastically, unable to contain herself.

Simon stared at her in a way that asked if she was a day short of a week, but she was too excited to care.

They made their way first to Judy's clinic, outside of which was a small queue of women and children. Inside was a brightly coloured, freshly painted room with two curtained off areas for examining patients. Judy could be heard behind one curtain speaking in soft English and a local nurse could be heard speaking in a language that wasn't English and didn't sound like Arabic either. Occasionally a third voice, presumably the patient's, could be heard.

When Judy had finished and the patient had left, she showed Martha behind the curtain where there was a small sink, a basic almost new hospital bed and a chair and a worktable. She then took Martha into a room next door which was drab and dirty looking. A coat of paint would have made a big difference to the apparent cleanliness of the room and she felt for the women sitting there with their sick children in the miserable space.

"This is what the other room was like before we did it up. To be honest, we hadn't planned on using this room yet so…But these women have walked miles and miles to get their sick children seen to and we felt that this was the best place to keep a close eye on their babies while we have no hospital."

Martha nodded and stood to one side, not knowing what to do, feeling like an intruder but nonetheless stuck to the ground taking the whole scene in.

One mother was sitting on the end of a low-lying bed, gently giving sips of Oral Rehydration Solution (ORS) from a teething cup to her small, thin toddler who lay listlessly in her arms. Another mother sat motionless on the side of a similar bed, looking at her baby who was lying in a small cot with a drip being fed into his tiny arm. The baby stirred gently and gurgled, its face breaking into a smile and its hands and arms lifting up off the mattress, asking the mother to be picked up, all the time keeping its eyes fixed on its mother's face. The mother half-smiled and looked anxiously over towards Judy.

Judy touched the baby's forehead with the back of her hand and the baby beamed up at her, waving its arms with determination.

"*Kwas*, good. I think he is getting better," she said, smiling too and nodding towards the mother and baby, indicating to the mother to lift him gently so as not to disturb the drip.

The mother smiled back and her face relaxed as if she understood that her baby would be well. She looked lovingly down at him, stroked his cheek and then gently picked him up. Judy carefully removed the drip and gave the mother a bottle with a few ounces of milk. He drank hungrily and the mother smiled, tears running down her face...and Martha's. There wasn't a more wonderful sight.

Judy looked over at the other mother and explained that she needed to go to wash her hands and would be back. When she returned, she walked over to the mother and child, put her hand on the toddler's forehead, then removed the cloth wrapped around his waist, turned him over gently in his mother's arms and took his temperature. She nodded at the mother and smiled.

"*Kwas, kwas*, the fever has passed. Let him sleep and he should be fine," she said as she nodded encouragingly. She then put her arms together as if holding a child and closed her eyes and pointed first at the little boy and then at the mother. The mother nodded hopefully as if understanding and redressed the small child. Judy took two blankets from the end of the bed and rolled them up and propped them against the wall at the top of the bed. She gestured to the woman to sit against the blankets and put her feet up on the bed and rest. Relief and gratitude filled the exhausted mother's face as she lay back against the blankets, hugged her baby to her and closed her eyes.

Martha caught herself thinking of all the things that are taken for granted back home and how, somehow, we don't seem to value African lives the way we value western lives. In some strange way, we think that death is a normal part of Africa, in a way that it is not in Ireland, Europe or America, yet a mother's love for a child is the same everywhere. If their baby is ill, they care as much as mothers do in the so-called developed world. They will sacrifice everything to save their children. With this dawning, she let out a long sigh and her face reddened with embarrassment.

"*Malesh*," she said and quietly left the room.

After the visit to the clinic, Simon re-joined Martha and Judy, and they walked back to the Help compound for some *fature* of sweet, spicy coffee and Kisra. Martha was processing all that she had seen and heard so she said little, but still listened. Judy and Simon talked about the hospital and how much it was needed and how soon it might be ready. Simon said that they were in the process of preparing a report to make a case to the funders for everything that they believed was needed to meet the needs of the community, and Martha took notes of each issue and the arguments to support each additional item. Her encounter that morning with the sick children had ignited a desire in her to do her part in getting Wadi Dabor a fully functioning hospital and clinic.

After *fature*, Simon and Martha walked to the hospital compound a couple of hundred yards past the clinic. The compound was empty and no work was happening as they awaited agreement from the funding agency as to what they would next finance. As it stood, the hospital was a series of old buildings that were currently no more than large empty rooms, set around three sides of a large walled courtyard. Help had only been able to renovate as fast as they could overcome certain bureaucratic hurdles and as funding became available. It had taken over a year to get initial agreement from the local administration as to how it would function and be financed following completion and that agreement had been known to change; Help saw no point in renovating if it wasn't going to be fully functional on an ongoing basis.

Simon had previous experience back in Ireland of working on hospital projects but clearly this was different and he had to work closely with the local administration to understand what would work in Wadi Dabor. At this stage nearly all of the buildings had been significantly renovated, repainted and rewired. The next stage was to equip them. Simon explained what equipment and beds were required and showed Martha detailed price lists that he had made. He had also listed where everything could be acquired and how much it would cost to get everything to Wadi Dabor, using experienced suppliers. It was all very precise and well considered. Martha was impressed. And later, when he took her through his engineer's reports on the work done and to be done, she was further impressed. It was clear that everything Simon had done was thoroughly and professionally prepared and Martha was greatly relieved that she would not have too much to do before she submitted it to the funding agency. She expressed this to Simon and he shrugged his thin shoulders. She would have been surprised if he had given her a more expressive response.

It had been a long day and Martha was glad to go to bed early that night. The next morning, she sat down with Judy and went through the running costs of her clinic. She had a reasonably clear idea of the costs involved from the previous year's report and from her work on the Khartoum clinics, so she and Judy were easily able to prepare a detailed budget for the current year. They also finalised the figures for the previous year, which were long overdue, but for which Martha had negotiated a reprieve on the basis of Liam's departure and the remote location.

After all the intense work, Martha decided to take a walk around the souks and streets of Wadi Dabor and experience it first-hand for the friendly town that it was. Although the people had very limited English and she had only limited Arabic, they still managed some engagement. She was, by this stage, very familiar with Arabic greetings and other much used Arabic phrases and enjoyed practising them in Khartoum, especially with the friendly waiters and doormen at the Sudan club. It made her feel more connected to the Sudanese. Despite knowing how to ask how much and knowing Arabic numbers and other phrases useful for doing business in the souks, she had found it difficult to engage with the mainly male stallholders in Khartoum. In Wadi Dabor, with more women stallholders, she enjoyed some relaxed banter, although it was mostly limited to *Salaam alaykum, Alaykum salaam, shokran, kwas, ma kwas, Hamdillallah* and other similar phrases combined with many hand gestures.

Martha had hardly seen Shelley since they'd arrived, except at the odd mealtimes. She had no idea what Shelley had been doing and over dinner that night Martha thought it better not to ask. Dinner was a chatty, relaxed affair and the meals served didn't vary much but were driven by what was available and in season locally. Martha was fine with whatever was going. Shelley on the other hand, in typical Shelley fashion, was inclined to moan a bit at the limited menu.

The next morning, they loaded up a pickup and Áine, Shelley, Martha and a driver, Ibrahim, headed off across the flat, dry land to visit Áine and Catherine's clinic and to bring much needed medical supplies. It was a long drive to the clinic which was on the other side of Darfur, near the border with Chad. They travelled on a bumpy and, at times, stony track, passing from one small settlement to another, with very little apart from scrub, bushes and the odd tree in between. The settlements were made up of a series of small grass-fenced areas each containing four or more *tukuls*. Inside the fences Martha could see goats, children and women and some small neatly planted areas. The children waved and jumped up and down as the pickup drove past. They saw very few men. Perhaps they had gone to Wadi Dabor or further afield to seek their fortune, or maybe to war.

They slowed down as they came near a large tent beside which was a long, narrow structure with straw walls and roof. Sitting on the ground outside, in neat rows, were forty or fifty boys, all with small blackboards on their knees. They were listening to a medium-built man who was talking while writing on a blackboard set up on an easel. There were no other buildings or structures and only some small trees and bushes. *What a strange place for a school, randomly plonked in the middle of nowhere!* Martha thought.

The pickup came to a stop beside the boys and they all stood up with excitement. Áine got out of the vehicle and the teacher greeted her warmly.

"*Salaam alaykum.*"

"*Alaykum salaam,*" he responded as he put his right hand to his heart.

"*Keef halak?*"

"*Kwas. Al Hamdillallah. Inti kwas?*"

"*Kwas. Al Hamdillallah.*"

Watching Áine's interaction with the teacher, Martha suspected that she shared her sense that speaking even limited Arabic to locals somehow gave a greater feeling of connection. It struck Martha that, by contrast, Shelley rarely spoke to anybody in Arabic.

Áine opened the back of the pickup and Ibrahim helped her lift out some boxes. One contained high energy biscuits and the other ORS. They gave the boxes to the teacher and he put his hand to his heart in gratitude.

"*Shokran.*"

"*Afwan, Ahlan wa sahlan*, you are welcome," Áine responded.

"*Al-Hamdillallah.*"

Áine turned and headed back to the pickup with Ibrahim following.

"*Ma'assalama, shokran*," the boys chorused as they waved goodbye.

Áine and Martha waved back. "*Ma'assalama.*"

Áine explained that the boys were all from the surrounding area, maybe twenty or more miles from the school. Each Sunday they walked from their homes to the school and then home again each Thursday evening. During the week they all slept in the tent or classroom. They arrived at school tired and hungry, having worked hard over the weekend at their villages to earn their keep and their small stipend which they paid to attend school. At weekends, they tended goats or helped grow small crops. The school received some resources from another charity but was short on food supplies.

They didn't stop for another break and it was mid-afternoon when they arrived at a large settlement of tukuls with various arrangements of grass fencing keeping animals and children in or out, or both…Martha couldn't tell. Children ran or sat around, women tended to pots on small fires, others walked straight carrying pots or urns or bunches of sticks on their heads while carrying buckets or baskets in their hands. Few of the women wore the traditional *thobes* and most were in normal, western dresses, all well-worn and faded.

Some of the women and children waved at the vehicle as it went past. Martha surmised that few vehicles travelled this far west; they had met not a single other one in their entire day's travel. She was amused that by the time they came to a stop at a metal gate set into a tall mud wall which surrounded the Help compound, the vehicle was surrounded by a herd of children shouting simply with the excitement of seeing the pickup. They didn't intrude nor put out their hands expecting anything. They simply looked on.

As they were unpacking, Catherine appeared. "Vaccinations, bandages, antibiotics, ORS, tea coffee, biscuits, sugar, baked beans, pasta. You'd think it was Christmas again," she said.

Unpacking done they sat down to a late lunch of pasta and tomatoes, followed by some biscuits and good old Irish tea with UHT milk.

The compound was simple. There was one small building containing a kitchen, store and living area with a table and chairs and a tall battered metal storage cupboard. It might have been blue some years previously but now there was more metal than paint visible. Outside the building were two simple ground-level wood-burning stoves, two pots and a neat pile of wood. The sleeping arrangements were similar to Wadi Dabor: small mud buildings each containing two beds and maybe a chair or a cupboard. Martha couldn't hide her horror when she saw and smelt the latrine: it was nothing more than a stinking hole in the ground inside a small corrugated hut that sat at a strange angle; its door shut only with much strong-armed manoeuvring. It was windowless, dark, hot and airless. The tight space was filled with a putrid smell that told Martha it was well-passed its properly functioning life.

"You get used to it," Catherine said seeing Martha wretch when she was shown it.

But Martha dreaded every time she had to use it; she could not get out of there fast enough.

Áine showed Martha the clinic which consisted of a room with an examination table, a chair and a storage press. Beside it, there was another room which was empty except for a desk and chair, a weighing scales on the floor and another suspended from the ceiling with a sling for holding a baby or young child.

"This was the assessment area and feeding centre during the famine but thankfully is little used now as food supplies are good," Áine explained. "Vaccinations and provision of primary healthcare are our main focus now and we have an outreach program too visiting the nearby villages. We are the area's only source of antibiotics and Catherine and I use them sparingly and only if we diagnose a bacterial infection. There are no doctors."

"I know," Martha responded, silently wondering at the wisdom of nurses acting as doctors, but knowing that there was no alternative.

Áine took out a packet of sterile blades from the locked storage cupboard. "Do you know why we keep a good supply of these?" she asked Martha.

"No. Why?"

"The local midwives ask us for them and use them to circumcise the young girls."

"And you give them to them?" Martha's response was spoken in clear horror.

"I was shocked too. But as Fiona, who was here when I first arrived, explained, what choice do we have? If we don't give them sterile blades, they will still get circumcised. It could be with any sharp object, even sharpened stones. The first time I saw a young girl with a fever and an infection down there, I knew we had no choice. I cried for days. She nearly died. The pet."

Martha went pale and put her hand down below her stomach protectively. "Oh my God. How can women do such barbaric things to little girls?" she said.

"It's a rite of passage, like an Irish Holy Communion, I suppose – but barbaric and destructive! It's all they know. They make a big fuss over the girl, usually she gets a new dress, and then all the women pin money to her new, fresh clothes, sometimes literally, as they hold her down, while the midwife goes about her business with the blade."

"That is so sick. The poor girls. The agony of it!" Martha said her voice quivering as she subconsciously clasped her thighs tight together under her skirt.

"It's horrible but no man will marry them if they are not circumcised. It seems that Sudanese men like their women dry and tight!"

"May they suffer in hell for it. God, I feel sick…the thought of it."

"I know. Catherine and I used to talk and talk about what we could do about it but we only ever went around in miserable circles. It beggars belief…Sorry I shouldn't have said anything but I still feel guilty every time I hand out the blades. And I dread that I might start to accept it. You know, as if it is okay…but it's not." Áine shook her head. "Come on, let's get a glass of water or something."

Martha followed her in silence, frantically contemplating what she might do about the situation to raise awareness of it, to change it. Shocked at her own ignorance and feeling totally inadequate, she considered how little, if anything, had changed for these women over recent years and with the current government, things weren't going to get better. They may get even worse. She felt angry and frustrated. The western world was just dabbling in the developing world. They were not really changing the situation for the better for the people who needed it most. It was a heartbreaking situation, made so much worse by how little Martha knew she could really do. *Plus ca change, plus c'est la même chose.*

Chapter 18

Sick and Flying

Before a meal of vegetable stew and bread, Martha started going through the figures for the clinic for the previous year with Áine and afterwards they finalised the budget for the year. Then they all sat around and chatted by candlelight. The relaxed, friendly atmosphere was spoilt by Shelley holding forth as if she was the big chief know-it-all, there to tell them all what to do.

Earlier, Áine had told Martha that Catherine's predecessor had warned her that Shelley always held forth and the thing to do was listen, say nothing and then do whatever you were going to do anyway. Shelley would hear their silence as agreement and that was fine by them. Martha wished that she had been given such good advice when she first arrived. She had had to bite her lip hard a number of times previously when Shelley had tried to assume full knowledge of, and responsibility for, Help's financial matters, though she showed little, if any, credible knowledge of the matter.

Shelley was talking now as if she could go on all night.

"I'm sorry to interrupt you, Shelley, but we all have an early start in the morning. Those small planes usually fly not long after dawn so we should go to bed very soon," Catherine suggested.

"We have to go out first thing and mark where to land for the pilot. We don't want him missing us…" Áine added.

Martha looked at her quizzically.

"There is a bit of a landing strip and we mark it by tying sheets to the bushes nearby."

"Oh, I see."

A German charity had chartered a plane to bring over some volunteers and supplies to a food and agricultural project they were setting up. For a small contribution to the cost, Help was using the plane to take Shelley and Martha back to Khartoum. The German food project had started as a response to the recent famine but, in the absence of proper roads, transportation had been and remained difficult, so a small runway of sorts had been constructed back at the height of the famine.

Martha and Áine were again sharing a room and, as they lay in their beds, Áine explained that the runway was nothing more than a levelled-off strip of dry land that, from the air, was indistinguishable from the land around it.

That night Martha was asleep just a few hours before she woke up with severe cramps, worse than she had ever experienced before. Bent double in pain, she found her torch and made her way quickly to the latrine. In her haste and given the darkness, she made no effort to close the door. As she was about to lower her bottom towards the hole in the ground, something scurried out of it. She would have screamed but she couldn't open her mouth; not alone did her bowels urgently want to empty themselves, but she was struggling not to throw up. When she thought that she had nothing more for her bowels to expel, she turned tentatively around and threw up into the stinking hole. In the brief moment that followed her vomiting, she felt sorry for any rats that might still be down there. But her sympathy was short-lived as she was back needing to go to the toilet again. She then threw up again, retching from the very depths of her stomach as if it might turn itself inside out in the process. By the fourth or fifth time, it took her all her strength to stay on her hunkers and not land plop on top of the rancid hole in the ground.

Eventually, she judged that she was done and she summoned up what she thought was the last of her energy to make her way back across the compound to the bedroom. She sat wearily on the bed and, using her torch for light, dug out two sachets of ORS from her backpack. She emptied these into her almost full water bottle and shook it. She took a few sips and lay back on the bed and hoped for sleep. No sooner had she shut her eyes than she was up again, grabbing her torch and rushing, as fast as her energy depleted body would allow, to the latrine. She wondered how there could be anything left in her stomach, which by this stage was aching with cramps and muscle strain. She slowly made her way back to the bedroom and rummaged for her small medical kit in her backpack. She got out some Imodium and Lomotil and took them with some ORS, hoping and praying for some relief. But none came, because as soon as she had taken them, she had to rush outside to retch again and then stumble on her wobbly legs across the compound to the latrine.

Sometime just before dawn, Áine woke up as Martha staggered again through the bedroom door.

"You okay?"

"No," Martha whispered. "Trots and vomiting all night…Can't hold anything down, even Lomotil."

Áine came over to Martha and took her pulse. "Oh dear, I'd better get you something. I'll be right back."

She returned after a few minutes to find Martha on her way back again from the latrine.

"Don't worry, we've all been there. This will help," she said, holding up a syringe and two vials. "One is for vomiting and the other for diarrhoea. Tablets are useless. You throw them up before they have a chance to work."

Martha nodded.

"If you turn over on your side and relax, you'll hardly feel a thing. They say I've a gentle touch with a needle."

Martha would have walked across hot coals if she thought that it would make a difference. A needle was nothing. She hardly felt Áine give her the injections and she just lay back and prayed hard that they would work. Right then she didn't think that she could raise her head off the pillow, never mind get up and get on a small toilet-less plane and fly to Khartoum.

Soon it was daylight and Catherine and Shelley drove out to the airstrip to tie sheets on the bushes. Áine stayed with Martha and left her mostly to sleep but woke her a couple of times to get her to sip some ORS to give her some energy. The injections seemed to have worked almost immediately and, while she was exhausted, she had at least stopped going to the toilet or throwing up.

She was fast asleep when Catherine opened the door.

"Sorry, Martha, but you have to get up fast! No time to waste. Where are your clothes? Here. Put them on quickly and I'll pack your stuff," Catherine said, moving Martha's clothes off the chair over to her on the bed.

Martha struggled to keep her eyes open and still felt as if she couldn't physically separate herself from the mattress. She mustered up whatever energy she could and took off her pyjamas and put on her skirt and top. Áine put on her sandals to save her having to bend down. Catherine put Martha's remaining things into her small holdall.

"Sorry about this, but the pilot is a nervous wreck! The Germans said that he was terrified he would overshoot and land in Chad. Now he wants to get back up in the air because he is scared silly that he will get caught in a haboob when the day heats up!" Catherine said.

They helped Martha out to the pickup and said goodbye to her with some gentle hugs. Martha thanked them for everything and Ibrahim then drove her out to where the small plane was waiting. Shelley was sitting up front beside the pilot, waiting impatiently. She didn't move when they arrived. Ibrahim kindly lifted Martha's holdall and backpack onto the plane and made sure that she was okay getting up the steps. Martha thanked him and said goodbye to him in both English and Arabic and he gave her a warm smile and said that she was welcome.

The pit of Martha's stomach felt as if a knife was piercing it and her bottom felt as if it would be dangerous to stand up. But she began to feel a bit perkier than she expected and was reasonably optimistic that she could last the journey without mishap. She even smiled to herself when she thought of the dreadful joke that her brother had told once in the months before she left. It was after she had fallen backwards hillwalking and had landed hard on a rock, badly bruising her bottom. He had laughed.

"Ha. You've got AIDS now!"

She had looked at him and he had said it again. "You've got AIDS, Martha, you know. Arse In a Diabolical State."

It wasn't funny then and it wasn't really funny now. But it was a relief to be able to think straight enough to remember it and not want to run for the toilet.

Martha had no sooner put her seatbelt on when the pilot took off. She sat back and closed her eyes for a few minutes but then decided that she didn't want to miss anything. Ever since seeing *Out of Africa* she had wanted to fly in a small plane, preferably an open biplane like the one in the film. The small five-seater wasn't a small open bi-plane, but it was much smaller than any other plane she had ever been in. She decided that she would sit back and take in the flying experience. Given their initial low altitude the panoramic views were more intimate than from a larger plane and Martha could see the women and children down below waving excitedly as the plane flew overhead. Once they hit higher altitude, the pilot put his head down on the dashboard and seemed to let the plane fly itself. *Do planes this small have autopilot?* Martha wondered as she watched the pilot, without lifting his head, chain smoke one cigarette after the other, dragging hard and frantically each time, as if his life depended on it. *And if his life depends on it, so do ours,* she thought.

Apart from the nervous pilot, Martha found the flight remarkably unexciting, with little more to see until they came in over the Nile, followed its path and headed in to land at Khartoum airport. She was dreading the airport as she hadn't the energy for anything demanding with regard to security or paperwork, but the gods must have favoured her as getting through it proved uneventful. *Al Hamdillallah,* she said to herself with a gentle smile.

Chapter 19

Home to Pigs and Stefan

Martha felt a brief moment of pleasure as she opened the front door of her flat. But it didn't last. In her absence, the replacement mechanic and administrator had arrived, as Molly had warned they would. The couple, Tom and Attracta, were moving into the spare bedroom in Martha's flat. *A couple, a couple of feckin' pigs,* Martha thought as she took in the state of the normally clean flat.

There were dirty dishes and cigarette butts on the table and the tiled floor was covered with butts, bits of food and spilled drinks. The smell of stale smoke and bad food hung in the airless sitting room. Butts floated in almost empty glasses. The shower room door was open and the stench of strong boozy piss wafted from the unflushed toilet. Martha covered her mouth with her arm and made her way across the sitting room, through the shower room doorway and tentatively over to the toilet. Trying not to gag on her still delicate stomach, she flushed the loo and threw some disinfectant down around the bowl. She closed the door and turned to review the sitting room. Her inclination was to sit down and cry. A nagging voice in her head told her to go into her bedroom and shut the door, but that wasn't in her already overtired psyche to do. Sleep would not come easy if she knew that she had to get up to such a mess.

She had cleaned and cleared the kitchen enough to make room for the dirty crockery from the sitting room when there was a knock on the flat door.

She cursed under her breath not feeling in the mood to greet the new arrivals, or anyone for that matter. She pulled open the door with a disgruntled frown, mumbling 'feck it' under her breath. Stefan stood looking at her with his fist poised to knock on the door again. His big brown eyes were full of concern looking at her pale, washed-out face.

"Are you okay?" he said as he took a small step towards her.

Martha didn't move but stood facing him, her eyes small in her head and her arms by her sides in exhausted exasperation. She felt him put his arms around the small of her back and pull her into him so that her face became buried in his chest. A wave of emotion rose up through her and she started to cry softly. With one arm he continued to hold her tight and with the other he stroked the back of her neck. Her crying started to build into uncontrollable sobbing and he gently nudged her further into the room and closed the door with his foot. She brought her arms up around his waist and clung to him. They stood that way for a few minutes and slowly her crying turned to barely audible sobs.

"It's okay, Martha. It's okay. Molly told me you were back and you had been sick."

Martha moved her head to meet his eyes and he bent down and kissed her forehead with a tenderness that sent a warm glow through her body.

"You don't want to catch what I had," she sighed as she looked up into his beautiful brown eyes.

"Don't worry. It was more likely something that you ate, I'll be fine."

He was still holding her tight when her involuntary sobs turned to hiccups that lifted her chest upwards and outwards in a jerky movement. They both laughed. She tried holding her breath but it made no difference.

"Sorry. Bad timing. I need a glass of water – if I can find a clean glass in this pig sty."

Stefan looked around them and took in the dirt of the room, the table and floor covered with spills and dirty dishes and stinking wet cigarette butts.

"My goodness, what happened here?"

"It seems some pigs moved in a few days ago. And when they ran out of clean saucepans, rather than wash one, they boiled onions in the kettle!"

"Disgusting. And they are not all ordinary cigarettes either, judging by the smell and some of the butts," Stefan said as he picked up a dirty glass and put his nose to it.

"I know. I've just cleaned up some of what they used for ashtrays and I cleaned the kitchen to make room for this mess," Martha said and she then sipped some water from her own bottle while bending her head and upper body forward in a U-shaped contortion.

"What are you doing?" Stefan laughed.

"I'm trying to cure my hiccups by drinking backwards – normally, I bend forward and drink out of the back of a glass – due to the lack of a clean glass, I'm using my bottle!"

"Looks a bit strange to me!" Stefan grinned.

He started lifting some of the dishes into the kitchen.

"I'll tell you what. I'll give you a hand cleaning up. Then you get some sleep and if you are up for it, I'll take you to the Italian night in the Hilton. How about that?"

"Sounds good but…I'm not sure if I will be up for it. Also isn't it a bit posh? I might not have any clothes here fit for the Hilton!"

As Martha was speaking, she felt herself getting excited and she remembered that she had some good clothes still left in her suitcase that hadn't yet faced the Sudanese sun and dust.

"I'm sure that you'll be fine," Stefan said running his fingertips down her arm.

His touch sent a tingling sensation around her body and lifted her fatigue in an unexpected and thrilling way. *Oh! What was that? Whatever it was, it felt good.*

Together they spent the next hour cleaning the flat. Stefan brought the dirty dishes into the kitchen from the living room and wiped the low table. Martha washed and Stefan dried. The tiny kitchen provided plenty of opportunity for intimacy and Stefan ran his hand gently across Martha's back as he passed behind her or touched her arm as he squeezed some more dirty dishes onto the bit of worktop at the side of the sink. Despite her lack of sleep, Martha experienced a sense of what might be happily called domestic bliss. Who would have thought that it could be found in a grotty kitchen in Sudan! She smiled to herself. Stefan told her how he had missed seeing her before she went to Wadi Dabor. He had been unable to fly back from the south because of the haboob. He had just taken off when he got a warning across the radio that a haboob had struck Khartoum and he had turned back. He asked Martha all about her trip to the west and what it was like. Despite being in Sudan for nearly eighteen months, he still hadn't flown to Darfur. She told him about Wadi Dabor, the hospital and the women and babies in the clinic. She got quite animated talking about how much we, in the so-called developed world, take for granted, how we undervalue African lives, but African mothers value their children as much as westerners value their children. African women sacrifice more for theirs, walking miles, carrying them in search of food, shelter or medical help.

She turned to look at Stefan to emphasise her point. "We don't appreciate that to a mother a child's precious life is a precious life, whether that mother is a wealthy European with all mod cons or a poor Sudanese woman with only the clothes on her back. Do you know what I mean?"

"I do...and I love how passionate you get about things!" Stefan said with a cheeky smile.

"Ah feck off. You're taking the proverbial!" Martha said splashing him with sudsy water.

"No, I'm not. It's that your passion is so sincere!" he said wiping his face, then taking her in his arms and kissing her briefly on the lips.

Martha looked at him wide-eyed.

"I used to get passionate about different issues too, but, as you know, half the time I was just trying to go against my father. Now my passions are definitely more sincere! Do *you* know what I mean?"

"Maybe," she said smiling.

"As a mark of my sincerity, how about I finish up here? You get some rest and I'll collect you at around six thirty. Okay?"

"You sure?"

"Sure," he said kissing her on the cheek.

Martha went to bed still smiling and closed her eyes visualising dinner with Stefan. Of course, there would be no wine as this was, after all, Sudan. But that didn't matter. They wouldn't be holding hands across the table or anything like that either. Still, if they were Sudanese, they couldn't even go out together at all, unless they were husband and wife or brother and sister or similarly close family. Perhaps they would go back to his flat afterwards, who knows? It was possible that they would. She didn't think that Stefan was shy in that way and he would probably ask her straight out. But if they did go back, what then? It would surely be awkward especially as she was fairly inexperienced and she wasn't going to take any chances especially as AIDS was a terrifying and very real prospect. But how would she express all this to Stefan?

Despite these very real concerns, she slept soundly for a few hours and was awoken by Tom and Attracta arriving back.

"Oh, the cleaners must have been here," Attracta exclaimed loudly.

They busied themselves clattering around the kitchen, making eggs and beans and coffee and giving out loudly about the Sudanese they had met that day. They referred to Khartoum as a dive and commented on how backward and ignorant everyone was.

These are the same people who boiled onions in a kettle, Martha thought. *I'm going to bite my lip, say a quick hello and walk straight through to the shower room, otherwise I will surely say the wrong thing.*

By the time Martha braved coming out of her bedroom to go through the living room to the shower, they had the kitchen back to being a mess again and were sitting on the couch. Attracta had her feet up on the coffee table beside their dirty cups and dishes and spilled coffee. They had already smoked at least two cigarettes each and were both pulling on another, filling the room with disgusting cigarette smoke. *Oh help, what am I going to be living with?*

She took a deep breath and regretted it as the smoke caught in her throat. She started coughing. They turned to look at her and she swallowed hard.

"Hi, I'm Martha."

She coughed again despite her best efforts not to.

"Sorry I missed your arrival," she mumbled, trying to catch her breath, while walking behind the couch that they were stretched out on.

Tom barely lifted his shaven head from Attracta's large stomach, where it was resting. He half-waved with his hand.

"Oh, hi, I'm Attracta and this is Tom," Attracta said flicking her straggly bleach blonde hair. "No bother, sure it gave us a chance to get settled in. Didn't it, Tom?"

Tom grunted.

"I suppose it did," Martha replied.

Her accent, bog Irish, working class, probably from the midlands, maybe Longford or Roscommon. Martha opened the door of the shower room. *Oh stop, Martha, stop. Stop making such judgements. You sound horribly like your snobby mother. Why are you thinking things like that anyway when you should be looking forward to a relaxing Italian dinner with Stefan?*

She stood for a long time under the warm shower, washing the dirt and grime of Darfur out of her skin and hair. She even took time to shave under her arms and her lower legs, remembering the sensation of Stefan's touch as she did so. She wondered what might happen that night between them and her body tingled. She thought that over the five months that she had known him, they had probably been coming to this day but she hadn't been prepared to admit it. She had needed to break things off with Patrick first. The reality was that she and Stefan had shared more honest insights into each other's personal life, especially their relationship with their families, than Martha had ever shared with Patrick. She suspected that he had been more open than she had, but, in her defence, that was partly because she was still trying to work some of it out for herself.

He was the eldest of a family of three children, two boys close in age and a sister six years younger. His father was an engineer who had spent a significant part of his career in the army, followed by the family spending a year with him on a consultancy contract in the UK, hence Stefan's perfect English. The father was militant to the core in everything he did: he wanted, no, commanded, that each of his sons do more than their obligatory time in the army. Stefan, in response, had declared himself a pacifist and had flat out refused. The six months compulsory service had been more than enough for him. He had worked part-time from the age of fourteen to earn money for flying lessons, which he started taking at the age of seventeen. His father told him that he was a fool and that he could have saved himself all that trouble and expense if he joined the army air force. The pressure from his father for Stefan to join the army never stopped, even when Stefan went to university and was studying electrical engineering, as his father had done. His brother, who could do no wrong in his father's eyes, had gone almost straight from his compulsory service to joining the army permanently.

As Stefan's rows with his father had grown in frequency and intensity, his mother said very little and focused her attention mainly on his little sister. She normally left the room when Stefan and his father were fighting. A couple of times she took Stefan aside and suggested that he join even for a year or two and that it might actually do him some good as clearly, in her opinion, he wasn't happy anyway and seemed to be permanently and habitually angry.

"Take a leaf out of your brother's book, this once maybe," she'd said, "it might give us all peace."

But as his father's favourite line was, "Why can't you be more like your brother?" his mother's comments only added fuel to Stefan's fire. He had decided to really drive home the point that he was never ever joining the army by joining a gay rights group in his final year in university, becoming one of their most outspoken members. One of his older professors, who was a good friend of his father's, got in touch with his father to express concern about Stefan being seen to be part of such a group; as he saw it, it had career-limiting implications. Stefan had expected this and had even orchestrated it. When he came home from college one evening, his father called him into his study and called him the Austrian equivalent of a dirty filthy faggot and a litany of other derogatory names. Stefan in return called his father a bloody bigoted bully and other heartfelt insults. His father punched him in the jaw, breaking a tooth, but leaving Stefan still standing. That was that, his father said, and told him to get out of his house and never show his faggot face there again. Stefan went and stayed with his girlfriend.

Out of sheer determination to show his father that he didn't need him, he finished his degree with first-class honours. He got a job with an international anti-nuclear charity and continued to take part in any other protests that he thought would annoy his father. He worked hard, including doing various nixers to enable him to keep up his flying and qualify as a pilot. The result was that he was seldom home and, when he was, he rarely did anything but sleep. Finding his girlfriend in bed with another man, late one night, was the start of his wake-up call and was ultimately what led him to Sudan. He said that after all that shit, he had decided it was time that he took a break from protesting. Sudan was his way of doing just that.

Destiny, Martha thought with a smile, as she pulled on a light, black fitted top, too warm for daytime wear in Sudan, and a calf-length fitted linen skirt. Trish, back home, called the outfit sexy and had encouraged Martha to bring it to Sudan, in case, *you know...*

Trish had never approved of Patrick. Martha remembered her saying, "He's too stiff and boring for you as far as I can see. I think you should find someone more exciting, unless, of course, you're going to tell me that, in bed, he's not at all stiff and boring!"

"Maybe he's not…boring!" Martha had responded.

Hmm wonder what Trish would make of Stefan, Martha thought as she caught her reflection in the mirror. It was a flattering outfit although it hung looser than she remembered. Hardly surprising, given the night that she'd had and that she'd had nothing but ORS, a slice of bread and a high energy biscuit all day.

Chapter 20

Hilton

Martha stayed in her bedroom, glancing over letters from friends, as she waited to hear Stefan knock on the flat door. She hoped he would be on time. She looked again and again from her watch to her clock. It was 6:25 p.m. when she heard a knock on the door and she got up from her desk and almost ran in front of the couch that Tom and Attracta were still sprawled on, slouched in the same position as she had seen them in earlier.

"Bye," she said, waving as she went past them, thinking to herself, *Don't wait up!*

"Hi there," she said, nearly pushing Stefan backwards as she shot out the door.

"Whoa!"

"Sorry. Sorry. I'm avoiding my new house-pigs, I mean mates."

"That good?"

"Better. You have no idea how glad I am that you asked me out tonight."

"You're welcome. I think!" He laughed that sincere laugh that she loved.

The Hilton was a far cry from the dated décor of the flat. It was a large, modern multi-storey hotel on the outskirts of Khartoum. It felt like stepping back into the developed world as soon as they walked through the door, a proper contrast to most of the buildings that Martha had reason to visit in Khartoum.

There was a large lobby, which was busy and noisy, filled with wealthy Arab men wearing starched, bright white *jallabiyahs* over equally white shirts and dark trousers which, Martha suspected, were expensive designer trousers.

On their heads many wore black-and-white Palestinian scarves as turbans, rather than the more usual loose white ones. Many of them also had heavy gold chains around their necks and gold rings on their fingers. Martha shivered a little as she sensed some of them eyeing her as she walked through the lobby towards the restaurant. Stefan noticed too and was about to put a protective arm around her back, but withdrew it remembering where they were.

The restaurant did different cuisine on different days, but Martha had never eaten there. She was impressed with the Italian bunting hanging around the restaurant and the red-and-white gingham tablecloths. She was standing at the entrance, taking in the room, when a waiter greeted Stefan by name. Stefan and the waiter exchanged pleasantries and the waiter showed them to a quiet table, all on its own, tucked discreetly away in the back corner beside a window. He handed them menus that were in both English and Arabic.

"I told you that I normally eat maybe once a week here with Michael or one of the guys I play tennis with," Stefan said. "But, believe it or not, this is the first time I've come with a woman."

"So, none of your previous girlfriends here qualified for the royal treatment?" Martha said, feeling chuffed and then only slightly embarrassed that she had effectively referred to herself as his girlfriend.

"None. I've been saving myself."

"That's not what you told me previously!" Martha teased, referring to the volunteer nurses that Stefan had told her about. "Seriously, this is great. It feels dangerously indulgent, especially after the wilds and wonders of western Sudan!"

"And it is great to dip back into a world outside of scruffy sandy Khartoum...So, what are you going to have?"

"I was thinking garlic mushrooms, followed by carbonara. What about you?"

"Garlic mushrooms followed by penne arrabiata."

"Gosh. I haven't had garlic mushrooms since forever," Martha said with a happy sigh.

"Well that's good. We'll both be stinking of garlic!"

"Getting a bit ahead of yourself now, aren't you?"

"Am I?"

"I wonder, as they don't eat pork, what meat they use for the carbonara."

"Probably some other smoked meat, goat or something."

They ordered juice cocktails with their food and two glasses arrived, fully dressed with cherries, colourful straws and paper umbrellas.

"To new beginnings," Stefan said as they clinked glasses.

"To new and happy beginnings," Martha replied as their starters arrived.

She tasted a mushroom. "Delicious. Little did I think earlier today that I'd be sitting eating Italian food here this evening!"

"I didn't dare dream that I'd be sitting here with you either. We never know what's around the next corner."

"I certainly don't and the more I try to figure it out, the more wrong I am," Martha said getting serious. "You know I broke it off with Patrick before I went to Wadi Dabor?"

"I know." Stefan nodded solemnly.

"Molly told you?"

"Yes. I hope you don't mind. I called around to her flat a few days ago and the two of us ended up sitting there having a long chat."

"Oh."

"She told me all about her boyfriend back home and how she missed him and was looking forward to going home to him and so on."

"He does sound lovely."

"So, then she said, what about you, and I told her that I had a big soft spot for you but that I knew that as long as Patrick was in the background, I had no hope…So, she told me that you had called him…"

"Hmm. I think I'd been postponing it, sort of dreading it. I always thought that proper relationships should be broken off face to face, rather than by phone."

"I've never really been faced with such dilemmas. I have this tremendous knack of driving the women to break it off with me. Of course, the nurses left the country, but Lena, she was different, as you know. I neglected her so thoroughly that I came home one evening to find her in bed with a stranger. I think that I might have preferred if she had broken it off by phone actually."

"A bit of a cruel awakening alright."

"I needed it." He sighed. "It was only after that that I came to realise I had pushed everyone that mattered away from me and, if I didn't get my act together, I'd become a sad, miserable, not-so-old man."

"*Laww smaht*, excuse me," the waiter said politely as he reached to clear away the starter plates.

"Sorry, thank you," Stefan responded.

"That was lovely, *temon*," Martha said glancing up at the waiter with a smile.

He put their main courses gently down in front of them.

"*Shokran*," Martha and Stefan said in unison. The waiter smiled and left them in peace to continue their conversation.

"So how did you react on the night you walked in on them?"

"Totally out of character for me then. I didn't scream or shout. At first, I stood there staring at them, saying nothing. It was as if I was immediately strangely resigned to it. Lena started apologising frantically. The two of them stayed under the covers, watching me, probably scared that I would burst into one of my tempers. Lena knew me when I was at the most angry stage of my life. Thinking back, I don't know how she put up with it. But that time, I didn't explode. I called my friends from college, Oskar and Malia, and asked if I could stay with them. Then I called a taxi and I went around the room packing all my things into every bag that I could lay my hands on. As I got to the apartment door, Lena came after me.

"'I'm sorry, Stefan, but you were never here…except when you were asleep,' she said.

"'I know. I'm sorry,' I said and I walked out the door. I never left Oskar and Malia's house over the next few days. I cried, I talked and then I hatched a plan. They were amazing even though I had neglected them too."

Martha reached over and squeezed his hand. He squeezed back.

"Good friends," Martha said, "how would we survive without them?"

"I know. And they had a new baby too! But that meant that Malia was at home. Dealing with people like me is well within her area of expertise, so I was really lucky. She was a rock of sense and it was she who suggested that, among other things, I make two lists side by side and put some order on my anger and chaos. On one side of the page I listed the things that I wanted to make better, and opposite them, I put things that I would do to make them better. Top of my list was reconnecting with my mother and my little sister, Marianna, who wasn't so little anymore as she was nearly nineteen. After that

I put more practical things down like qualify as a pilot, which I was very close to doing, change jobs, give up protesting…"

"That was quite a list! And it sounds like such incredibly practical advice. Fair play to Malia."

"She was truly amazing."

"What did she suggest regarding your father?"

"I put him on the list too, with a big question mark opposite. But every time I thought about him, I couldn't get beyond the anger that I felt towards him. I'm afraid that question mark is still there and truth is that, even now, I still feel angry when I think of him. But I am going home on leave in the next month or so, so who knows."

"Who knows! Perhaps you have both moved on. Hopefully. And your brother, where's he in the scheme of things?"

"Mark, as I said before, he's a good guy, the opposite of me. Non-confrontational. I started meeting him regularly for coffee and the odd meal. He's rising up through the ranks in the army. We are as different as chalk and cheese but I love him. There is a real soft side to him, while he is macho in that army way."

"Oh, I like the sound of him," Martha said teasingly, "soft but macho!"

Stefan's voice grew quiet. "I haven't actually said this out loud before but since I've been here, I've been thinking about things and, I don't know…it may be a mad thought but I wouldn't be surprised if it turned out that he's gay. He's nearly twenty-six now and he hasn't had a girlfriend, even though girls love him. Can you imagine the implications if I'm right?"

"Oh, Stefan, that would be tough, given your dad and all that."

"It would be tough but Austria is getting better all the time. And I'm certain that most people don't think like my father!"

"What about your mother and your sister, have either of them said anything? Mothers usually know, they say."

"If my mother thought it, she wouldn't say a thing. She has never been one to rock the boat. Anyway, it was only after breaking up with Lena that I started seeing her again regularly. I'd visit her at home when I knew Dad was at work. We don't mention the army but she does talk about Mark and Marianna. She says that she worries he won't find a nice girl to settle down with because he never really goes out."

152

"And did she try to persuade you to see your father?"

"Oh, she did. Before I left, she suggested that I come over for dinner with them. But I said not yet, next time. I couldn't face it then. Hopefully when I go home...I don't know."

"Maybe. It's worth a try, although I'm not the best ad for it. Oh, I really hope that it works out for you. It can be shit when it doesn't."

Stefan nodded. "At least I have a good relationship with Marianna now. She is great, arty and very creative. She has even dragged me to some museums and is doing art in university. Dad adores her and Mum says that she brings the best out in him and reminds her of the man she married. Mum is arty too, she used to do lovely paintings and is very creative."

"Stefan, I think it is so amazing that you have built up good relationships with most of your family. I wish that I could do the same with even one of mine."

He took her hand. "Keep the faith, who knows what life will bring."

"That's what I keep telling myself. But I haven't seen many possibilities. And believe me, I've tried."

"It may be a long road."

"Or a *cul de sac*," Martha said. She hadn't told Stefan about the therapy, nor about how her mother and each of her siblings denied that she had been treated any differently from the rest of them. The counsellor had said none of them could face admitting that what they had done was wrong, it was their problem, not Martha's. The counsellor and Mrs Connolly both believed that Martha would find a way to rise above it. Sitting in Sudan, over dinner with Stefan, Martha was starting to believe that she might do that, she might well rise above it. She realised that she had gone unusually silent and that Stefan was looking at her in that *are you okay?* way that he had.

"Enough about my family. How about a lighter subject? A couple of weeks ago, you were about to tell me how you know Ireland's winning entries from the Eurovision Song Contests, but we got interrupted. Out with it. I mean I don't think of you as a Eurovision kind of guy!"

Stefan paused at the change of tone but chose to go with the flow. "So, you don't see me as Europe's next Johnny Logan?"

"No, funny enough, I don't."

"I think I would actually look great in a nice pair of tight white jeans singing…" He paused and then quietly sang the words of Ireland's last winning entry 'Hold me now'. His facial expression reminded Martha of Johnny Logan's particular expressive way of singing.

She burst out laughing and almost choked on her drink. "Stop, stop," she said between coughs.

"Oh, you prefer 'What's another year'?"

Martha shook her head.

"I've been waiting…"

"Enough," she said, still laughing, "I think you should tell me what caused this affliction and then we should get out of here before we are thrown out."

"Okay. Do you remember ABBA's song 'Waterloo', way back in 1974?"

"Yes, but don't sing it, not now anyway."

"Well my father hated the Eurovision, and he really hated that song. So, needless to say, I took to singing it. Even back then I liked to provoke him. And I learned nearly every other Eurovision winning song after that. Drove my father mad. Thinking back on it, my whole family must have dreaded the Eurovision every year," he said as he stood up.

While Stefan was paying the bill, Martha paid a visit to what she considered to be the loveliest, poshest, cleanest toilets in Sudan – a far cry from the smelly tin hut of earlier that day! Stefan waited for her at the entrance to the restaurant and they made their way back out through the lobby where many men were still standing and sitting, talking and gazing as Martha followed Stefan out to his truck.

"Do you want to risk going to my place for a while?" he asked as they were about to put on their seat belts.

"I think actually that it has to be your place." Martha laughed. "Unless, of course, you fancy some more cleaning up at mine!"

Chapter 21

Stefan's Apartment

Stefan saluted the security guard cheerfully as they made their way over to the front door of the small, modern apartment block. He took Martha's hand as they entered the hallway and they walked together up two flights of stairs onto a small landing and then into his apartment. It was a far cry from Martha's dreary place. He closed the door and jokingly broke again into singing 'Hold me now' as he took Martha in his arms, lifting her onto her tippy toes. He then kissed her on the lips sending blood raising around her body. Their tongues moved together as if dancing in unison to the one tune. They kissed long and deep to the point that they were both breathless but reluctant to pause for air. Stefan's hands made their way up the back of her top and pulled her tight to him. She untucked the back of his shirt and moved both her hands up his back, willing him as close as humanly possible. She felt his hips move against hers and felt his arousal pressed firmly against her navel. Her head was light and her body tingled with pleasure. Their kissing gently slowed to nibbling each other's lips. Their eyes exchanged unspoken words of love and longing. In one movement he brought his hands down to her bottom and lifted her up onto his hips and carried her over to the soft couch where they stretched out, entwined in a tight embrace, moving their hands up and around each other's backs. They paused, locking their eyes long enough to catch their breaths before re-engaging in deep, arousing kissing. Martha had never experienced such incredible prolonged excitement before and, after a particularly long, passionate kiss, she let out an involuntary giggle. Stefan looked at her momentarily perplexed and then smiled as he looked into her face.

"Sorry, that was just wow."

"For me too. Even better than I dreamed."

"Unreal," Martha said with a happy sigh.

"What next?" Stefan responded with an anticipatory shrug of his shoulders.

The large clock on the wall looked down at them.

"Well, it appears that you're stuck with me, for the night anyway."

Stefan contemplated the clock which said 11:05 p.m., five minutes after curfew.

"It appears that you're stuck with me too – I couldn't have planned it better!" he said, shaking his head with a smile and kissing her on the lips. "I don't know about you, but I need a glass of water."

"Me too."

He walked over to the small open kitchen in the corner of the spacious living room, took a large jug of water from the fridge, poured two glasses and handed her one.

"Think you'll have to lend me a T-shirt," Martha said, looking down at her crumpled top and skirt.

"That won't be a problem, follow me," he said, leading her by the hand across the living room into a small square hall and through a door into a large bedroom. He turned on the light to reveal an airy white bedroom with a king-sized bed, two bedside lockers, two chairs and a large storage unit the length of one wall. Balcony doors were open behind a mosquito net, allowing a gentle breeze to cool the room.

"Would you like white with a girl's face, white with a tiger, white with 'no to nuclear power'…?"

"I think I'll go for white…with the tiger. Might reflect my mood more than the others, don't you think?" she said, holding the T-shirt up to herself and opening her mouth in a tiger impression. "Bathroom please?"

He pointed to a door across the small hall.

The bathroom was spacious luxury with fresh, white tiled walls and all the comforts one might need in a posh hotel but more. There was even a small window. Thick, white cotton towels hung on a rail. Pure opulence, Martha thought as she stripped down to her underwear, shook out her clothes, folded them on the chair and put on the T-shirt. She caught a glimpse of herself in the mirror and pinched herself. Not a drop of alcohol consumed and she felt as high as a kite. She smiled as she was about to go out the door and had second thoughts. She stopped, took off her bra and left it with her clothes. As she walked back into the bedroom, Stefan, who was stripped down to his T-shirt and underpants, was putting his trousers on a chair. He glanced across at her and gave a little wolf whistle. She smiled and made to smack him with the back of her hand but he dodged it, grabbed her and landed them both on the large bed. They laughed and then kissed once more.

"Stefan," Martha said, looking at him imploringly.

"Yes?"

"You know…I am more than happy to stay over but…I'm not sure how to make this come out right…I don't want to disappoint you or anything…"

He held her eye contact, his face full of concern. "I don't think that you are likely to disappoint me…"

"I don't want to rush anything. I know it sounds weird but I'm not sure if I'm ready. Not tonight, I mean. Another night. Soonish, I mean. I'm sorry."

"Martha, Martha, please don't be sorry. It's okay. I understand. For goodness sake, I've waited months to kiss you. I can wait longer for, you know, the rest…" he said, taken aback.

"I'm really sorry."

"It's okay, honest…would it help if I slept on the couch?"

"No," Martha said aghast, "no, definitely not. I do want to sleep with you. I want to be held by you. It's just that, how will I put it…it may take me some time to be ready to make love with you."

"That's fine with me, honestly. It will be worth the wait," Stefan said with relief and he took her in his arms and gave her a long reassuring kiss, before heading for the bathroom.

When he returned, Martha was under the light cotton sheet, half sitting up against some of the pillows.

He got into bed beside her and she moved to lie in the crook of his right arm with her head resting on his chest and her right leg wrapped across his legs. She put her hand up his T-shirt and played with the hair on his chest.

"It's a hard body to resist all the same," she said.

"What about yours? Your long, sexy legs, your sexy little bottom, your lovely flat stomach and, dare I say it, your pert breasts…" he said as he brought his left hand up her thigh to hold her bottom and then moved it around to rub her stomach, edging his hand slightly up nearer her breasts.

"You teasing me?"

"A bit."

"I suppose I deserve it." She paused and sighed. "Okay, here goes. I've pretty limited experience. Patrick was the only one I ever actually, you know, slept with as such..."

Stefan squeezed her in his arms to say that he was listening.

"I suppose...I'm kinda nervous and I don't want to spoil something by rushing into it."

"It's okay, Martha. I understand." He kissed the top of her head and wrapped her in his arms.

"I know you've a lot more experience than me," she said, and then added in a rush, "and also we need to talk about contraception and you know, all the other risks?"

"Okay. I see. Fair enough. What can I say?"

Martha shrugged.

"Well, apart from with Lena, I've always used a condom, even if the girl was on the pill. To be honest I was scared silly of AIDs. And after I found Lena in bed with the other guy, I went for a check up to be sure I was clean, which I was. I am reasonably confident that I still am. I haven't been going wild, by any stretch of the imagination, I promise. And I've been careful."

"Patrick did the same thing after he discovered that his girlfriend before me had been sleeping around. He said that the doctor had him tested under a false name – for life insurance purposes, it can go against you to even admit that you had an AIDs test! He was given the all clear too. I started on the pill a few years ago because of gynaecological problems. After I met Patrick, I stayed on the pill but we still used a condom, even though I'd been with no one else...Patrick is the cautious type – and, I guess, so am I!"

"I'm pretty cautious myself, you know. It goes with being a pilot!"

"Well, I'm still on the pill for fear of a repeat of previous problems. I used to lose two or three days every month, getting my period twice a month. It wasn't pretty and I couldn't possibly manage it that way in Sudan."

"That sounds rough," he said pulling her into a hug.

"It was."

She looked up at him. "I'm sorry, I'm going on a bit. I just feel that I want you to understand some of my hang ups, I suppose."

"Martha, please, stop saying that you're sorry. I'm glad that we are talking about it. If there is one thing that I have learned, it's that it's good to talk."

He held her tight in both his arms and kissed her on the forehead and then her cheeks and then her lips.

"I love how we've been able to have open and honest conversations right from when I first met you. You say it as it is, no pretence," he added.

They fell into a comfortable silence and Martha fell asleep smiling to herself at how easy it was to talk to Stefan about such personal things. She woke up hours later with her right arm dead underneath her and she turned over to her left side with her head half on Stefan's shoulder and half on a pillow. Stefan turned onto his left side too and his chest pressed against her back holding her with his right arm around her tummy, up her T-shirt, his hand nearly touching her left breast. She fell back asleep, wishing that he would touch it.

It was bright on Friday morning when they awoke, still in that position, and Stefan snuggled his face into the back and side of her neck, nuzzling her as he did. She was immediately aroused and as she turned gently their lips met. As they kissed their bodies became more entwined. His right hand found her already aroused nipple and gently caressed it. Her hand reached inside his underpants. He ran his hand down from her nipple to her underwear and ran his finger along the front waistband, edging his hand into her pants.

"May I?"

"Yes. Yes please," she said, guiding his hand between her legs. He touched her exploringly in all the right places, finding the right balance between applying pressure and being gentle. He seemed to grow in her hand and this further increased her own excitement. As their bodies moved in unison she felt as if she was soaring to a height never experienced before. They were at one in their excitement and when they reached their pinnacle, they didn't pull apart but stayed locked in each other's arms, holding the feeling tight, imprinting it on their bodies and minds.

"Have you any idea what you do to me?" Stefan whispered into her ear.

"What about what you do to me...I've never experienced anything like it," she said, still holding his body close and feeling the heat rise between them. They lay together for a few more minutes until their combined body temperatures became too much.

"You're so hot. In more ways than one! I'm in danger of dissolving into a puddle," Stefan said. "I need a shower."

"Me too. I think I'm going to dissolve any minute now too...Together?" she suggested, to her surprise, and his.

Chapter 22

Molly Leaving

It was almost midday when Stefan drove Martha back to her flat to get a change of clothes more suitable for a hot Sudanese afternoon, one which they planned to spend visiting Tuti Island. As she walked through the sitting room, Martha put her hands up on either side of her face as blinkers from the dirty dishes, spillages and cigarette butts. She went straight to her bedroom, got changed quickly into a light, casual blue dress and grabbed a swimsuit, towel and a change of clothes for later. Stefan sat on the ugly couch in the sitting room and waited for her, taking in the mess; butt ends of what he took to be more joints, the slightly aromatic smell of which still lingered in the room, mingled with the smell of stale food and cigarettes. Martha assumed that the happy couple were asleep, or quietly otherwise in their own bedroom.

As they were about to leave, Martha heard, through the open hatch between the two kitchens, Molly and Siobhán in the flat next door.

"Oh, I think I'd better say hello to the girls next door."

"Of course."

"I haven't seen them since before I left for Wadi Dabor and Molly is heading home to Ireland soon." Martha went up behind Stefan on the couch and put her arms around him and kissed him on the top of his curly dark head.

"Good morning Molly, Siobhán," Martha said putting her head through the hatch.

"Oh, good morning, Martha, and how are *you* this fine afternoon?" Molly replied teasingly, coming over to her side of the hatch.

"Any chance of coffee for two more in there?" Martha said as her face went bright red.

"Come on around. I see you've made a miraculous recovery."

"Miraculous!" Martha winked and quietly closed the hatch.

"I went into your flat the other day, in search of some rather scarce sugar, and I really don't envy you coming home sick to that mess. If my mam saw that, she'd have picked up every dirty dish and pot and moved them all straight into their bedroom. That's what she used to do if my brothers left a mess. They weren't long about learning, I can tell you!" Siobhán said, as they all sat together enjoying Kisra and coffee.

"No accounting for how some people live! Stefan and I did a big clean-up yesterday and it's back to square one today!"

"Molly and I were saying that, if you like, you could share my room. The two new nurses who are coming the day after tomorrow will be taking the room Molly is currently in."

"You should think about it, Martha," Molly added.

"Oh. Thank you. I appreciate it. We'll work something out. I'm sure…But Siobhán, more importantly, what are we going to do without our Molly?"

"I don't know. I'm dreading her leaving. We will surely miss her. You'd better not desert me now that you have your man over there," Siobhán said nodding in Stefan's direction.

"I won't, I promise. And we promised that we'd resume those driving lessons this week too. So, how about I give you a lesson tomorrow night and then we treat Molly to a farewell ice cream in that little place up the hill. What do you think, Molly?"

"Good idea. I like that place. It feels different to the usual haunts, and we can sit outside."

"I like it too," said Siobhán. "It's not as dusty and post-colonial as the Sudan Club or as full of wealthy Arabs as some of the other places. But we need to do a proper group night too. How about the Chinese for a big gang, including Sister Shelley, the new nurses, Stefan and whoever else you'd like Molly?"

"Excellent. And of course, Michael too. I will think of who else should be there but I'll probably stick to the ones we've mentioned. I'll book it when

I'm passing. Thursday night would be good as it will give you guys Friday off to recover. I'll be flying home then." Molly's whole face smiled as she said 'flying home' and Martha felt happy for her.

Martha and Stefan headed off and spent a leisurely afternoon on Tuti Island, followed by a swim and dinner at the Sudan Club. There they bumped into a number of friends and acquaintances, who stopped and chatted with them or saluted them from a distance with, what felt to Martha to be, knowing smiles.

Somehow, without express comment, they had both assumed that Martha would stay at Stefan's that night and that he would drop her off early the next morning on his way to the airport. They enjoyed another intimate evening and fell asleep together early, making up for the previous night's lack of sleep and allowing for an early start.

Arriving into her flat, wide awake at 6:30 a.m., Martha couldn't resist cleaning up a bit and even dug out a sack of flour, sifted out the usual wiggling white creatures, and made some fresh bread rolls, which she left first to prove and then bake, while she cleaned and showered. When she heard Molly and Siobhán moving about next door, she brought some bread rolls in to eat with them and left two for the couple, who still hadn't surfaced, despite being expected at the office at 8:30.

Over breakfast, Molly commented that they were not early risers and rarely made it into the office much before 9:30 a.m. This was almost tolerable while Molly was around to do the work that was to become Attracta's but wouldn't wash after she left. Plus, the vehicles needed to be ready to be on the road promptly. Molly and Martha had both observed that Dahab, the Sudanese mechanic whom they all really liked and trusted, seemed well able to take care of the vehicles as he had been doing without an expat mechanic for quite some months. Molly had tried speaking to Attracta and Tom about their responsibilities but she wasn't convinced that she was getting through to them and had suggested that Shelley might talk directly to them. Shelley had shrugged her shoulders.

"Well at least they are only on a few months' contract to cover until the other mechanic arrives on a year's contract."

"*Al-Hamdillallah*. But why are they here at all?" Martha said, wishing them gone already.

"Head office and Shelley decided we needed someone to fill in but there weren't many mechanics coming forward and Tom knew someone who knew someone in Help. The problem was that he only agreed to come if his girlfriend could too. And head office, in their wisdom, agreed to it despite Attracta not having any particularly relevant experience or qualifications!" Molly explained.

"Wearing my accountant's hat, it seems to me that, at an exorbitant cost to Help, Attracta and Tom are getting a fully paid holiday, with all their considerable expenses covered by hard-earned donations. Wearing my personal hat, on top of that they are getting a full-time resident cleaner, me! The mess they create can't wait until the cleaner comes in once a week."

"I can't disagree with you on either front but perhaps, when they settle in, things will get better. If not, there is always the offer of the spare bed in Siobhán's room," Molly said optimistically.

"And I only snore some of the time," Siobhán said laughing. "But Martha, maybe *you* have a better offer elsewhere!"

Molly had left the table and reappeared from her bedroom carrying a bundle of envelopes.

"Martha, I didn't get a chance yesterday to give you your post that came over with Tom and Attracta. Quite a little bundle for you."

"Thanks, Molly. I'll leave them in my room for later."

Martha headed back her flat flicking through the pile to see who might have written to her. There was a thick envelope from Mrs Connolly which Martha suspected included some bars of chocolate. There was another from Trish with cheeky love hearts and smileys on it and there were a couple from the office. Finally, there was one from Patrick which, by Martha's calculations, had been posted to head office in Dublin before her phone call to him. She looked at his familiar neat handwriting on the envelope and was surprised at how it touched her heart. A mixture of emotions played inside her chest as she visualised him sitting down to write it with no anticipation of that phone call. She ran her finger along the name and address of the firm he worked for which was printed boldly on the envelope, Delaney, Robertson and Co.; she shrugged as she considered that he had written the letter in between doing his work at the office. Still too busy to write a proper letter, she thought as she shoved the envelope to the back of her underwear drawer, before putting the other letters on her bed for reading later.

She was a good hour working at her desk in the office that morning, going through the figures for the previous week that Dawit had put together, when Attracta sauntered past her and greeted her with a grunt. As Attracta returned from the kitchen with two cups of coffee, Dawit looked at Martha and, to her surprise, rolled his eyes to heaven and shook his head. Dahab, the mechanic, had already been in to Dawit with a list of parts that he needed and had got a float from Dawit and headed off to make his purchases. Molly was off somewhere else. Their absences didn't seem to bother Tom or Attracta, who just sat at Molly's desk and drank their coffee and chatted away.

Martha went over to Dawit's desk and discussed various expenditure items with him, to make sure that it had all been charged to the correct budget.

Dawit nodded in the direction of Molly's desk. "That's all that they have done since they got here."

Martha shook her head in agreement as she glanced over at them, wondering how they had the brass neck to be so lazy and apathetic. She saw no point in dwelling on the matter and instead chose to concentrate on the Khartoum figures for the various projects and, with some small adjustments, she finalised them with Dawit. She then spent the rest of the day working on completing the reports and budgets for Wadi Dabor and putting them into the different formats required by the funding agencies and making as strong a case as possible for the proposed additional expenditure. In between times, Molly returned to the office and she and Attracta and Fuad had a meeting with Shelley to agree what admin work needed to be done over the next few weeks. Martha could sense Molly's rising frustration at Attracta's apparent disinterest and she suggested to Molly that they take some time out together and have lunch in Molly's flat.

"What a pair of lousy useless lumps!" Molly said as they walked down the road.

"Don't get me started, please. I know many volunteers are fabulous and make genuine sacrifices to come here, like yourself and Siobhán of course. But I do think that we have far too many expensive expats doing jobs that locals could do just as well or even better and at a fraction of the cost. I don't know why we need an expat mechanic at all, never mind the useless Tom. Dahab seems to do just fine left to run the vehicles on his own with local staff and he knows where to buy parts and get others repaired."

"I hear you, and I have sometimes thought like that too, in terms of giving more responsibility to local nurses and leaving expats in a purely supervisory role. I do feel that certain roles have to be expats though, especially the administrator."

"The way I see it a good accountant could do the administrator's role and the accountant's role with a few well-trained locals as support, of which there seem to be plenty of suitable candidates. As long as adequate controls are put in place, there is no reason why this can't work effectively. That would be one less expat, one less big expense...if properly implemented. And Dahab is well able to fill the mechanic's role, which makes two less. Mind you, I'm not looking for the accountant–administrator job myself!"

"Well, Attracta won't be any use on that front, that's for sure. I wish that I wasn't going back and leaving her to take over."

"I wish you weren't leaving full stop," Martha said putting an arm around Molly. "I'll miss you."

"Ah well, at least you now have Stefan as a distraction," Molly responded with a wink. "He adores you, you know?"

"I've no idea why or how. I keep thinking that I'm dreaming and I'm going to wake up soon. Bet you are dying to see John when you get back."

"I sure am. Oh, it's been far too long," Molly said, with a longing look in her eyes that said she was already half-way home.

Chapter 23

Orphanage Chinese

Martha made her usual trip to the orphanage that Thursday after a busy week finalising budgets and reports, meeting funding agencies about future and current year's funding and submitting the Wadi Dabor reports and budgets for approval. She had worked hard and late to make time for her day at the orphanage and was, as always, grateful that she had it to look forward to at the end of the week.

Before she had left for Wadi Dabor, she had been aware that little Kamil was not well and she was fearful of what she might find when she entered the babies' room. He was lying listless in a cot on his own and, in the two weeks since she last saw him, he had been slowly disappearing, back to where his life began. Soon he will be gone, she thought as she picked him up carefully, scared that she would break his thin, protruding bones. As she cuddled what was left of his little body, he gave her a weak smile. She held him to her chest, praying that he wasn't suffering, wishing that she could have been there for him for more of his short life. 'Slimming sickness', she had heard AIDS called. She had never before seen its effects but she supposed that was what it was. Poor innocent little Kamil was dying before her eyes and there was nothing that she could do about it, except hold him briefly in her arms. It broke her heart a thousand times over. She fed and cuddled a number of the other babies too but she returned a number of times to hold or stroke Kamil.

She moved on to the toddlers' room and spent some time playing with them. But, despite their cheerful little ways and their obvious enthusiasm, her heart wasn't in it the way it normally was. After lunch, she spent the afternoon with Layla and the older children and was grateful for Ghaliya's demands for chasing and hugging. There was no outburst from the sometimes wild Ghaliya that day, as if she sensed Martha's sad mood. When Martha took Emir outside to play ball, he gave her a big hug wrapping his legs around her body and hugging her neck. As he had done so many times before, he ran his finger down her arm, checked his finger to see if the white had come off and laughed when he confirmed that it hadn't. Martha ran her fingers down his arm too, looked at them as if for traces of brown and shook her head when there was none. They laughed together and then she smiled at him as she tickled his little tummy. He giggled and wiggled and laughed heartedly some more with the innocence of an unspoilt child. She was drawn into his laughter and found herself giggling and wiggling too as he reached and tickled her down her side. *Laughter really is the best medicine.* She hugged him with gratitude and then pointed towards the ball lying on the ground. He let go, jumped down and picked it up. He then took great pleasure in showing her how much his kicking had improved in her absence. He carefully chose various positions in the yard and aimed at the back of the gate from different angles. He was successful more times than not and Martha laughed and clapped at his success. When he had tired of kicking, they played throw and catch and whenever she dropped the ball he said, "It's okay," and picked it up for her.

"*Shokran Emir, Ma'assalama Emir,*" she said when she had to go and she gave him a big hug which he returned with a cheeky grin that brought a smile to her face.

Before going to the office to say goodbye, Martha stopped off to say goodbye to Kamil. She held him gently, stroking his thin cheek, looking down at his tired young eyes looming large on his little old face.

"*Ma'assalama* Kamil, may God give you peace," she said and kissed him on his forehead and sunken cheeks before putting him down softly on his mattress.

She then put her head around the office door to tell Abdel that she would see him next week but as she turned to leave, he called her back.

"Good news, Martha."

"Oh?"

"Emir is going to a new home soon," he said enthusiastically. "It is another orphanage but much better for him. It has a number of houses together. Each house has its own mother and there's even a school."

"Oh, I see. It sounds really good, I'm glad for him," Martha said quietly, taken aback, knowing that she would miss him terribly.

"We are visiting it next Thursday. Would you like to come?"

Martha paused before answering, still trying to process that her Emir was leaving. She hoped that it was a better place. He deserved it.

"Sorry. Yes, I'd like that. Thank you. I would really like to go. What time?"

"If you are here by about ten. Okay?"

"Grand. Would you like me to drive?" Martha said, remembering that the orphanage had only limited access to borrowed vehicles.

"I was hoping that you would say that," Abdel responded with a smile.

"No problem."

She headed back to the Help office to leave the bicycle and borrow a vehicle so she could go to the Sudan Club for a swim before getting ready to go out. Stefan had called in one evening for a couple of hours earlier in the week and had hung out with her and the newcomers, Mary and Connie, and Molly and Siobhán in their flat. Other than that, they hadn't seen each other as he had been away with work as was his norm. In the meantime, Martha had spent as little time as possible in her flat, other than in her own room, to avoid feeling the urge to keep cleaning up after The Couple.

Stefan had said that he would collect her that evening at around quarter to seven and then collect Michael on the way to the restaurant for Molly's farewell meal. Molly, Siobhán and the new nurses would travel separately and there was talk that Shelley and The Couple, as Martha had taken to calling them to stop herself calling them The Pigs, would join them later. When Molly told Siobhán that Michael was definitely coming along, her face had reddened and Molly and Martha had exchanged winks.

The Chinese restaurant could have been described as having subdued or dimmed lighting. It gave it a certain dark mood and barely hid its scruffy colourless interior. The menu was limited but it made a pleasant change from the Sudan Club's British fare and the home cooking, which usually fell to

169

Martha, which was limited by what was available in the few shops and the souks.

Since their arrival a few days previously, Martha hadn't had much of a chance to really talk properly to Mary and Connie, so she deliberately sat beside them. In the middle of the table sat Molly and Stefan, with Michael and Siobhán at the opposite end to Martha, engaged in some light-hearted banter, judging by their smiles and laughter. Molly had quietly orchestrated that they sat together.

"Bit of a matchmaker in you Molly?" Martha said, not loud enough for an already red-faced Siobhán to hear.

"Yes," she said and turned to Mary and Connie, "I played my part in getting Stefan and Martha together, you know. And with me gone, it will be up to Martha to take over the matchmaker mantle and get you guys some men! I hope she does as good a job!"

They had starters of wonton soup, which was a bit watery but otherwise fine, Martha thought. They were halfway through their main courses when Shelley swanned through the door in full Sexy Shelley guise, with her hair tied in a lose bun and a low-cut top that went beyond normal western decency, never mind Sudanese modesty. Behind her sauntered Tom and Attracta. With plenty of shuffling of chairs, room was made at the table.

Martha watched as Shelley squeezed a chair for herself in beside Stefan. Molly, who was sitting opposite Stefan, turned and winked at Martha. Martha smiled and shrugged her shoulders as Shelley put her hand on Stefan's arm, leaned forward and puffed out her well-endowed and exposed chest, which, Martha thought, needed no puffing out. Shelley launched into a diatribe about the bureaucracy of the Sudanese government and the international funding agencies. Stefan turned around to catch Martha's eye and, just as he mouthed the word 'help' to her, Shelley dropped her hand onto his knee and squeezed it. He jumped slightly and turned around to face her and her over-exposed credentials, leaving Martha trying to contain herself from either choking on her food or spraying it in a snort of laughter. Molly had caught the gesture too and glanced Martha's way with a massive grin. Martha lost the battle and just managed to get her napkin up to her mouth, to turn her suppressed laugh into a loud grunt followed by a coughing and choking fit.

This sent first Molly, and then Connie and Mary, into fits of laughter. Martha mumbled her excuses and made her way in the direction of the bathroom.

"I better see if she's okay," Molly said, trying to regain a straight face, and got up and followed Martha, leaving Shelley staring after them both and Stefan, sitting beside her, struggling to contain himself.

"What was that about?" Shelley asked, turning to Connie and Mary.

"Eh, I'm not really sure, I think Martha started choking, or something…" said Connie.

After almost collapsing with laughter in the bathroom, Martha and Molly re-joined the group and sat down quietly. Martha tried not to look left or right in case something or someone set her off again. But as she sat down, Molly threw a knowing grin Stefan's way and wagged her finger at him, while mouthing, "It's all your fault!" Stefan smiled back and shrugged his shoulders before turning his attention to accept from Shelley some of the extra food that Molly had ordered when the latecomers had arrived. He immediately started to eat it slowly and deliberately, as if he was following the old mantra that each bite should be chewed at least sixteen times. Martha turned towards Mary and Connie and concentrated hard on finding out what they thought of Sudan so far.

They finished the food between bursts of conversation and then Shelley announced, that after all Molly's hard work, Help would pay the bill. There was a round of applause for Molly, but no speeches – Siobhán and Martha had been well warned not to dare.

"Look after Martha, Stefan, she's a keeper," Molly whispered as she hugged Stefan before they all went their separate ways.

"I know," he said, "and thanks."

Martha hugged Molly and said that she'd see her for coffee in the morning before taking her to the airport.

"Mind you, Siobhán's driving is coming on so well that she might even drive you to the airport!" Martha suggested.

"No chance – there's no point in taking unnecessary risks just when you are going safely home!" Siobhán said.

Martha was delighted to overhear Michael and Siobhán arranging to meet up the next day, before Michael headed out to Stefan's car to get a lift home. As she walked to the door Martha felt Stefan's arm around her back. She turned to look at him and caught sight of Shelley standing alone, watching them, with her mouth hanging open, looking like someone had stolen her ice cream from under her nose. A small part of Martha felt sorry for her.

"So, what exactly was all that choking about?" Michael asked as he got into the back of Stefan's pickup.

"Oh Stefan, let me tell you about Sudanese bureaucracy," Martha said in response to Michael's question as she puffed out her chest and touched Stefan's arm and then moved her hand down to his knee, copying Shelley's voice and gestures from earlier.

Stefan burst out laughing and Michael seemed a bit baffled.

"You'd better tell him, Martha."

"Basically," Martha said, "you may have noticed, Shelley has had the hots for Stefan from before I first met him on Christmas day. She always goes out of her way to sit beside him and flirt with him, as she did tonight. Unfortunately, until we walked out the door together, she had no idea that we had, had…become an item!"

"Oh, I see. Hmm. That's you fecked now – there goes your career prospects in Help so. I hope you hadn't any big plans like!"

"You could say that Shelley wasn't my biggest fan even before I stole her man from under her nose!"

"Hey, I was never her man!" Stefan protested.

After they dropped Michael off, Stefan reached across and put his hand on Martha's knee and ran it up the inside of her thigh.

"Whoa," she said closing her eyes and grinning.

"It's been a long week."

They greeted the security guard at Stefan's apartments and then Stefan grabbed Martha's hand and they ran up the stairs laughing. Martha flopped down on the couch expecting Stefan to flop beside her but he went over to the fridge and pulled out a bottle of white wine.

"*Voila*," he said holding it up.

"I'm impressed! Where did you get it?"

"Ask me no questions and I'll tell you no lies. Let's say that it pays to work at the airport!" he said as he pulled the cork and poured two generous glasses.

"I hope that you are not planning on taking advantage of me!" Martha said as they raised their glasses to each other with a soft clink.

"Of course I am," he said as he sat down and put his feet up beside hers on the coffee table.

"Good…I'd be disappointed if you weren't!"

She settled her hand slightly up his long, loose shorts. He edged her skirt up to above her knees and rested his hand on her bare leg. They sat in that position sipping their wine, laughing at how the night had unfolded, sharing small titbits from their week. Stefan had finally flown west to Wadi Dabor and they exchanged views on how different it was from Khartoum. Martha brought his hand up to her lips and kissed first the back of it and then his palm before returning it to rest on her bare leg. He held her gaze while he spoke of southern Sudan which was pretty inaccessible, except by air, not just because of the poor roads but also significantly because of the many land mines. To Martha's horror, Stefan said that even accessing the south by air was scary as there was always the risk of being shot out of the sky as you came in to land. He and other pilots chose to land in the war zones, not in the normal slow gradual landing, but a more vertical almost corkscrew descent. He'd sooner fly to Wadi Dabor any day.

The people in the south were starving despite the good land. He confirmed what Martha had heard, they couldn't farm safely because of the landmines and equally tragically most of the men and boys had been pulled away, willingly or unwillingly, into the war. He thought that the south and its people felt more African than Arab and, in some ways, felt more colourful. It was definitely greener and lusher but a much harder place to live being dominated and decimated by war and fear.

As they talked their hands seemed to join in in the conversation: they held hands and intertwined their wrists; they rubbed palms; they touched fingers and hands; they moved their fingers up each other's arms, feeling the baby soft flesh on the inside of their wrists. It was as if their hands were moving to the lyrics of their conversation.

Martha told him about her sad day at the orphanage, about little Kamil in particular. Stefan reached for her, holding her in his arms without saying anything. When the tears streamed down her face, he kissed them and then kissed her eyes and then her lips. Martha closed her eyes and kissed him back.

Chapter 24

Village Talking

Everything felt very different in the office with Molly gone. First thing in the morning before Siobhán, Connie and Mary left for their clinics or after they returned in the afternoons, the atmosphere was fine, but in between times it was best described as awkward and uncomfortable. Tom and Attracta continued to keep their own time and what either of them did during the day, other than drinking coffee and smoking, was a mystery. Perhaps Shelley knew. But Shelley wasn't saying much, least of all to Martha, except when absolutely necessary for work purposes. Thankfully, Martha's relationship with Dawit was good and that helped her to stay sane. Mostly Martha kept herself busy making sure that financial matters were kept properly in order, as far as it was possible for her to do so. She was grateful for the computers which had made keeping the financial records and preparing reports much easier. She was impressed by Dawit's computing competence and that he had found somewhere to learn more spreadsheet skills. There were times when the erratic electricity nearly got the better of them and, while they saved their work regularly, they lost an hour or more of computer work every two or three days. Whenever there was an accumulation of things going wrong, Martha remembered Molly's IBM policy: *Inshallah, Bukhara, Mumbkin.*

Martha spent less and less time in her flat in the evenings as she spent more time in Stefan's; he had given her a key to let herself in whenever she wished. If he was away with work or doing his own thing with Michael or other friends, she went out with the girls or went swimming in the Sudan Club or took Siobhán for driving lessons which, Martha reckoned, she soon wouldn't need at all. Sometimes Siobhán herself wasn't free when Martha

174

was, as she was off with Michael. Martha continued her weekly Hash runs and après Hash outings with Máire. On these evenings and others that she knew that Stefan was likely to be at home before curfew, she would call over to his place and stay the night. They were as good as living together except that Martha continued to keep the bulk of her belongings in her own dreary room, in the dirty flat that she continued to share with The Couple.

Martha made her weekly visit to the orphanage on the Thursday following Molly's departure, driving over there that week as she was expecting to visit what was to become Emir's new home. But, when she arrived, Abdel explained that the charity running the home had postponed the visit as the new houses were not yet finished. Martha took a deep breath and started about her normal routine feeding and playing with some of the babies. She had chosen not to ask Abdel if Kamil had died as she felt that she knew the answer. She swallowed hard when she approached his cot, knowing it wouldn't be his little face looking back up at her. A beautiful little baby girl looked up at her with big, smiling brown eyes. *As one life ends, a new one begins,* she thought as she lifted the baby out of the cot. She tickled the baby's chubby legs and arms and received a big smile in return.

She took a bottle from the shelf and pulled up a chair beside the Sudanese women who had greeted her warmly each Thursday for a long time now, after the initial few weeks of coolness. Martha wondered if they had softened in how they were with the babies or if her initial impression had been too judgmental. Who could blame them for being uncomfortable with a blow-in *Khawaji* coming into their space? Her experience was similar in the toddlers' room. Perhaps they realised that Martha didn't want to intrude but to spend time with the children and be of help. The language barrier meant that there were no great conversations, but Martha had learnt enough Arabic to get by and to show respect and gratitude to the women for accepting her. She was starting to appreciate that it must be difficult for them, working each day with children who were the outcasts of the society into which they, in their innocence, had been born.

A couple of weeks after the original scheduled date, Martha drove Abdel and Layla, the warm Sudanese woman who worked most frequently in Emir's room, to the outskirts of Khartoum where the children's charity SOS had built a small village on land donated by the Sudanese government. They were greeted by a tall, welcoming Sudanese man who was responsible for the overall running of the village. Martha didn't catch his name but she observed that he was greeted warmly by the women and the few small children they met as he showed them around. He was the "father" of the village and he seemed to fit the role well. The village was made up of ten individual brick houses set around a communal building. Each house had a "mother" and was a self-contained home with running water and electricity and with its own kitchen, bathroom, living room and bedrooms. As far as Martha could work out, but she didn't like to ask straight out, the house mothers were older Sudanese women who were maybe widowed and had their families reared. They were no longer tied to demands of minding their own children and were therefore free to live in these beautiful homes as full-time mothers to the orphaned children. The absence of older children during their visit, it was explained, was because they were at a school nearby which had also been set up by SOS. Emir, so far, had had very little schooling but moving to the SOS village would give him not only a chance of an almost normal family life, but a chance of an education too. Abdel and Layla were genuinely excited that Emir would have these opportunities. Martha knew that it was the right thing for Emir, and she was very happy for him, but she couldn't stop herself from feeling sad at the thought that he would no longer be at the orphanage when she visited. There was no denying that she would miss playing with him, but most of all she would miss his hugs and smiles.

After their visit to the village, on their way back to the orphanage, they stopped at a food stall and bought some hot grilled chicken legs. Beside the stall were thin ragged children begging in the street and Martha felt the usual wave of guilt at seeing their suffering but feeling so impotent to ease it. Places like the SOS village gave her hope and she expressed her thoughts to Abdel who smiled in agreement.

"*Soya, soya*, slowly, slowly," he said hopefully.

As Abdel spoke, Martha drove around a corner and there, looming large in front of them was a most unexpected sight: a fairground. Martha stopped the Land Cruiser and laughed at how out of context it seemed. It was like any fairground that you might see in Ireland, with dodgems, chair-o-planes and a roller coaster. Martha read the billboard to see if it might be open the next day, Friday, their one full day off, and the billboard indicated that it would. That was Friday planned, she decided.

Abdel laughed at her childlike giddiness at seeing it.

"Imagine what I'll be like tomorrow," she said, knowing that she would be laughing as much out of fear as pleasure.

Later that afternoon, when Martha called into the girls' flat, it took no effort to convince Siobhán, Connie and Mary to plan a trip the next day to the fair and they expected Michael and Stefan to be equally enthusiastic.

Stefan collected Martha as planned early that evening and, as they made their way to the Hilton, she filled Stefan in on her trip to the SOS village and the planned outing to the fairground the next day, which Stefan quickly agreed to.

It was their third time together at the Hilton and the waiter greeted them warmly and showed them to what Martha referred to as their secret table because of the privacy it afforded them.

They sat down and gave their order for two large glasses of fruit juice cocktail and garlic mushrooms followed by penne arrabiata and pizza.

"Oh Stefan, I'm sorry. I haven't shut up since you collected me," Martha said.

"That's okay, I'm getting used to it!"

"Feck off," she whispered with a grin. "But what about you? What have you been up to these last few days?"

"Well, the big news is that when I got back yesterday, there was a letter from my mother. After reading it I decided to bite the bullet and book my flights home…" he said before pausing, waiting for Martha's response.

Martha felt her heart sinking at the thought of him being gone for a couple of weeks. He had quickly become part of her life, her rock in both calm and troubled waters. She stopped herself thinking that way, admonishing herself for being so selfish.

"What did your mother's letter say?"

"Nothing specific really, I suppose. Everyone is well. She and Marianna are looking forward to seeing me soon. It's been too long. Some news about neighbours. That sort of thing."

"And your dad?"

"He's well but he's not getting any younger, she says. Of course, he's a lot older than her. Ten years to be precise."

"She was maybe trying to nudge you to talk to him?"

Stefan nodded. "I think she is suggesting that I shouldn't leave it too long to see him."

"Well, you had planned already to try to talk to him when you go home, so you're both thinking the same way really."

"True," he said pensively.

"How are you feeling about it?" Martha reached across the table and held his hand discreetly.

"Nervous. Really nervous. I have to do it but I'm struggling with imagining a good response. I think I'll break the ice by holding up my hands to being the difficult, contrary so-and-so that I was to rear…"

"It's hard to argue with that!" Martha said teasingly.

"Are you calling me difficult?"

"You're only in the ha'penny place beside me!"

"Hey, I like you just the way you are."

"There is one problem."

"Oh?"

"I'm going to really miss you when you're away," Martha said, feeling her eyes well up and a tear run down her face.

"I'm going to miss you too…a lot," Stefan said gently wiping her tear away with his thumb and then bringing his hand back down to the table to hold hers.

"I actually can't believe that I said that out loud. I was scared that it would sound selfish," Martha said between quiet sniffles.

"I'm glad you did. When I was booking the flights, the one thing bothering me was that I will miss you and I wanted to tell you that."

She looked at his wonderful big brown eyes and ignored the tears running down her cheeks.

"Martha, you're the first person who has made me really determined not to repeat my mistakes. You've helped me to speak up and be honest. Malia, back home, always says, 'Speak up, say what needs to be said and say it soon because the longer you leave it, the harder it is to say'."

"Funny, I've often thought that too. Years ago, I saw a few plays by Brian Friel, an Irish playwright, *The Communication Chord*, *Translations* and another one, I forget the name. Rightly or wrongly, it seemed that there was one big message, well one that resonated with me anyway. Bad communication can ruin lives. You know, words unspoken, lies told, pasts denied or buried, love not expressed…"

"I know. Look at my own family. We could certainly do with talking more. Now that I've retired from protesting, maybe I should work on communicating. Maybe I've started already with you," he said.

"We could try not to fall into the family trap, you know, break the cycle, by being open and honest with each other. No doubt I'll make some mistakes along the way. I'll say too much or it will come out wrong…but I'll try," Martha said.

"I am sure that we'll both make mistakes. But look at it another way, we are reasonably good at talking already!"

As they talked, the waiter had discreetly served them their food and they had eaten it. Martha only realised this as he reappeared to clear their empty plates. Stefan politely asked for the bill and they got up to leave.

On the journey home Martha was quiet, churning over the implications of their dinner conversation.

When they got to Stefan's apartment, she went over to the fridge to get a drink. She contemplated the orange juice but felt all juiced out. She was considering opening a bottle of white wine when Stefan produced a bottle of red wine and a bar of dark chocolate from a cupboard under the sink.

"How about something different?" he said with a smile.

"Oh, you know me so well. Chocolate and red wine, life's wicked pleasures!"

They sat down together on the couch, clinked glasses and shared a warm kiss on the lips. Then Martha paused and put on her serious expression, as was her way, Stefan would say.

"I went for therapy, you know, counselling," she said staring into her glass, waiting for Stefan's reaction.

He paused, then gently put his hand under her chin, lifted up her head and kissed her on each cheek and then on the lips, closing his eyes momentarily and then opening them to look into hers.

179

"That was amazingly brave of you. It must have been difficult."

Martha nodded. "Nobody goes to counselling in Ireland unless they are mentally ill, an alcoholic, a gambler, a sex maniac or something a bit mad. It makes me feel like a bit of a freak. I feel mortified even mentioning it," Martha said rubbing her face anxiously with her hand.

"I might have gone for therapy too if I hadn't had Malia and Oskar to guide and support me. They were amazing. Did the counselling help you?"

"I suppose. A bit. It sorted out some things in my head. I felt emotionally stronger. It made me more aware of myself and why I get so negative about myself at times. I suppose the more I understood, the less negative I felt...but that was until the counsellor suggested that I talk to my mother and my siblings about my childhood..."

"And what happened then?"

Martha told Stefan about her mother's and her siblings' sneering responses and effective denials that she had any reason to feel that she had been badly treated.

"Their responses make me feel like a fraud, as if I don't know my past or who I really am. I wonder if I've made it all up. It wrecks my head sometimes."

"So, it all still bothers you?"

"Yes. It does. It's like having a large chunk of self-doubt stuck inside me, pulling me down when I should be feeling content or even high. I want to put it behind me. Being away from home has helped. But...well how do I know what's the truth and what my brain has made up?"

"That's a tricky one..."

"And you know Máire here, well she and her mum were always so good to me when I was growing up. Sometimes I feel the urge to ask her about what she remembers so that I can compare it with my memory."

"But why haven't you?"

He took her hand and held it firmly in his, both of them staring at their joined fingers.

"What if she too says that I misremember it? I might really crack up, knowing that I've created some made-up past that never actually happened!"

"That seems unlikely, Martha. Perhaps go for it, you know, as you would tell someone else to do?"

"I know. I know. Do you know the film *The World According to Garp*? In it the child is scared of the 'undertoad', you know the undertow, which can pull you down no matter how strong a swimmer you are. I feel like my confused memories of my past are my undertow pulling me down."

"Martha, the person that I'm looking at doesn't appear confused. What if you are right and they are making you wrong? You are a wonderful person, somebody who is more sympathetic and empathetic than anyone else I know. You are so much more than your family and your past."

He held both her hands in his and kissed each one in turn, then he looked into her eyes and the warmth of his brown eyes penetrated deep inside her pushing out her lingering self-doubt.

"I love you, Martha, like I've never loved anyone else."

"I love you too, Stefan." And as she closed her eyes and kissed him, she knew in that moment, it was scarily true.

"Hmm. It seems that we've learned a lot already about being open and honest."

"I've never felt more open and honest in my life," she whispered in his ear as she felt a desire rise within her, filling every fibre of her being. In the heat of that feeling she stood up, took his hand, pulled him gently off the couch and led him into the bedroom.

At the end of the bed they stood facing each other and he reached and kissed her on the lips, holding the moment. She kissed him back and, as he watched, she opened the button and zip of her skirt and let it fall to the floor. He reached out and rested his hands on her hips, anchoring their bodies firmly together. She opened the button and zip of his trousers and eased them off his hips so they fell to the floor too. He lifted her shirt up over her head and together they did the same with his. She watched and felt his every move as if it touched the very essence of her being. Her breathing was heavy but her head felt light. He lowered one bra strap down her shoulder and then the other, kissing her down the side of the neck and shoulders. She purred with excitement as her body tingled with each touch. Slowly he reached behind her back and undid the clasp of her bra and let it fall to the ground. She danced her hands around to the small of his back, moving them with gentle pressure lower and lower. He moved his mouth gently down her body and kissed her on one nipple, sucking it gently. The purity of the pleasure stopped her breath and she closed her eyes and breathed deeply as he pulled her to him. Her heart pounded as if it had grown too large for her chest. She could feel his heart, too, thumping excitedly in her ear as he held her head to his chest. She turned her head to look up at him and their eyes locked in mutual love and understanding.

"Tonight," she said.

"You're sure?" he whispered.

"Never more sure," she said, bringing his underpants gently and lovingly past his erection and down his legs to join the other clothes on the floor.

He moved his hands further down her back and pulled her towards him. She kissed his chest and snuggled into it still feeling the thump, thump of his heart in her ear. His leg moved between hers and both her legs wrapped around his thigh.

"Slowly," she whispered as she pulled him tight to her.

"Slowly," he said, kissing her and gently sucking her lips as her tongue slipped into his mouth. His hands were on her bottom, pulling her to him and she reached with one hand and moved her pants down her legs and wriggled out of them. A little voice inside her was still saying slowly but her whole body was racing and roaring with excitement as his hands glided around it, down the side of her neck, toying with her excited nipples. Her hands moved around his body too, touching him, tracing his contours, pulling him to her, loving the feeling of his arousal, wanting him...They seemed to gasp in unison when he reached between her legs and touched her. Then in one fluid movement he lifted her up onto his hips and lowered the two of them together onto the bed where they kissed and touched and held each other to the point where they couldn't and didn't hold back.

"I love you, Martha."

"I love you too, Stefan."

They lay in each other's arms embracing the moment but then before they knew it, they were kissing and touching and their excitement was building all over again.

"Just a minute," Stefan whispered, untangling himself momentarily to reach into his bedside drawer and take out a condom which he put under the pillow. As he did so, Martha knew that this was it and she felt a brief flash of dread, remembering the first time with Patrick, her first time ever. *Relax*, she told herself, *this couldn't be more different.*

As Stefan turned back to face her, he seemed to catch her moment of fear.

"We don't have to do anything that you're not ready for," he said, kissing each of her eyes and then her lips.

With his words her fear left her and she kissed him back, easing herself on top of him, moving her body in between his legs, as her lips moved slowly around his body, telling him with gentle gliding kisses that she loved every part of him. As she moved up his body, he touched her gently between the legs, feeling her dripping wet with excitement. She moved onto her side and reached for him. With her other hand she fumbled under the pillow and found the condom and opened it carefully with her teeth. He watched her with a smile that said, *I love you and I want you.* She gently put the condom on him and he kissed her and moved on top of her, touching her between her legs, making her feel out of control with desire.

"I love how excited you get, I can feel it," he gasped, locking his eyes on hers as he entered her. Then starting slowly and building up to a unified crescendo, they made love together for the first time.

Chapter 25

Fairground

In the morning, Martha woke up in Stefan's arms. She took stock of where she was, then closed her eyes again to savour the memories of the previous evening. She felt Stefan's stomach press against her back and hugged his arm around her. He stirred behind her, hugged her close and kissed the side of her neck. She knew that she couldn't resist him and she didn't want to.

Later, after they had showered and dressed, they sat on the couch eating breakfast.

"I look like something that the cat dragged in," Martha said feeling tired but noticing that she couldn't stop smiling.

"I look like the cat that got the cream," Stefan replied snuggling into her neck and nibbling it teasingly.

A sense of happy anticipation prevailed at the girls' flat when they went to collect them for the fair, but, when they got to the fairground and stared at the rides, doubts crept in.

"Are we feckin' mad?" Michael said, looking up at the chair-o-planes as they whirled and spun in the air. "They are not known to be overly fussy about their airplane maintenance here and we are thinking of getting up on that!"

"Is that a normal whirring noise coming from the motor? Should it shudder like that?" Martha asked.

"What about the roller coaster over there, should it rattle so much?" Mary asked.

"Should we risk it?" Martha said.

"I'm in," said Connie.

"Me too," said Siobhán and Stefan.

"Ah feck it," said Michael, "when your time is up, it's up. I'm up for it too."

"Sure, in the scheme of living here it's no major risk, really – but can we start with the dodgems, maybe?" suggested Martha, noticing that there was currently only one lonely looking car being driven around sedately by a quiet Sudanese teenager.

They took three dodgems between them and as soon as they sat into their cars, the Sudanese teenager drove away from them. Initially, as the ticket seller watched them, they drove around the platform sedately, but, when he headed off to chat to his friend, they quickly changed pace and started ramming each other with as much gusto as the cars would allow. As Martha and Stefan were reversing from ramming Mary and Connie, they felt themselves being rammed from behind and they turned around to see the Sudanese guy grinning at them as he rammed them again and then turned to head in the opposite direction. They went after him and, together with Michael and Siobhán, cornered him. They deliberately didn't hit him with full force but enough to say, 'You're on!' The four cars were quickly engaged in a ramming and chasing game but before they knew it, the ride was up. They paid for another and switched drivers and this time they were joined by a few more young Sudanese drivers. Having taken their money, the ticket collector again went off chatting to his friend. The dodgems became a free for all with crashes and bangs and whoops of laughter until the ticket collector noticed and blew his whistle and stopped the ride. He shouted something in Arabic that needed no interpretation, as he waved his arms crossly telling them to get out of the cars.

"Whoops," said Mary, "kicked off our first ride!"

"I feel like a bold child." Michael put on a big pout.

"And so you are," said Siobhán, giving him a smack on his thigh.

"How about the chair-o-planes next?" Stefan said, taking Martha by the elbow to lead her in that direction.

"Oh help, I can't believe I'm doing this," Martha said, praying hard that she wouldn't throw up when the ride started.

The chairs quickly rose up into the air and were soon going around in a circle.

I can do this, I can do this, Martha thought as she clung to Stefan and the bar in front of them. But then each chair started spinning separately and everything was spinning. Martha shut her eyes tight, willing it to stop. Then she shut her mouth tight, convinced that she would throw up at any moment. When the spinning slowed down, Martha wasn't sure if it felt less or more nauseous, she just wanted it to end. When it did, her eyes were still shut tight and it took her a while to realise that the chair was actually at a standstill. She opened her eyes, everything was still moving and, when she went to stand up, her legs were wobbly and wouldn't quite hold her up.

"You okay?" Stefan said as he helped her off the ride.

Martha nodded, scared to open her mouth until the feeling of nausea subsided. She sat down on the ground and pulled her knees up to her chest and rested her head on them.

"I'm not doing that again," she said as she eventually stood up to join the others.

"Let's get a Pepsi or something," Stefan suggested, nodding in the direction of a drink stall with a few tables and chairs in front of it.

Over drinks, Connie said that she had no interest in doing the ride again either and it was decided that Stefan, Mary, Siobhán and Michael would do it while Martha and Connie would sit and watch the world go by. Then they would all have a go on the roller coaster.

By the time they made their way over to the roller coaster, there was a long queue and as they waited, they watched two full runs of the shuddering, shaky ride.

"I'm not even going to think about it," Martha said. "I'll be fine."

"Me too," said Connie, "it's the spinning that kills me, I can hack the going up and down."

"I can too," Martha said, trying not to remember the Fokker 50 flight.

They piled into their seats and the ride started gently, then sped up and tilted slightly as it went around first one and then a second tight corner, then it rose steadily to a gentle peak and went at speed down again and around another two tight corners with even more of a tilt. It rose slowly up to its highest point and Martha braced herself for a rapid drop, but the drop was slow and devoid of exhilaration, and, after a short straight run, the ride was over.

"That was nothing," Martha said with a mixture of relief and disappointment.

They walked around to see if there were any other rides worth considering but the rest were children's carousels so they dismissed them. Michael couldn't resist buying some pink candy floss and Siobhán told him that she would give him another smack if he didn't keep it away from her hair. They decided to head to the Sudan Club for a swim and an early dinner.

After a leisurely swim, Martha stretched out on a sun lounger by the pool and quickly fell asleep. She woke after maybe an hour or so with her hat over her face and, as she lifted her head, it fell to the ground.

"Well sleeping beauty, I put your hat over your face so you wouldn't burn," Siobhán said, "and your beast is over there almost snoring!"

"Late night last night." Martha grinned and reddened.

"I guessed."

"We need an early one tonight. I think I'll have another swim and then dinner."

Later, as they walked across the lawn to go for dinner, Martha spotted Máire about to leave the Club and went after her as she appeared to be alone.

"Do you want to join us for dinner?" Martha asked, nodding in the direction of the others. "You know everyone."

"Perfect timing, I will," Máire replied.

The seven of them enjoyed a relaxed chatty dinner, then said their goodbyes and Máire gave the others a lift home on the way back to her place.

When they got back to Stefan's apartment, they sat end to end on the couch, drinking juice, rubbing each other's feet and lower legs, chatting.

"Do you know I've never fancied a guy until I got to know and like him a bit first?"

"Really?" Stefan said raising an eyebrow.

"Yeah. I think it makes everything seem easier and more natural or something."

"I can't say that I've always been that discerning." Stefan laughed.

"I don't think it's easy to get really intimate with someone until you know them a bit personally – at least it isn't for me."

"You mean that laying bare our souls, makes it easier to lay bare our bodies?"

"Yeah, I do actually!"

"I can't disagree with that," Stefan said lifting her foot and kissing it.

"I never knew touching feet could be so…I don't know…sensual."

"I am starting to think that touching you anywhere is dangerous."

"Do you think that you should give it up so, just to be safe?" Martha said laughingly.

"No, I think that I should do more of it!" he said, running his hand gently up her leg.

"I feel like this can't be happening to me," Martha said later as they lay back on the bed trying to cool down after making love. "I keep thinking that I'm going to wake up and find that I'm just Martha Hyland, the boring accountant, who struggles with her family and who ran away to Sudan…where she was still a boring accountant!"

"Hanging out with a boring dysfunctional pilot…Is that what you'll wake up to?"

"That's not what I meant, and you know it."

"Well, you are much more than a boring accountant. You are a beautiful, passionate woman with a big heart and this boring pilot loves you. Molly, Siobhán, Mary, Connie, Máire, they all love you too."

"Well, there's Liam, Shelley, Attracta and Tom, I certainly can't say that they love me."

"But that's it, look at them. Do you want to be like them? I don't. If they don't like you, that's their problem, not yours."

"And what about my family? When I lived in Dublin every time I thought that I was getting my shit together and starting to feel good about myself, I would go home and straight away, I was back to being the old me again. I'm the invisible one, the one nobody sees or hears, unless they need something done, like a cup of tea or coffee made or the dinner cooked and then it's 'Martha this, Martha that…'"

"And what do you do?"

"That's the sad thing, isn't it? I do it. I say nothing and do it and then I hate myself for not standing up to them. Away from home, I'm quite confident and successful and sometimes even regarded as funny. But at home, I'm the family doormat and I let them use me as they see fit. Sad or what?"

"Do you want my honest opinion?" Stefan said, putting his arm around her as she snuggled into him and rested her head on his chest.

"Yeah, I guess."

"I think they sound like a miserable, shallow bunch who know you not at all. It seems to me that your mother set the standard and they followed. I imagine them too busy driving their fancy cars and going on their fancy holidays to notice the beauty of the world in front of them. Take Sligo, where you grew up, you describe beautiful beaches, mountains, sunsets. Based on everything you've told me about them, I doubt that they would see the beauty that you talk about even if it was to get up and bite them."

Martha thought for a while. She could never remember them actually looking or commenting on any of it.

"I can only remember Jim and his wife, Martina, bringing their kids to the beach once in all the times that they came home, and all they did was make a song and dance about getting sand in their precious BMW. The first thing they did when they got back to the house, before they even greeted my mother, was get out the vacuum cleaner and clean the car."

"And you go swimming alone under the stars in the Sudan Club and think that you are in heaven. Do you want to identify with that person who is vacuuming the sand out of their car or the one enjoying the feeling of warm sand between their toes?"

"I don't like vacuuming!" Martha grinned.

"Or do you think that they make love the way you do? Or is it more like, what's that expression you used when you were talking about sex in holy Ireland? I know – wham, bam, thank you, ma'am!"

"Okay, okay, I get it. You're right," Martha said between giggles. "They're miserable. And while we might share some genes, the reality is that we have little else in common. Hmm, I think that I need to hold that thought!"

Chapter 26

Meroë and the Polish Driver

How time flies when you're having fun, Martha thought two days after she left Stefan at the airport to fly home. It seemed like only last week that he said he was going home late next month and now he was gone two days and it felt like a week. Two whole weeks without him. She sighed, clattering dirty dishes noisily together as she picked them up off the coffee table, hoping that Attracta or Tom would hear her from their bedroom. She decided to wait to wash them equally noisily later when they had resumed their normal position stretched out on the dirty couch, in hope, rather than expectation, that they might take the hint and offer to wash their own dirty dishes.

She had a few plans made before Stefan left and now, out of the blue, she also had a trip to Meroé to look forward to on the following Friday. Connie had met an Irish woman, Sally-Ann, working on an electricity project in Sudan with some Irish and Polish engineers. They had permits to take five vehicles to visit Sudan's pyramids at Meroé a mere one hundred and twenty-five miles north-east of Khartoum. Connie had been offered a place in a pickup with a Polish driver, who had virtually no English, and she was keen for someone to come along for moral support.

"Why not?" Martha said. "What about the others though?"

"Well there's room for a few of them too but I warned them that this Polish guy, Michal, is a bit of a lunatic driver, and they declined!"

In the meantime, before Friday, Martha's other big plan was to catch up on her letter writing. She had written recently to Mrs Connolly but she definitely owed Trish a letter. She had already given Trish a light-hearted version of the challenges of her trip to the west and coming home to the pigsty, to be happily rescued by Stefan. Trish had enjoyed hearing that the 'sexy outfit' that she had made Martha pack had been put to good use. She had finished her last letter with 'Next instalment soon please on the adventures of Martha and Stefan in Sudan, henceforth to be known as M & S in S!' When Martha sat down to write her letter the first thing she wrote was that in future she intended to refer to Trish, (Patricia), and Páidí who lived in Phibsboro as P & P in P, which she claimed had a much better ring to it than M & S in S!

Martha wasn't quite ready to give Trish the full insight into the depth of her feelings for Stefan, partly out of fear of fully admitting it to herself but, if she was to be honest with herself, more out of fear that it would turn out to be an illusion, a mirage in the desert. She still bought into the adage that if it sounded too good to be true then it probably was too good to be true. The chances were that all she had with Stefan wouldn't last. It would end as unexpectedly as it had begun. If she allowed herself to analyse why she felt like this, she might have considered that her fears ultimately stemmed from her deeply embedded feeling of being unworthy of his lasting love. If he was all he was cracked up to be, then he wouldn't stick with her and sometime in the future, he would wake up and realise that she was not the person he thought that she was, or even the person she thought she was. She still had a nagging feeling that her mother, brother and sisters couldn't all be wrong and that it was she who had a distorted version of her youth forever stuck in her head.

There was nobody there to argue with these thoughts and so she parked them and went back to writing to Trish, telling her about the sickening fairground ride and how *I am never getting up on anything like that again. Although, actually, on Friday, Connie and I are taking a seven hour or more trip on an unmarked desert track to visit Sudan's pyramids with a lunatic Polish driver at the wheel! Why do I agree to these things? Saner people would say "no" and stay in Phibsboro!*

Friday arrived and Connie and Martha went to the Acropole Hotel very early to meet Michal, their driver. Not alone did he not speak English but he didn't speak any Arabic either. *This is going to be fun.* They set off without comment and drove through Khartoum North and out to the edge of the desert where they met up with the four other pickups. Sally-Ann and four Irish engineers occupied one pickup and the others were filled with Polish men and women.

191

Martha wondered if Michal's reputation was well established, given how full the other vehicles were and how there was only Michal, Connie and herself in theirs! From her previous conversation with Máire, and from listening to the Irish engineers, Martha understood it would be hard to see where to drive at times as there was no proper road, just a rough track. Dan, one of the Irish engineers, said the idea was to keep the Nile on their left but know that the Nile would not always be visible, which sounded more than a little vague to Martha. The driving time each way was expected to be three and a half to four hours, all going according to plan. They were to travel in convoy and another Polish driver, who was to lead, seemed confident that he knew the way.

The idea of the convoy seemed reasonable until they took off at race speed, driving along a track that was nothing more than two parallel grooves in the sand with a mound of sand running down the middle. Whichever way they looked the scenery was the same, miles and miles of desert. Michal continuously drove right up the rear end of the vehicle in front of them resulting in continuous braking and accelerating. Within a half an hour they met their first colourful souk truck coming straight against them. It was not for turning. It held its ground and its horn roared. All five vehicles were forced off the track and each one struggled to get back on again through the heavy, soft sand.

Martha thought travelling in a convoy meant that the vehicles would wait for each other. But this was more like a testosterone-fuelled competition to see if the drivers in front could shake off the drivers behind. On they raced: accelerating, braking, veering out of the way of oncoming souk trucks with their loud honking horns…The trucks owned the track and none of them were for turning. They always forced the other vehicles off onto the soft sand. After three hours they were still at the very back of the convoy and were going full throttle when Michal was forced to brake hard, rather than rear-end the vehicle in front. Their pickup stopped, stuck, perched on the mound of sand that ran between the two parallel grooves. All four wheels were spinning but bringing them nowhere. They got out and, without a word, Michal produced three shovels from the back. They started digging in the scorching heat, slowly moving the sand from under the base of the pickup to under and in front of the tyres. The other vehicles had continued on regardless. Neither

Martha nor Connie knew what was going to happen next. Between nervousness and the heat, Martha didn't know whether to laugh or cry, so she started singing.

"Don't forget your shovel if you want to go to work."

Connie joined in, glad of a way to relieve the tension that had been building up from when they first met Michal. He left them digging and got into the vehicle. They just jumped clear as he drove on along the track. They looked at each other aghast.

"For fuck's sake!" they said, believing in that moment that he was a big enough feckin' lunatic to leave them both there, abandoned in the scorching heat without so much as a tree in sight for shade. He stopped just as suddenly and waited for them to run the couple of hundred yards to the truck and get in. He took off at startling speed, it was as if he planned to fly across the desert to avoid getting stuck again in the sand. There was an oncoming blue-and-pink souk truck heading straight for them; it kept coming and they kept going. The two drivers were playing chicken. Who was going to move last? Just as the souk truck's presence filled their wind screen and its horn roared in their ears, Michal swerved off the track and kept going for a couple of hundred yards. He swerved again, back in the direction of the track and kept driving at breakneck speed on no particular track but going rapidly uphill. Then he braked, causing Connie and Martha to lurch forward feeling their seatbelts scar their shoulders. They were a few feet away from the edge of a sand cliff.

"Fuck," said Martha.

"Holy fuck," said Connie, "I thought we were goners."

They both started laughing and Michal threw them a filthy look before he got out of the pickup. They followed and stood at the top of the cliff, staring around them to see if they could see the track, the Nile or anything useful.

"*Al Hamdillallah, Al Hamdillallah!*" Martha and Connie screamed and clapped when they saw the other four pickups waiting for them in the distance. Michal reversed back down the hill and then turned and sped in the direction of the others. Martha wondered if he would be able to stop without hitting one of them, but, at the last second, he braked and swerved around them, threw up a spray of sand and came to an abrupt halt. Martha and Connie got out of the pickup and ran over to Sally-Ann.

"*Is amadán mór é*," Martha said speaking in Irish in case the other Poles spoke English.

"He's the biggest feckin' eejit that I've ever had the horror of meeting. He's nearly got us killed more times than I can count and we are running out of lives!" Connie declared.

"I did warn you! Michal is a known lunatic…We've had our hairy moments too. I didn't think that it was meant to be a race," Sally-Ann said defensively.

"Perhaps you could ask Dan if the other pickups could drive a bit slower, so that, maybe, all our lives might be spared," Martha suggested hopefully.

"I'll try. But he fancies himself as a bit of a boy-racer too, though he's long past that age!"

"Look." Martha pointed over Sally-Ann's shoulder and they all turned around. Within a few hundred yards of them a long train rolled past. A few people were hanging out of the doors and windows of the carriages but, stranger still, on the roof of the train were dozens of men in white *jallabiyahs* sitting on their hunkers, chatting in little groups, like they did at the souks.

"The train driver must be more reliable than our fella!" Martha said.

"Dan says that the passengers often fall off and when they do, the train stops and waits for them to run and catch up and get back on! Mustn't hurt them too much to fall in the sand at that speed – they're tough people!"

After the train had passed, they were all glad to get out of the heat and back into their vehicles. Connie and Martha were grateful that the last leg of the journey to Meroé was without any scary incidents. And what a strange sight it was. After miles and miles of virtually nothing but sand, there, out in the middle of the desert, stood big and proud some two hundred pyramids, many nearly complete and with almost intact large, elaborate stone entrance porches. There were three distinct groups of pyramids, divided and surrounded by hot, dry sand. All that was between Martha and these ancient structures were random hills of soft, hot sand. These weren't dunes held together by clumps of marram grass and other growth. These were hills, maybe twenty feet or more high, with not a blade of greenery in sight, just scorching hot brown sand that gave way with every step. They stepped out of their vehicles to take it all in and planned to eat their lunch before having a closer look. The heat quickly caused them to revise their plans and eat their lunches and drink thirstily in their vehicles.

"Fifty-seven degrees centigrade or one hundred and thirty-five Fahrenheit, according to my thermometer. Dangerously hot," Dan said as the women hopped and skipped across the sand trying not to burn their feet through their sandals, wishing that they had worn something more sensible, as the men had. The small group of women scurried into the shade of the pyramid doorways, took a closer look at the old carved wood and wondered was it really two thousand years old too. As Martha sheltered with Connie in a doorway, she could see that many of the pyramids had been decapitated. Máire had told her about a treasure-hunting Italian who had got permission from the Sudanese government to explore the pyramids on condition that any treasure found would be shared. But seemingly whatever was found had ended up in museums in Berlin or Munich, or so the story went. Martha shared this story only with Connie, as the Polish women had little or no English. They hopped along from one doorway to another, trying not to sink or burn themselves in the roasting sand. They had caught up with Dan, Sally-Ann and the other Irish, when a tall Sudanese man in a long off-white *jallabiyah* and a lose turban emerged from out of the hazy heat, appearing like a strange ghostly apparition gliding across the sand as if the searing heat caused him to levitate.

"*Salaam alaykum,*" he said by way of greeting.

"*Alaykum salaam,*" Dan replied first and the others echoed his response. Martha was still taking in that the man who appeared before them was indeed a real live human being.

"English?" he asked.

"No, Irish."

"Ah Ireland. Big trouble. English out. English *ma kwas*, not good. Out, out, out." He laughed.

They looked at him baffled. The 'out, out, out' could only refer to the famous speech of perhaps five years previously, in which the British prime minister, Margaret Thatcher, dismissed, in no uncertain terms, the New Ireland Forum's alternative proposals for Northern Ireland. Who was this strange Sudanese man standing in the middle of ancient pyramids, surrounded by sand, speaking in broken English about Irish politics?

After a long pause Dan spoke. "Yes, *ma kwas*. In Sudan, English out. Sudanese government in. *Kwas*."

The Sudanese man moved closer and slapped Dan on the shoulder in solidarity for their situation.

"*Insha'Allah*. You follow me. I show you more things."

He took them over to some large cut stones that must have formed part of a significant building at some time, perhaps another pyramid. With his foot he brushed away some sand and revealed part of a pristine, elaborate, coloured tiled mosaic floor. He moved a few feet along and revealed more of it, clearly all forming part of some grand design. They looked at it in awe and thanked him for showing it to them, but indicated that they were all anxious to get out from under the hot sun.

"You want to visit caves? Many bats. Cold. *Kwas*," he said, pointing into the distance.

"No thank you, we must get back to Khartoum. Long journey before the sun goes down," Dan said pointing at the sun as if moving it below the horizon.

"I understand, *Ma'assalama*." He touched his right hand to his heart, turned and left them, gliding off across the sand, disappearing back into the barely present haze, as surreal in his departure as he had been in his arrival.

They made their way back to their vehicles, shaking their heads at the strangeness of it all. The others were waiting impatiently with their engines already on and the air conditioning running.

When Connie and Martha sat in the pickup they squealed as they felt the cold seats under them.

"Hi Michal," they chorused. He turned and looked at them with unveiled disdain.

"Do you think he actually wants to kill us?" Martha whispered to Connie.

"Sure felt like it on the way here. But I spoke to Dan again and he promises not to abandon us this time. Here's hoping."

Dan was true to his word, and while the journey back was still at speed, there wasn't quite the same lunatic braking and accelerating and they all managed to stay together. In addition, they only had to leave the track twice as they only met two souk trucks.

When they finally sat in their own Help pickup back at the Acropole Hotel, they laughed with relief as the hot seats burned their bruised bottoms. Despite having worn their seatbelts, they felt thoroughly bumped and battered by their journey.

"Where to now?" Martha asked.

"I suggest straight to the Sudan Club as planned. A shower, a swim, a shower, food and then home. I need to see and feel water."

"Great minds think alike. But remind me to never again get into a vehicle with a known madman."

"Agreed. It was worth it though, wasn't it?"

Chapter 27
Aid and Memos

After Meroé, Martha felt that she'd had enough excitement to do her for the rest of the time Stefan was away. She anticipated him getting all protective when he heard about what she referred to as her 'near-death experiences'. For a few days afterwards she was almost glad of the peace of the office but then, as she found that she had more and more free time on her hands, she became further convinced that a financially trained administrator could do her job and the administrator's. And she still couldn't figure out what work, if any, Attracta the acting administrator was actually doing.

With Stefan away, Martha spent more evenings in the Sudan Club mixing with a variety of experienced expats. She found herself picking their brains as she tried to understand how things really worked with foreign aid in Sudan. The government-enforced exchange rate was still a major bugbear of hers. Although she worked her way around it in as many legal ways as possible, she realised that in the scheme of the total foreign aid programme, Help's in-country expenditure was a drop in the ocean. She also learned that the army often creamed off food and supplies brought in by the agencies for the poor and the hungry. There were more rumours too that the northern government was supplying arms to certain rival tribes in southern Sudan, aiming to keep the south divided and weak with the hope that this weakness would ultimately allow the northern government access to the oil and other resources in the south.

One evening Máire and Martha were having dinner at the Sudan Club when Susannah, whom Máire knew well and Martha knew in passing, joined them. Knowing that Susannah specialised in development aid and had worked with various agencies for some twenty years, Martha was curious to know her views on the Sudanese aid situation.

"There is an old proverb, *give a man a fish and you feed him for a day, teach a man to fish and you feed him for a lifetime*. Well it's not quite that simple, is it?" Susannah said.

Máire and Martha nodded in agreement.

"One agency I know recently decided that the Sudanese didn't fish enough so they replaced their traditional manual pole-driven boats with imported boats with imported engines, which required imported parts and fuel. The Sudanese fishermen then caught as many fish in three days as they had previously caught in six and now only fish three days a week."

Martha and Máire laughed knowingly.

"I know a similar story," Máire said. "In recent years, one of the large aid agencies, in their wisdom, decided that Sudan could grow more rice in the north-west so they introduced new systems, including large storage silos and brought in fertiliser from Europe, all the way by sea to Port Sudan and then the whole way across the desert to north-western Sudan. The crops increased threefold – some of the Sudanese didn't plant any rice for the next two years as, the way they saw it, they didn't need to."

"So," Martha said, "the Sudanese were expected to sell their surplus fish or rice and make a profit and expand their businesses."

"Exactly. In other words, the big wigs in the so-called developed world expected the Sudanese to share their capitalist values: they totally failed to understand the Sudanese subsistence ways of thinking and living," Máire added.

"It would be funny if it wasn't actually true!" Susannah said.

These conversations made Martha think even more about the way that Help was set up in Sudan. Help's aim was to expand its operations through continuously opening new clinics and with each new clinic came another expatriate and the huge costs that went with it. Shelley had already prepared budgets for two additional clinics on the outskirts of Khartoum. Based on her own observations and from long discussions with Siobhán and Molly, Martha's opinion was that the existing clinics could all be run, on a day-to-day basis, by local staff with some overall supervision from an expat. In time, with proper training and structures, four or more clinics could be overseen by one expat, not one expat per clinic. If Help regarded themselves as engaging in development work, then surely that meant training local staff and making clinics more self-sustaining over time.

With Martha's background working not just as an accountant but also as a business consultant, she decided to put her thoughts on paper. She prepared a detailed memo with a myriad of suggestions: reduce expatriate costs and requirements through merging the accountant and administrator roles; do away with an expat mechanic; bring a number of clinics under local staff with one overall expat supervisor and have a long-term plan for Help's involvement in Sudan with a view to making the clinics more sustainable with less involvement from Help, and in particular requiring less Help funding over time. She believed that Help's ultimate goal should be to make the clinics self-sufficient. She set out how such an approach could free up Help donations to be utilised in other areas of Sudan or other countries more desperately in need of primary health care. She also felt that, with head office support, there were more ways to tackle the exchange rate issue and to reduce further monies being brought into Sudan directly. She approached Shelley and asked to meet to discuss her thoughts.

"Martha, why don't you stick to accounts and I'll stick to running the place. As an accountant, I can't see what you could possibly know about running clinics."

"Well, yes, you see, you're right, to a point, but I can't separate the two. How things are organised currently costs a lot of hard-earned money and I'm just trying to find ways to save Help some of its limited resources," Martha responded quietly but firmly.

"Martha, let me put it another way, you stick to your knitting and I'll stick to mine."

"It's not as simple as that – finance is my knitting, you see…"

But Shelley had already turned her back on Martha and strutted away as fast as her little legs would allow her.

Martha made another attempt that afternoon to get Shelley's input into the memo but Shelley told her that it was her memo and she could do what she liked with it.

Two days later, with some trepidation, Martha knocked on Shelley's door. Shelley looked up with a scowl that said *take a hike* but Martha inhaled a deep breath and issued her prepared speech.

"I don't presume to know how to run the organisation but it is my job to consider Help's finances. I have prepared this memo for the Board's consideration. I did ask you for your input and I have noted on it that the memo is mine and mine alone and that you declined to read it or express your opinion on it. I just want you to know that I have sent it home for distribution to the Board. Here is a copy of it as it was sent."

Shelley's face turned red with rage but Martha didn't wait for a response. She put the memo on Shelley's desk and walked out shutting the office door quietly behind her. She had already sent the memo the previous day with a returning expat to Trish in Ireland and she knew that she could rely on her to distribute it to Help's listed Board members.

Having handed Shelley the memo, Martha headed back to her flat an hour or so earlier than usual. She was relieved to know that she could comfortably avoid Shelley the next day as she was going to the orphanage. She sat in her room and read for a while and then headed to the Sudan Club. Luckily, Máire was there too and they enjoyed a hot and heavy game of squash after which Martha went for a swim to clear her head. Despite the pool being busier than it was during her late evening swims, Martha switched out of the world around her and got lost in her thoughts. She worried that, with so much time on her hands, she had become like a demented woman with a bee in her bonnet about how Help was run. She had probably been too blunt and too gung ho. She should have waited for Stefan to return and sought his advice on how to handle the whole thing in a more diplomatic and effective way. But Stefan was more a rebel than a corporate man who specialised in diplomacy, as he would have been quick to tell her. The truth was that he was probably too like her, too confrontational! What might that mean for their future relationship when the honeymoon period was over? Patrick understood office politics and how to play them. He was unconfrontational to a fault. She could learn from him. The more she thought about it all, the more she felt disillusioned with the whole foreign aid business and started to really question her motives for coming to Sudan. She had come with an expectation of contributing something but now she felt that she was part of a team of western interferers who failed to understand the people that they claimed to be here to help. She had never thought of herself as an idealist before but looking back on how she had jumped into taking the job with Help, she now saw how naïve and idealistic she had been.

Where did philanthropy and development aid end and where did world politics and world economics begin? Were countries giving aid to Sudan for genuine altruistic reasons or were they just trying to stay close to Sudan as an Arab country and as a country with good natural resources? She didn't know. It was all more complex than she had the knowledge or the intellect to get her head around but she knew that she wasn't comfortable with it, in as far as she did understand it. She wished that Stefan would hurry back so that he might help her thrash out some of these issues. He wasn't due back for another week and he had a history of being too idealistic himself. Plus, finances and related areas weren't really his thing. Patrick always had a great mind to help her look at business problems from different angles. *Oh Patrick, I'm sorry*, she thought remembering the unopened letter from him stuffed at the back of her drawer.

Martha's apprehension about how the board might react to her memo was building to serious anxiety and she blurted her worries out to Máire as they sat talking by the pool on Saturday afternoon.

"Don't worry, Martha. Something had to be done and clearly Shelley wasn't going to do anything. You've done the right thing." Máire looked at her watch. "I'm really sorry, I hate to cut you short but I need to get home soon to get ready to go to Mass."

"Mass? You go to Mass in Sudan?" Martha couldn't believe that she had spent nearly nine months in Sudan and she had never known that anyone, never mind Máire, went to mass there.

"Oh yes, there are plenty of Christian services in Khartoum," said Máire.

Martha thought for a moment. "Perhaps it might be something that I need. Can I go with you?"

"Of course, of course. Come. But you must be ready in thirty minutes flat," Máire said looking again at her watch.

In the car on the way, Máire told Martha that her Sudanese colleagues were intrigued that men and women stood beside each other in church and this did not distract them from their prayers.

"If I thought that the men at church back home would be a distraction to me, I'd have gone more often!" Martha joked.

"They were also surprised that not even the women covered themselves at Mass and I told them that, when I was growing up in Ireland, women had covered their heads, normally with black lace mantillas but few do nowadays."

"I remember seeing older women going to Mass wearing mantillas in Sligo right up to before I left Ireland but I don't remember women in our protestant churches ever covering their heads."

The church that Máire normally attended was one of a number of impressive churches left over from when Sudan was colonised. It was a large and imposing building with bright red-and-yellow stonework, large stained-glass windows and statues of Mary and Jesus. Paintings of the Stations of the Cross hung on the walls around the sides of the church. It was like many Roman Catholic churches in Ireland. Martha was surprised at how full it was, with mainly white expatriates attending. Although baptised and confirmed a protestant, Martha went to Mass in a Catholic church at home as often as to service in a protestant church, which wasn't more than five or six times a year for both.

She was pleased to find the Mass in Khartoum pleasantly slow and not lacking in some good hearty singing.

"I enjoyed that Máire, thank you. Even the singing was good and I knew most of the hymns."

"Yes, unlike at home, there is lots of singing at Mass here. I must say that I like it too."

"I find Mass normally very similar to a protestant communion service in the words used and the general lack of singing but at home my biggest problem is that I can't keep up – you guys say the words at least twice the speed we do!"

"I know we do." Máire laughed. "Maybe it stems from men being in a hurry to sneak off to the pub afterwards!"

"Sometimes it feels like the object is to say as many prayers as possible as quickly as possible! And, with little or no singing, you can be in and out in half an hour as opposed to the normal one hour or more for our good old protestant services!"

"I like the slower speed of your services. I've gone to protestant services abroad and even in Ireland. I like that everyone joins in the singing even if they haven't a note in their head! I even join in myself," Máire said.

"Sure, if you ignore transubstantiation, which most of my Roman Catholic friends have never even heard of, then, apart from the lesser role of Mary in the protestant churches, let's face it, there isn't much dividing the Christian churches except men, money and power!" Martha said with a long sigh.

"The root of all evil at every level, when you think of it!" Máire added.

Martha struggled to sleep that night and in the small hours she again remembered the unopened letter from Patrick hidden away in the drawer. She got out of bed, turned on the light and rummaged in the drawer until she found it just as she had remembered it, her name written neatly on a business envelope with Delaney Robertson & Co, the name of the law firm where Patrick worked, printed boldly on the lower right-hand corner. She sat back into bed and opened the envelope. It was handwritten on headed work paper. It was a longer letter than any of his previous ones.

Dearest Martha,

Apologies for my poor letter writing over the last number of months. Work has been more manic than ever with two significant projects apart from my usual commercial work. It is a weak excuse and I know that I should have made it my business to write better and more frequent letters.

It may seem strange to say but as time goes by, I miss you more rather than less. I find myself rereading your long letters and wishing that I was there to share some of your experiences with you. You certainly have faced many challenges but, true to form, I suspect that you have risen to them. Sudan is a huge leap from any country that we have experienced and you have given me a very personal and real sense of it.

Please do not forget to let me know when you are able to take your volunteer's break in Kenya as I am so looking forward to us spending time there together. I have warned work that this is one holiday I will not miss.

I am sorry to hear that your brothers and sisters continue to give you grief even all the way to Sudan. You don't deserve it. You have been a dedicated daughter, aunt and sibling – above and beyond duty.

There have been many changes here in work and I too face some new challenges. Hopefully I will rise to them. I was at a dinner the other evening in the partners' dining room on the top floor. I would have loved if you could have been there as you would have loved the food. However, I suspect that you would have hated some of the shenanigans. Despite the room being like an overheated greenhouse, we all had to keep our jackets on until the Managing Partner took his off. I was fit to collapse and you know how much I sweat. I was fully expecting my shirt to be indecent by the time I took my jacket off. Really some of the older partners are incredibly stuffy.

Not much other news except that soccer fever has taken over the country. I have even caught the disease and plan to go to some matches.

My family all send their regards, very specifically my mother. She says that she realises that you are a good influence on me and are great at getting me out doing all sorts of things. She says that in your absence I am in danger of turning into a workaholic. She sees less of me since you left!

I promise to write more often from now on. Maybe even a letter a week! But I had better get a life outside work so that I've something more interesting than contract and commercial law to write about!

I love you lots and I should say it more often,
Patrick

Martha was shocked. The letter was so different from all of Patrick's previous letters. It said more than he'd ever said to her face to face. If she had got it sooner how would she have felt towards him? Would she be with Stefan? She wasn't sure. She still had feelings for him but was it as a friend? Was it love? Was it that he was a rock she could anchor herself to? He could be a better rock if they both learned to be more open and honest with each other. She felt confused and guilty. Patrick was a good soul. She must have broken his heart with her phone call. She folded the letter back into the envelope and put it under her pillow. She turned off the light and closed her eyes. She tried not to cry. She saw his words near the end of the page.

I love you lots and I should say it more often,
Patrick

The end of the page, the partners' dining room, the older partners, the headed note paper…

She was a fool.

She took the envelope out from under the pillow and pulled open the two sheets of paper. On the bottom of each was a list of the firm's partners, twelve of them. And there in amongst them *Patrick J. O'Sullivan*.

Oh, Patrick, now I understand. You have been at home building a future not just for yourself but, you thought, for me too. That's why you have been so busy and so distracted. You decided to tell me in your own way that you had made it. You wanted me to share your success, to be by your side, but instead I slammed a door in your face. I'm sorry, Patrick. I don't know what love is. I don't know how to do relationships. I want to know. I thought I knew but really…I know nothing.

Chapter 28

Letter from Home

The trip to mass had been a refreshing change and between it and Patrick's letter Martha felt a huge pang of yearning for home, real home, her friends, the familiar, Ireland. But her nostalgia got a jolt with the letter that arrived the next day.

Dear Martha,

It seems that you have chosen to ignore our last letter which was sent to you several months ago. We know that you are alive and well as Mother still receives your occasional letters and our children receive cards and other things from you, but this does not absolve you from your responsibility to Mother.

At this stage, we all feel that we will have to put our feet down and insist that you come home. Three times in the last two months alone, one of the carers has let us down and we have had to ask neighbours to look in. Can you imagine how embarrassing it was, having to ring Mrs O'Reilly and ask her to check on Mother and bring her in some dinner, as happened again only last Saturday.

Máire's mother, Mrs O'Reilly, would have helped out with a heart and a half, but Martha did smile at the thought of her siblings and her mother calling on her for help – when they hadn't had a good word to say about her for years.

We have considered a nursing home but as the cost of it would be almost 80% of what Mother receives from Father's pension, this wouldn't leave much money for anything else.

What else would that be, Martha thought. The accountant in her wanted to point out to them that the tax breaks on the nursing home costs would significantly reduce the actual net cost. Perhaps she'd tell them this when she wrote back: if she wrote back.

After much consideration, we have decided that the best thing would be for you to move back to Sligo and get a job here. Given your line of work this should not be a problem. You could live with Mother at no expense to yourself and it would mean that if a carer let us down, there would always be a back-up. Think of the money that you would save, not having to rent an apartment in Dublin or incur any other household expenses.

We know that your contract with Help is up in a few months and we expect that they will be willing to release you sooner, given that your Mother needs you at home.

We are concerned that you may refuse this generous offer because we have a very different memory, to your distorted one, of your childhood but we assure you that we have put all that behind us and we won't mention it again.

Now that you have had some time away, we expect that you will see where your duty lies and that you will come home.

Your brother and sisters,

Jim, Margaret and Robyn

Martha was surprised at her reaction to the current letter. On getting Jim's letter after Christmas, she had been very upset and had worked hard over the following months to put it behind her while still doing what she felt was right for herself, as an aunt and a daughter. She had sent cards and photos to her nieces and nephews, marking their birthdays, Easter and other random occasions. She had purchased some little treats in the over-priced Khartoum duty-free and included them with the cards. And she had written a number of times to her mother giving her select insights into her life in Sudan, her work and her visits to the orphanage, but nothing too personal. She had not received a single letter or card in return, not even on her birthday. She had decided that it was a relief not to receive any correspondence because it put her in control of her relationship with her family and spared her any upset correspondence from them might have caused.

Unlike her emotional response to the previous letter, Martha found herself reading the current letter mostly calmly and without serious rancour. Stefan was right, they knew her so little, if at all. *I may have been the family doormat before I left, but I won't let myself be it anymore*, she thought. To use her sister Margaret's expression, they could build their own bridge and get over it. But there was one thing that rankled her and that was the reference to her distorted version of her childhood. As she stared at the letter, she decided that it was the impetus she needed to go and talk to Máire about how Máire remembered Martha's childhood, and in particular remembered her relationship with her family.

She decided that she would write a response to the letter but what exactly that response would be, she would only decide after she talked to Máire.

The following evening, not long after Máire was due home from work, Martha called to her apartment with the letter in her backpack. She had never called uninvited before and knew that Máire would be surprised to see her. Máire answered the door, immediately invited her in and told her to sit down while she poured them each a glass of water from the fridge. She sat down beside Martha at the kitchen-cum-dining table which looked out onto the balcony where a lovely array of well-tended potted plants was displayed. As Martha was trying to fathom out how to open the conversation, the plants caught her eye.

"Máire, your plants are really lovely. I've never noticed them before…"

"All credit to my cleaner, I'm afraid. Her pride and joy. I kill everything."

Martha wasn't really listening.

"I guess you're wondering why I'm here."

Máire nodded.

"Well, you see, I got a letter from my siblings and I need to talk to you about it. I've been wanting to talk to you for a long time, but truth is, I've been avoiding it," Martha said before rummaging in her backpack and taking the letter from it.

"I understand. I really do. I think I've been avoiding talking about your family too," Máire said, gently nodding her head and putting her hand on Martha's shoulder in a way that said what Martha already knew, Máire cared about her.

Martha nodded in response and looked up at Máire.

"Well, do you want to show me the letter and then we can talk as much as you want?" Máire continued softly.

Martha handed over the letter and watched as she read it slowly, shaking her head from time to time as she took in its contents. When she had finished, she paused, gathering her thoughts.

"I've no plans to go home any time soon," Martha said, "it's the reference to my distorted memory of my childhood that bothers me…" And for the second time in two months Martha found herself telling someone how she had gone to a counsellor and that she had confronted each of her siblings and her mother about how she felt about her childhood. When she started to tell Máire about their sneering responses, Máire reached across the table and took her hand, shaking her head in obvious disbelief. Martha's eyes filled with tears which streamed unimpeded down her face.

"When I met you that first day at the UNICEF offices, I wanted to reach across the table and say thank you, thank you to you and to your mother for all your kindnesses, for making me feel that you cared."

Máire handed Martha a tissue from a box on the counter and took one herself and dabbed her own eyes.

"Oh, I am so sorry, Martha. We let you down. We did so little relative to what we should have done."

Martha shook her head. "You did so much, more than you will ever know."

"It broke Mammy's heart. I should have talked to you sooner here. I nearly did…I should have…It goes back years…You see, Mammy was always resolved to say something, do something and my father was always telling her to stay out of it or she could make things worse. Finally, it all got to Mammy when one day she and your mother took all the children for a picnic on the beach, as they sometimes did. It was your mother's turn to provide the picnic and while Mammy and your mother sat and chatted, your brother and sisters and mine played beach ball and swam in the water. You were told to sit a bit away, out of earshot on the sand and your mother would call you when you could move. Then the others started saying that they were hungry and you were sent to get the picnic things out of the boot of the car. I was a bit of a Mammy's girl and anyway I thought that I was getting too old for beach games. Also, I was an eavesdropper so I was sitting nearby and I saw you struggling to carry the picnic bags over to the rugs. I went over to help you. Then, as I was happily helping you to unpack the food and put out the plates and cups, your mother noticed. 'Leave her alone, Máire, she's well able to do it herself,' she said. 'And when you are done, Martha, you go back and sit in the car while we eat. Will you go and call the others in a few minutes please, Máire?'"

Martha let out a quiet sob and Máire paused and looked at her, her face full of concern.

"Go on Máire, please, I need you to go on."

"Well your mother turned and resumed chatting to my mother but I could see my mother's agitation. I stayed and helped you and when we had everything laid out, you got up and walked back towards the car with your head down. I watched you until I heard my mother's deep voice rising and I stood transfixed. My mother was standing up watching you walking towards the carpark and she looked then at your mother, sitting comfortably on a rug.

"'Julie, I cannot stand idly by any longer and let you treat that child the way you do. It's wrong. It's cruel. If I say nothing and do nothing, I might as well be doing it myself. You make her do non-stop jobs for you, for all of you. She cooks dinners, she cleans the house, and she hardly ever gets out to play – she is eight years old, for goodness sake, it has to stop.'

"Your mother stood up and put her hands on her hips. She stood her full height, but she was still a good foot shorter than my mother.

"'You're wrong! She's nine years old. And it's none of your business, I'll have you know. How dare you? Have you any idea of the sacrifices that I've made for that child? She's a spoilt little brat, she is.' Your mother gave a sneering cackle – I'll never forget it. 'You think you know it all. You O'Reillys know nothing.'

"'Well, I know what I see and it is wrong. Surely, Julie, you yourself know that it is wrong?'

"'How dare you? Who do you think you are – telling me how to rear my children? I would be happier if I never had to see, or hear, from you again, ever.'"

Máire was surprisingly animated as she relayed the story as if she was re-living it. She paused and took Martha's hand again, looked with concern at Martha's face, worried that she might have said too much.

"I'm fine, Máire. Honest. Please don't stop." Martha was no longer crying, she was just taking it all in, feeling as if a light was being shone on some dark place within her. She half smiled when she visualised Máire's mother, standing tall and regal over her own smaller mother. Her own mother would have jumped up and down with anger and yelped like a Pekinese while Máire's mother was, by contrast, a more sedate large lovable golden retriever. Martha had made this strange comparison before when she was telling Mrs Connolly about Máire's mother and it fitted right in with what Máire was telling her.

"Well, my mother was exasperated and just repeated firmly 'it's wrong, pure wrong'. By that time a few people were starting to stare in their direction and my mother thought better of saying anything further. She turned and saw me standing there. 'Máire, could you please ask your brothers and sister to gather their things quickly together and come now. I'll be waiting in the car in the car park. Okay?'

"They were all starving and fit to be tied when they saw all the food laid out and they couldn't have any of it. But, on the way back to the car, when I told them a little bit about what had happened, they knew there was no arguing with the situation.

"'I can't believe that Julie would treat her own child like that. It's not natural. I had to say something, didn't I?' Mammy said.

"'You did, Mammy, you did,' I said.

"'But what are we going to do for food?' Seán said.

"'There you go, always thinking of your stomach. Do you think that poor Martha will get much to eat tonight?'

"'Dad's away, can't we stop at the chippers? Please, Mammy?' Martin said.

"Mammy sighed and brought us all to the chippers but gave her burger to the boys to share and only picked at her chips. 'What if your father's right? What if I've made things worse for Martha? What am I going to do?'"

Martha thought that she remembered what had happened that night but she didn't say anything. Máire seemed to sense her thoughts.

"I know, Martha. I know. When we got home, Mammy was up to ninety with worry about you so she sent my brother Martin around to your house on the pretext of looking to see if your brother had his ball or if it had been left behind at the beach. As he got to your front door, he heard your mother screaming at you. He peered through the glass at the side and could see your mother walloping you hard on your bare legs with a wooden spoon. He got such a fright that he ran straight home and told Mammy.

"'It's all my fault. I have made things worse. What will I do? What will I do?' she said over and over."

As Martha sat listening to Máire she felt like a vulnerable child again, the lonely beaten child at the heart of the story. She remembered the wooden spoons in their house. She had felt the force of them being broken on her many times. Her mother never wasted them though. When they got broken, she had Martha's father saw them down and sand the top of the handle. The shortened spoons were used in the kitchen still. As an adult, Martha had on occasion held them in her hand and considered that her memories of the full impact of them hitting her bare bottom, legs or her body must have been accurate – the bruises often took weeks to fade and in boarding school she had found them hard to hide and even harder to explain. It must have taken one hell of a force to break those spoons across her.

"By the next day, Mammy had hatched a plan. She was going to be there for you whenever possible. We may all have been either almost reared or off at boarding school, so she was going to look out for you, come hell or high water. That's Mammy for you, always seeking to resolve situations and when she makes up her mind that's that. She sticks to her guns."

Remembering all Mrs O'Reilly had done for her, the feeling of being that vulnerable child was leaving Martha and she started to feel more like an on-looker watching it all happen to someone else.

"That explains it. That explains why your mother was always there for me, even when it didn't make any sense." Martha smiled and squeezed Máire's hand. "She's a good woman, your mother. And you're a good woman too. Thank you. Thank you from the very core of my being," Martha said between gentle sobs of relief.

"We are so sorry, so sorry that we didn't do more."

"What more could you have done? You did so much," Martha said shaking her head gently. "Oh, Máire, now you have helped me again. It means so much to have heard that story."

"Martha, I'm sorry."

"Please, don't feel sorry. You have freed me from the one thing that I couldn't free myself from," Martha said, her smile twinkling in her eyes. "I finally feel that I'm going to be free of the undertow of my memories, because now I know they are true. Thank you. Thank you."

Chapter 29

Response

Martha and Máire had stayed chatting for another few hours that night and along the way Máire had produced some vegetable stew from the fridge that she had made the previous day. Máire's story explained why Mrs O'Reilly had so often been in the right place at the right time for Martha. The weight of some of Martha's self-doubt had finally been lifted. She couldn't believe her new feeling of almost lightness and she kept checking in with herself, in case it was all a dream. It was as if she had been dragging a weight behind her for years and she had finally managed to cut the chain. She imagined herself telling Stefan and how pleased he would be for her. She anticipated hearing about how he had got on with his family and, in particular, his father. She could see them together raising a glass to their great unburdenings. In between these imaginings, she felt pangs of tenderness and sadness thinking of Patrick and how she had wronged him. She wanted to tell him too. She knew he would want to know and he deserved to, she knew that he too would be pleased for her. But Patrick was in the past. Her phone call to him had made sure of that. Whenever the Patrick–Stefan dilemma reared its head, she reminded herself that there was no going back, Stefan was her man. Stefan didn't just love her, he understood her and she understood him; when he arrived back, they would only have to look into each other's eyes to acknowledge that they had each unburdened themselves of the weight of their particular family dysfunction. Words would not be necessary.

In the days after her conversation with Máire, Martha sailed around the place with a brazen smile. She greeted everyone cheerfully, even Shelley, who threw her a filthy scowl on the few occasions that their paths crossed. She even smiled at Attracta and Tom when they made their way into the office an hour or more late for work each day. Two days after her conversation with Máire, she cleaned up after them in the flat and they immediately messed it up again. She looked at them and at the mess.

"Can we make a deal? If you guys make a mess, can you please clean up after yourselves? Okay?"

They stared at her blankly so she continued. "You know there is no daily cleaner, only me. Do you think that I like coming in to your mess? No, I don't. So, can you please wash your dishes, your mugs and your saucepans, empty your ashtrays, you know, simple things like that?"

They slowly nodded, looking at her as if they had never seen her before.

"Thanks. That would be great because I am actually sick of cleaning up after you. Right?"

They nodded again and Martha picked up a pile of dishes from the coffee table and handed them to Attracta and pointed her in the direction of the kitchen. She then picked up another pile and handed them to Tom, who stood gawking at her as she walked out the flat door. She headed straight to collect Siobhán to go for a swim and dinner. When Siobhán opened her flat door with her bag on her shoulder, Martha dragged her quickly out to the pickup, got into it and burst out laughing.

"Okay, Martha. You've lost it this time. What was all that about?"

"Well, you're right. I have lost it. I just told Attracta and Tom that I'm sick of cleaning up after them and I handed them each some dishes to go and wash. They are still looking after me. I'm not going to be anyone's dogsbody anymore and that's that." Martha smiled triumphantly. "In fact, I'm not putting up with crap from anyone anymore. End of story."

Siobhán burst out laughing, visualising Martha getting all bossy with Attracta and Tom and they not knowing what had hit them.

"But what sparked all this? I mean you've been walking around as if you are on a high for the last couple of days. You're not smoking their bang or anything?"

"God no. Nothing like that." Martha laughed. "I had an amazing conversation with Máire the other night and let's just say it lifted a weight off my shoulders. I'll tell you about it another time," Martha said. She didn't want to tell anyone else until she had told Stefan.

"Well, in the meantime, let's go for a celebratory swim and dinner."

The next day, as Martha was passing the fax machine, she heard the rare sound of it ringing and she stopped to see a memo, addressed to her and copied to Shelley, from the Chair of the Board of Directors. She waited for it to finish coming through, glancing around fearing that Shelley would arrive at any time, which thankfully she didn't. Martha took the pages to her desk and sat down to read them.

It acknowledged with thanks her 'well-prepared memo of the previous week' and said…

"…the Board consider that many of the points raised are worthy of further detailed consideration and action.

"We have therefore requested Mr Daniel O'Meara, an experienced Foreign Development Consultant, take up the new position of Executive Head of Mission for Help in Sudan within the next month, or as soon as a visa can be arranged. Mr O'Meara's initial contract will be for a period of three months after which it may be extended. During this initial period, he will carry out a full review of operations. Mr O'Meara will report directly to the Board and all senior staff in Sudan will report directly to him. We attach his passport details so that a visa can be applied for as soon as possible."

Martha smiled nervously to herself. Shelley would go mad. Martha knew this. Given that a number of the board members were known to rarely attend meetings and were members in name only, Martha had not expected such a decisive response. Somebody must have taken her memo seriously and now the proverbial was going to hit the fan. And some of it was definitely going to hit her when Shelley saw the memo.

She swallowed hard. No time like the present to get the ball rolling. She and Fuad were already heading to the Foreign Ministry that morning to finalise the visas for the new administrator and mechanic, who were due in a few weeks. Martha decided she would use the opportunity to immediately start applying for the new Executive Head of Mission's visa. Before heading off she nervously left a copy of the faxed memo on Shelley's desk with a note to say that she would start the visa application straight away.

As she sat in the car on the way to the Foreign Ministry, Martha said little as she considered that maybe changes will happen after all and that, whatever happened, it was going to have big implications for her. On the one hand, if her recommendation to merge the administrator's and the accountant's jobs was to go ahead then she would soon be out of a job. On the other hand, if Mr O'Meara disagreed with many of her recommendations, then staying on in Sudan as the accountant would be untenable with Shelley still in charge. Either way Martha reckoned she could expect to be leaving Sudan within the next couple of months. *Where and what next?* she thought. One thing she knew for sure, she was not going back to Ireland yet. She was not ready to face her siblings and the purgatory that would bring. She would get in touch with her old practise in Ireland and see what other possibilities they might know of elsewhere in Africa. She had still a number of months to run on her career break and could negotiate more. They had connections with international firms and were bound to find her something. She had loved Zimbabwe except that it was landlocked. She craved the sea. She would look for somewhere with an accessible coast.

Later, when she returned to the office after a surprisingly speedy and efficient trip to the Foreign Ministry, Dawit made a face, stamped his feet and pointed towards Shelley's office. Martha nodded, understanding that Dawit was telling her that Shelley had had a meltdown when she arrived and saw the memo. Shelley came out of her office only once that afternoon to get herself a cup of coffee. Martha kept her head down as she passed but she felt 'the look' burning into the back of her head and it raised the hairs on the back of her neck. After Shelley's office door had slammed shut, Dawit and Hakim, the office secretary, glanced from the closed door to Martha, raised their eyebrows slightly and gave her a half smile of sympathy. Neither had much fondness for Shelley having been at the receiving end of her rudeness on too many occasions.

"I think I'm in trouble," Martha said quietly to them. *I sure hope that the visas go through fast and I get the administrator trained quicker than Shelley has my guts for garters.*

A few evenings later, having spent the previous few days avoiding Shelley as much as possible, Martha drove, with a smile the width of her face to the airport, as planned, to collect Stefan. She had not let her differences with Shelley spoil her relief at having spoken to Máire or her happy anticipation of seeing Stefan. Every so often Patrick would come to mind; reading his last letter had reminded her why she had loved him and why she had believed their relationship could survive her year away. If only he'd given her signs earlier that he missed her or even cared about her, things might have been different, very different. But she was lucky, she reminded herself, she had Stefan and when she thought of him, her body tingled in all the right places, places that Stefan had revealed to her.

She arrived early and checked at the desk to see if and when his flight was due in. She took a seat in the unusually quiet airport and tried to read her book. She had an hour to wait and, in that time, she got very little reading done as she was too full of anticipation. She promised herself that she was going to say very little and let him tell her how his trip had gone first. She wasn't going to jump in feet first as was her habit. She imagined their first embrace. If this wasn't Sudan she'd be ready to jump into his arms but she couldn't greet him with even a small hug right there in the middle of Khartoum airport. But when they got back to his apartment, there would be nothing stopping them.

Finally, there was activity in the airport that indicated the flight had landed and Martha watched for him coming through the exit door. As she stood there, she started to feel restless and anxious that all would not be as she hoped and planned. *What's the worst thing that can happen?* she asked herself as she had so many times before. Before she could answer her own question, there he was, walking through the doorway. Her heart gave a brief happy beat. But he stared straight ahead, wearing an expression she didn't recognise. There was something impenetrable about it. Was it anger? Frustration? Upset? Or all of those things? She was almost in front of him but he didn't see her. How could he not see her? Her heart felt punched to silence.

She said his name. "Stefan."

"Martha," he responded in a flat tone.

"Stefan, how are you? How was your flight?"

"Fine."

"At least it was on time." Martha caught herself making small-talk as she struggled to find her footing.

"Yes. It was on time."

He stopped and looked in the direction of the car park. "Where are you parked?"

"Over here." Martha said, biting her lip and holding back tears of disappointment and frustration but still resolving to stick to the plan and let him speak.

He didn't utter one complete sentence during the short journey to his apartment. She attempted more small talk, asking some carefully chosen questions: 'When are you back at work?' 'Had you a horribly early start?' All she got back was, 'Don't know', 'Suppose so'. And, despite having the windows open, Martha was certain there was a strong smell of booze coming from his breath. *Well,* she thought, *if one is in a bad mood, there's nothing like a few drinks to make the mood even worse.* She pursed her lips for fear of making some sarcastic comment along that line. His bad mood was proving increasingly contagious; how dare he have taken the wind out of her happy anticipation and good spirits. Part of her wanted to stop and tell him if that was how he was going to be he should just make his own way home. *Be patient, be patient, maybe when we get back into his apartment, it will be different.*

She parked the Land Cruiser beside his pickup and saluted the security guard. Stefan took his bag from the back and to Martha's embarrassment, didn't respond to the man's friendly greeting of "*Salaam Alaykum.*" Martha responded loud enough for both of them, "*Alaykum Salaam.*"

They made their way upstairs and into the bright apartment where Martha had the table nicely laid, ready for the meal which she had put in the fridge after she had prepared it the previous evening. Stefan passed no comment and went straight into the bedroom. Martha slumped down on the couch feeling angry and totally dejected. She listened to him thump and thud around the bedroom, presumably unpacking. He hadn't bothered to ask her anything, how she was, what had happened, any news, nothing. *How do I attract such guys?* she thought with a sigh. *Next thing he will be telling me that he was at the best gig ever. Well, feck him. I'm not going to be his or anybody's dogsbody ever again. I've been kicked around for more than enough of my life already. This is where it ends.*

After a few minutes of silence from the bedroom, she decided he could have two choices: he could talk to her or he could stew in his own misery – alone. She got up from the couch and marched over to the bedroom to tell him just that. He was sitting on the side of the bed, with his feet on the ground, wearing that same mad-as-hell expression. Despite his obvious ire, she felt drawn towards him, drawn to putting her arms around him, to comfort him. She desperately wanted to see his face relaxed and his eyes smiling the way she knew them. She took a deep breath.

"Stefan, I just can't do this…I won't do this…you've a choice; you can talk to me right now or I can just leave…"

His facial expression changed to aghast. "Martha, don't go. Please don't go," he said, grabbing her by the wrist.

"Well, what would you have me do, Stefan? Stay here until you cool off and decide you want to talk to me? I won't do that."

"I don't know. I don't know what I would have you do…I don't want to lose you."

He released her wrist and reached tentatively for her hand. She turned and faced him and found his brown eyes peering directly at her, imploringly. The tightness in her face and body relaxed. She brought her free hand up to his face and ran the tips of her fingers gently up the side of his cheek, tracing a line across the top of one eye, down his nose, then slowly across his lips, letting her fingers linger there momentarily.

He closed his eyes and gasped softly.

"Did you miss me, Martha? Did you really miss me?"

"Yes. You know I missed you. Of course, I did."

He pulled her to sit down beside him. She let herself fall back on the bed leaving her feet on the floor. He lay beside her in the same position. Martha stared up at the ceiling. This wasn't how she'd dreamt it. *We make plans, God laughs. It sucks.* As the tears fell down her face, annoyance built up inside her again. She deserved the lovely romantic reunion she had envisaged.

"I'm so sorry, Martha. This isn't how it was meant to be. I totally screwed up. I was going to sort everything out at home and then…" He was sobbing.

"No this isn't how it was meant to be. This is not it at all." She shook her head and leaned up on her elbow; tears were streaming down the side of his face, into his hairline. Her heart softened.

"I've really messed it up this time. I'm sorry," he said.

"You messed it up all right. I didn't know who or what it was that had arrived into that airport." She kissed him lightly on the lips.

"I messed it up with my father. I can't do things right with him. I get so furious. And now I come back here and take it out on you. I'm so sorry."

"Stefan, please stop saying sorry and just tell me what happened? How bad can it be? What about the others, your mother, your sister, your brother?"

"Things are fine with them."

"That's good because I thought that I'd love to meet them sometime which, you know, would be kind of difficult if you weren't talking to them!" She was trying to make her voice sound light.

"I want you to meet them. I really do," he said, sounding slightly desperate, taking her hand again. "For the first few days, I kept wishing that you were there with me. I told Mutti, Marianna and Mark all about you. Marianna teased me about being in love. She said she could tell because I seemed different. She said that I smiled more. Mutti said that I seemed happier and I said that I was. I suppose that was what gave me the confidence to speak to my father."

Martha was still leaning on her elbow observing him and she noticed that his face and voice changed from almost cheerful to forlorn as soon as he mentioned his father.

"One evening I went over to our house. I was staying with Oskar and Malia as planned. I knocked on Father's study door and asked if we could talk. He answered 'yes'. He was expecting me as Mutti had told him that I was coming. I went in and sat down opposite him. He looked at me as if I was a stranger.

"'Well?' he said.

"'I am sorry Father; I am sorry for being a difficult child. I am sorry that I have disappointed you.'"

Martha ran her hand down Stefan's face tenderly, encouraging him to go on.

"For some reason I thought that he would meet me halfway, you know, say that he was difficult too or something.

"'Yes, you were,' he said, 'you made all our lives very difficult, especially your poor Mutti's.'

"'I've said sorry to Mutti already,' I said.

"'Well, I hope that you have seen the error of your ways and will behave better in future.'

"'Yes, Father,' I said. I paused for a long time, peering at him, still expecting him to say something about how he had been as a father. But nothing. Something inside me snapped.

"'But you made things difficult too, Father.'

"Still no response.

"'I was never good enough for you no matter what I did, unless I was willing to join your bloody army!' I said, louder than I meant to.

"'Do you think so, Stefan, and is that the way you see fit to talk to me?' He spoke in that clipped monotone way that he has. It made me worse."

Martha stroked Stefan's face with the palm of her hand, dreading what he might say next.

"I wanted him to show some emotion, shout, anything. 'Yes, I do think so and I wish that you would admit it – just once!' I shouted."

"'I think that you should leave now, Stefan,' he said, shaking with fury as he held the door open for me.

"I walked out of his office and out the front door of our house, slamming it loudly behind me. I was so angry; I strode the whole way over to Oskar and Malia's place without stopping."

"Wow. What did they say?"

"It's a very long walk. By the time I got back, they were in bed and I went straight to my room and went to bed. I spent most of the night remembering the conversation and getting even angrier, remembering all the other rows that I'd had with him over the years. I didn't see Oskar or Malia before they went to work the next morning and so I spoke to them after their children were in bed the following evening. Malia made me promise not to leave Austria without making up with him. She said that I'd regret it. The next evening, I went over to our house. But there was nobody there. I waited outside expecting someone to return. Eventually a neighbour saw me and said that she had seen an ambulance there. She had seen my mother very upset so she assumed that something had happened to my father. She let me use her phone and eventually I tracked them down to a hospital on the outskirts of the city. I met my sister in the corridor there. 'Dad had a stroke,' she said – imagine, Martha, Mr Exercise Every Day had a stroke!"

"I'm sorry, Stefan," Martha said lowering her head on to his chest and hugging him. He wrapped his arms around her and clung to her.

"I'm sorry, Martha. I thought that I had left all that anger behind me since moving here and especially since meeting you, then I go home and I'm back to where I was before."

"Oh, Stefan, I know. I know that families can do that to us…"

"You know better than anyone else I know."

"Well, I think I know and then again I think that I don't know," Martha said, pondering her own situation. "Being over here in Sudan, I was starting to think that I had it nearly all worked out but it's never that simple, is it?"

"No, it never is."

"What happened next? At the hospital I mean," she said.

"Marianna and I sat and waited and eventually Mutti appeared. She said that he was stable and that time would tell. The doctors said that we should go home and get some rest and they would call if there was any change. I wanted to stay. I don't know why. We went back the next morning. Mutti went into see him, then Marianna. I thought that I would go in next. Mutti said that she didn't think that it would be a good idea. She said, 'Give him time, Stefan, he needs a bit of time.' 'But I don't have time,' I said. It was only when I pressed her that she admitted that he refused to see me. Even from his bed in intensive care he was determined to control me and make me suffer. It's as if he knew that I wanted to come back here, back to you, and say that I did it, I made up with my father. But he wouldn't let me – I don't think he ever will."

"I'm sorry, so sorry."

"And what do I do? I come back here and I act like as big a bastard as he ever was. I don't want to be that person, Martha. I don't."

"I know. I don't want it either. I'm not ready to go home, not for a very long time anyway. But I can't stay here much longer."

She started to cry and she buried her face in the crook of his arm.

"What do you mean you can't stay here?"

She stopped crying and lay back on the bed looking at the ceiling again. He did the same and they lay in their own silence for a while.

"A lot has happened since you left…I need to leave."

"But where will you go?"

"I don't know, I think somewhere in Africa still." She stared at the shadows on the ceiling and imagined they were a map of Africa and all she had to do was pick a country. She chose somewhere with a coast. That was what mattered most to her. She needed the familiar comfort of the sea. She didn't tell him she had already started making enquiries through the office back home. She didn't tell him that she had imagined them both on a beach together, holding hands as they ran into the sea, laughing at the sheer joy of it. Now she saw herself on the same sandy beach, paddling alone, in quiet contemplation, as she had so many times before.

"Why Africa?"

"I don't know, Stefan. It's far from home."

"That's a good reason."

"I think so."

"Can I come with you?"

"Maybe. We'll have to see."

He reached his fingers up to her face and ran them along her lips.

"Yes," she said. "We will have to talk. There's so much to think and talk about."

Chapter 30

Families

As they ate dinner, she talked and he listened. At times he nodded and occasionally he reached over and took her hand for a moment. He refused to say anything further about his trip home, he said he just wanted to hear all that had happened in Martha's life while he was away. But for all that, his eyes told her that his mind was somewhere else.

They tidied up in silence and afterwards she took him by the hand and led him back into the bedroom. She lifted his T-shirt over his head and her own over hers. He unclasped her bra and let it fall to the floor before opening his trousers and stepping out of them. She stepped out of her skirt and pants in one slow movement. She moved closer to him and looked up into his face, hoping to see some of the old light and passion she had known before he left, but in his eyes, she saw sadness lingering like a dense fog. She kissed each of his eye lids, kissed each cheek, then down the side of his neck, pulling him to her as she did so, her fingers moving in a gentle dance up his back, playing to the same inner tune as her lips.

"I love you, Stefan. I love you," she whispered.

"I love you too, Martha." He was crying again.

"We can work it out," she said, hugging him close, doubting her words, doubting her feelings. *Whatever happened to our 'marriage of true minds'? Do I love him? 'Love is not love that alters when it alteration finds'…I think I love him, before he left, I knew…*Her mind jumped to thoughts of Patrick's letter. The more she thought, the more she doubted.

Their love making that night started tenderly but Stefan soon brought to it an uncomfortable urgency that left Martha feeling devoid of the sense of unity she had always treasured with him. After he rolled onto his back, she kissed him, turned on her side with her back to him and lay awake wondering, *Was this it, was this how it was going to be, had the time before he left been their honeymoon period?*

In the morning, when she woke, she felt no urge to reach for him. *The ball's in his court now, he should reach for me.* She felt him stir beside her. He gave her one quick kiss on her back between her shoulders.

"I'd better go to the airport and check my roster," he said, getting out of bed and heading for the bathroom.

Bullshit, Martha thought as she lay back on the bed. *Feck him and his dark mood.*

He reappeared a few minutes later and started to get dressed.

"What's going on, Stefan?" she asked through gritted teeth.

"Nothing. I just need to find out when I'm next flying."

Martha took a deep breath before speaking again. "Stefan."

"Yes."

"I know all the shit with your dad is hard…"

"You could say that!"

"And I know it's not easy to get your ahead around…"

"You could say that too!"

"Stefan, I'm trying!"

He came over to beside the bed, bent down and kissed her on the lips. "I know that, Martha. But I think I've a lot of working out still to do. When it comes to you and your family, you're a bit further on with knowing where you're at than I am with mine."

"It's early days yet, you know?"

"I know. Gotta go."

The next day Stefan called into Martha at the Help office – something he'd never done before. He'd always called to her flat, or if she wasn't there to the girls' flat.

"Just wanted to let you know, one of the other pilots has gone on leave now that I'm back so I'll be flat out for the next week or so."

They were standing in the middle of the main office with Dawit looking up at them from his desk. There wasn't much she could say. She swallowed hard.

"Okay, so…that's a pity. I thought…I…"

"I know. Sorry. I'll see you soon though."

Feck it, Stefan, avoiding me isn't going to solve anything.

A long week of anticipation, tears and trying to keep busy passed and then, one evening, just as Martha was heading off for a swim in the Sudan Club, there was a knock on her flat door. Attracta and Tom didn't move from the couch, they remained stretched out as usual, taking slow deep drags on a joint. Martha was nearly at the door anyway. She opened it and there stood Stefan. Her heart leapt.

"Stefan!" She smiled and thought perhaps she saw a hint of a smile on his face too.

"Fancy dinner at the Hilton?" he said.

"Now?"

"Now. If you're not busy?"

"I was just going swimming. Come in while I change."

While they waited for their food, Stefan told Martha more about his trip home and especially some of things he'd got up to with his siblings; the galleries they'd seen, the music they'd heard, the coffee shops they'd visited…He told her that he'd got on well with Marianna's boyfriend although he'd thought his long heavy dreadlocks were a bit much and no, Marianna's boyfriend hadn't been introduced yet to Stefan's father! He'd also met one particular friend of Mark's, Ben, a couple of times and yes, he still suspected that Mark was gay; he was even more convinced now he'd met Ben! Martha loved hearing about it all. *Now he was talking!*

They ate without much chat and when their plates had been cleared off the table, Stefan cleared his throat.

"I suppose you guessed, I wasn't asked to do the extra flights this week, I volunteered to do them! I'm sorry. I was doing what I've always done, I was running away from an emotional overload."

"Yes, I guessed. But feck it, Stefan, I was so pissed off with you for not at least trying to talk to me about it. Whatever happened to better communication? I nearly told you to go take a running jump – it's as well I'd a week to calm down or I'd have given you a bullet myself!"

"Fair enough. I'd have deserved it."

"So, what's the story now? I can't and I won't take any more of those long silences and dark moods."

"I don't blame you…Look, I know I had some lovely times with Mark and Marianna, but do you know what I realise I felt more than anything else when I was home? I never put a finger on it before but it's how I think I've always felt; I am an outsider in my own family. I want to belong but I don't."

"Seriously, Stefan, who are you telling? I'm the queen of outsiders! By my standards you have bloody good relationships with your brother and sister and even with your mother. I envy that but I'm happy for you."

"I know and I am grateful for what I have but don't you see? I still feel like an outsider and as long as my father is alive, he'll make sure I always will be. That's what gets to me."

"For goodness sake, you've told me about some of their letters to you, they love you, they care about you…"

"Yes, when there's distance between us and when *he's* not on the sidelines, it all feels fine. But when *he's* anywhere nearby, it's all completely different."

"I hate to say it, but *he* won't be on the sidelines for a whole lot longer, you'll only have to work around him for another few years!"

"That's true, I guess."

"Don't get me wrong, I'm not saying it will be easy but he won't last forever, not like my lot."

"I'm sorry your family are such shits. Where do you think that leaves you, Martha? What now?"

Martha shook her head and sighed. "There's no easy way to tell you. I know you think I've it all worked out but, to be honest, in some ways, I feel more confused than ever. I've a bit more working myself out to do and I intend to do it elsewhere. All I know at this stage is I'm leaving Sudan, probably for Kenya and probably in the next month or two. I heard this week from the office at home that I've been offered a management consultant contract in Nairobi."

Stefan grimaced and tried to turn it to a smile. "That was quick. Not much breathing space there! Where does that leaves us?"

Martha rubbed her forehead with both hands. "Oh shit, Stefan. I really don't know. That depends on many things, including you! I care about you. I really do but you've got to think about what you want. I can't answer for you." Martha gave a half-laugh. "I've plenty of my own shit to deal with!"

"Too much shit to be shovelled," Stefan said, quoting Martha from a previous discussion.

They both laughed.

"Let's give it our best shovelling though...At least we're back talking and sure you never know where that might get us," Martha said, giving him a dramatic wink while rubbing her leg against his under the table.

"And on that note, I think I'll ask for the bill!"

Over the next few weeks, they fell back into the habit of seeing each other regularly with Martha staying over at his place a couple of nights each week. A wedge of uncertainty had settled between them but both of them accepted rather than fought it.

Daniel, the Executive Head of Mission arrived less than a month after the memo had arrived from the board. Between times, tensions with Shelley had been horrendous and mostly they had avoided each other. In fact, Shelley had mostly avoided all the volunteers and when she wasn't in her office with the door shut, she was often in her bedroom in her flat. Nobody was surprised when she chose to terminate her contract three months early; just days before Daniel arrived in Khartoum, she left. Tom and Attracta flew out on the same day. Despite, or maybe because of Shelley's absence, Daniel quickly got to grips with improving the efficiency and effectiveness of Help Sudan, both operationally and financially. Martha liked his thorough and professional ways; she liked that he listened to her; he agreed with the need for a plan to rely less on expats and more on locals; he understood the exchange situation; he confirmed combining the roles of accountant and administrator and a suitable candidate was recruited. Following a thorough handover, Martha would fly to Nairobi to take up the offer of a year's contract there as a management consultant.

The week after Daniel arrived, when Martha was still working flat out bringing him up to speed on everything, Stefan arrived at her office, for only the second time ever. But this time, she could see, his mood was high.

"Martha, Martha, can you finish early please? Can you come and grab a bite with me at the Sudan Club? There's something I want to show you." Martha looked from Stefan to Daniel before answering.

"Impossible to say no to that," Daniel said with a soft, knowing twinkle in his eyes.

As soon as they sat down at a table in the Sudan Club, Stefan took two folded pages from his pocket and handed them to Martha. She opened them and looked at him and laughed.

"I haven't suddenly learned how to read German," she said. "What is it?"

"It's a letter from Mark. Here let me tell you what it says…"

Mark started the letter by apologising for the horrible way their father, Vater, had treated Stefan for as long as he could remember and also for the fact that he had never challenged him about it. He said that he had just let it happen, feeling scared to rock his own relationship with Vater, which Mark said was on shaky foundations of its own, given that Mark had his own struggles, more about those later…After Stefan had left, Marianna told him about Stefan's apology, the argument which followed and then how Vater had refused to see Stefan before he flew back to Sudan. When Mark had heard all this, he was furious. Being fit and stubborn, Vater had made a remarkable recovery and after he had had a few days at home, Mark decided to finally challenge him on his treatment of Stefan. Vater refused to admit any fault and told Mark that he had always been such a good son and he shouldn't allow himself to be poisoned by Stefan's way of dealing with the world; fighting against anything and everything that he didn't like in it. Mark told Vater that Stefan had always fought for what he believed was right; Stefan had values and he had lived by them; Stefan had courage. Mark told their father that he wished he'd had half of Stefan's values, courage and honesty. "Now that I have Ben in my life, *yes Ben*, Vater, I am going to have courage and I am going to live a more open and honest life, *with Ben*." Vater had made to say something a couple of times but something had stopped him, maybe some new dawning. Mark told him that he would leave him to think about whether he wanted to run both his sons out of his life and his daughter too. Marianna knew the story and had said that if Vater chose to have nothing more to do with her two beloved brothers, then she would have nothing more to do with him. Mark heard nothing for a week and then he got a note from Vater saying that it was a good conversation the other night and that he hoped that Mark would come for dinner soon. Mark did go for dinner and a number of times since when his off duty allowed it. He had introduced Ben to Mutti and they had got on well and had even ganged up on him, teasing him about how fussy he was about his pet motorbikes.

In the closing paragraphs Mark said he was sorry, such a letter wasn't how he had planned on telling Stefan that Ben was his boyfriend. He suspected that Stefan had worked all that out for himself anyway! Mark also said that Vater's health wasn't good and he didn't expect him to have too long ahead of him. Mark signed the letter, *With love from your admiring brother.*

Martha cried and cried as Stefan talked her through the contents of the letter. Stefan couldn't hold back the tears either.

"Stefan, I'm so happy for you. That's fantastic."

"There's more," he said as she went to hug him.

He held up a short note in very shaky writing, also in German.

"Is that from your father? What does it say?"

"Son, I am sorry. I hope you will come home soon again and you will spend some time with your bad-tempered father." Stefan grinned wider than Martha thought she'd ever seen him grin. Well, maybe not the widest he'd ever grinned, she later teased him, after their shared joy and excitement had led them to re-find perfect, if temporary, unity in Stefan's bedroom!

"Stefan, there's hope for us all!"

"After getting Vater's note, Martha, I really do believe there is…"

Epilogue

Stefan's contract in Sudan was due to end a month after Martha moved to Nairobi. He had decided that he was going to finish it out and then fly home, where he would spend at least a month before deciding what he wanted to do next. Martha and he hadn't ruled out the possibility of him joining her in Kenya, but in their own hearts, neither of them expected it to happen. They both felt the need for fresh breathing space.

Sudan was the start of Martha shedding new light on her childhood and all that had shaped her, but it was not enough; she needed to process what these revelations really meant for her. To do this she needed physical and emotional distance between her and her family. So she decided to send them back a letter.

She had drafted it many times. The first drafts were short and to the point:

Dear Siblings, it is time for you to build your own effing bridges and for once to do your duties. I've taken enough crap from you all for too long already...

The final draft was equally succinct:

Dear Jim, Margaret and Robyn,
Thank you for your letter. I am not in a position to come home as I've taken a long management consultancy contract with a firm operating in a number of countries in Africa. Fortunately, there are three of you who, between you, should be able to do at least a fraction of what you expect of me.
Good Luck,
Martha

When Martha had moved to Sudan, nobody, other than Máire, had known her; nobody had pre-conceived ideas of who she was as a person; nobody could dictate to her what they expected of her. With this had come a certain freedom to find out for herself who she might be. Now that Máire had given credence to Martha's previously denied memories, she wanted to start again, somewhere nobody knew her or thought that they knew her; somewhere where she could reinvent herself, if she wished.

But before she reinvented herself, she was going to reconnect with Trish on a girls' adventure. They had a wonderful holiday planned to kickstart Martha's time in Kenya. Padraic was not invited, Trish had told him. How would she ever squeeze all the gories out of Martha if there was a man on board? In between chats, they would probably see all of the big five: elephants, lions, leopard, rhino and cape buffalo. They were going to have ten days of safari; Tsavo, then Amboseli, then the best of all, the great plains of the Maasai Mara.

Martha arrived in Nairobi a day earlier than Trish and as she walked the streets, she popped into shops and stared in awe at their full shelves; the choices of shampoos and soaps, the full range of spices, the colourful clothes. She wandered into a fruit and vegetable market and she thought she had died and gone to heaven, such were the beautiful shiny displays of fresh produce: apples, oranges, bananas, pineapples, peppers, avocadoes, carrots, onions…After Sudan, she was blown away by the variety and abundance of it all.

Martha expected after Trish left, she would be lonely in Kenya but it had promises of new people and so many exciting new experiences. And it had sea. Growing up, she had always had the sea.

She found solace in its ebb and flow.

About the Author

After thirty years as a reluctant accountant, Vanessa retired from figures to focus on writing and over the last seven years has taken part in writing workshops at Bantry Literary Festivals, The Irish Writers Centre and The Big Smoke Writing Factory.

When not escaping to West Cork or further afield, the author lies in Clontarf, with her husband, three of their four children – one has flown the nest – her black dog Yoda and her black, epileptic cat named Cat.

Find her on Twitter @VanessaPearse1